ENDING THE EXPLOSION

ENDING THE EXPLOSION

Population Policies and Ethics for a Humane Future

by William G. Hollingsworth

SEVEN LOCKS PRESS
Santa Ana, California
Minneapolis, Minnesota
Washington, D.C.

Library of Congress Cataloging-in-Publication Data

Hollingsworth, William G., 1937-
     Ending the Explosion: Population Policies and Ethics for a Humane Future / by William G. Hollingsworth.
          p.   cm.
     Includes bibliographical references and index.
     ISBN 0-929765-44-3. -- ISBN 0-929765-42-7 (pbk.)
     1. Birth control--Moral and ethical aspects.   2. Population policy.
3. Overpopulation.   I. Title.
HQ766.15.H65   1996
363.9'1--dc20   96-7741
                                                                                      CIP

Manufactured in the United States of America

SEVEN LOCKS PRESS
P.O. Box 25689
Santa Ana, CA 92799
(800) 354-5348

To Pat,
Jana, Steve,
Thelma and Holly

CONTENTS

Medical and Professional Disclaimer

Because they pertain to some of the policy and ethical issues dealt with in this book, medical and medical-related matters are sometimes mentioned or discussed. However, no part of this book is intended as medical or other professional advice. Nor should any part of this book be at all regarded as, or in any way be used as a substitute for, medical or other professional advice.

Acknowledgments

Only partly because writing this book took more years than I care to admit, it is impossible for me to name all of the individuals who provided helping words and deeds. Numerous demographers and other expert witnesses graciously endured pertinent and impertinent questions by a stranger trespassing upon their fields. Three who deserve special medals for long-term helpfulness are Ansley Coale, Paul Demeny, and Carl Haub. Among others owed extra thanks are Stan Bernstein, John Bongaarts, Mary Kritz, Parker Mauldin, John Ross, Robert Sendek, My T. Vu, and Charles Westoff.

While the book's flaws are entirely mine, many persons have read and commented upon all or part of one or more drafts. Though my forgetfulness may make it incomplete, the list of helpful readers surely includes, besides Coale, Demeny, Haub, and Ross, the following: Virginia Abernethy, Joseph Allen, Leon Bouvier, Ambrose Ekpu, Step Feldman, Lindsey Grant, Lakshman Guruswamy, Gail Herman, Pat Hollingsworth, Cynthia Lloyd, Donald Mann, Phyllis Piotrow, Virginia Richard, Jim Martin-Schramm, and Joseph Speidel.

I am indebted to a long list of persons for library or secretarial support; among them are Carol Arnold, Cathey Banks, Ann Hail, Carolyn James, Cyndee Jones, Sharon Miller, Melanie Nelson, and Sue Sark. Other staff and faculty colleagues and numerous students at the University of Tulsa and its College of Law also have my thanks for their encouragement, understanding, and good cheer.

Speaking of students, I am deeply grateful to a long line of student research assistants for source-gathering, proofreading, and other tasks. With respect to this book, I should especially mention Scott Davenport,

Eric Eighmy, Eddie Erwin, Gretchen Garner, Lyn Grikis, Christie Hadder, Louise Michels, Bill Redell, and Donna Thompson-Schneider.

My very deep gratitude is also owed editor Sharon Goldinger and her associates at PeopleSpeak and publisher Jim Riordan and his associates at Seven Locks Press. The same is owed Donald Mann for his extraordinary kindness.

I am also privileged to thank special loved ones, to whom I am most profoundly in debt: my parents, my wife, and our children. The impossible and happy task of trying to repay such immeasurably immense debt brings great joy, and freedom, to my life.

We travel together, passengers on a little space ship, dependent on its vulnerable resources of air and soil; all committed for our safety to its security and peace; preserved from annihilation only by the work, the care and, I will say, the love we give our fragile craft.

— Adlai Stevenson

Over the bleached bones and jumbled residues of numerous civilizations are written the pathetic words: "Too late." There is an invisible book of life that faithfully records our vigilance or our neglect. . . . This may well be mankind's last chance to choose between chaos and community.

— Martin Luther King, Jr.

INTRODUCTION

Humankind could cherish and conserve the planet's wondrously diverse community of life. We humans could help build a future in which both natural splendor and human dignity would flourish.

We could help create a world that affords freedom and ample sustenance to every person, a world where the windows and doors of education are open to every child, a world where everyone can share in the dignity of work and play, a world where all creeds, races, tribes, and nationalities celebrate their differences and commonality as one human family. At long, long last.

None of this will be easy, but all of it is possible. If we are willing — very willing. Our helping to create a sustainably bountiful future will require studious attentiveness, inspired dedication, moral courage, tireless perseverance, exuberant creativity, sufficient wisdom, and a laugh-at-ourselves sense of humor.

COMPONENTS

The difficulty of the enterprise is matched only by its complexity. The project of building a sustainable humane future is essentially a union of numerous component tasks, large and small, all interrelated.

Among those tasks are arms control and peacekeeping, preservation of remaining natural ecosystems, reforestation, ecologically sound water management and agricultural development, soil conservation and restoration, land reform, pollution abatement and waste management, development of environmentally sound energy systems, energy conservation, other-scarce-resources frugality, preservation of cultural diversity, respect for human rights, attainment of economic and social justice — and prevention of overpopulation.

REASONS FOR FOCUS

This book concentrates upon the world population crisis not because resolving that crisis is somehow humanity's only needed step toward a future of sustainable well-being. Instead, the book's focus on population results from the coalescence of three considerations:

First, without an early end to the population explosion, building a humane future becomes a virtually impossible undertaking rather than remaining merely a terribly difficult and complex one.

Second, ending untenable population growth is the task whose probable imperative even the saints (meaning everyone who cares) — and sometimes especially the saints — seem most inclined to discount or deny.

Third, humanity's denying or disparaging the prospect of massive over-population is matched only by a reluctance to devise policies adequate to prevent that immeasurably tragic outcome. We and our governments still love to imagine that halfhearted efforts will somehow suffice.

PERSPECTIVE

The controversies surrounding and within the 1994 International Conference on Population and Development showed how disinclined we humans are to confront the population crisis with clear and steady focus. How readily, for example, is attention diverted by ideological battles between conservative religious forces and liberal feminist forces over abortion, sexual morality, and perhaps even a perceived general conflict between women's rights and some nations' cultural integrity.

The point is hardly that the just-stated issues are unimportant. As relevant parts of this book acknowledge, cultural integrity, women's rights, sexual morality, and the prevention of abortion are matters of profound ethical concern.

The problem is how often the discussion of those and other valid ethical issues causes people to forget how indescribably cruel an enemy of children, women, and men (and of a culture's survival) massive overpopulation would be. The problem is how easily we forget that preventing massively tragic overpopulation is itself a primary ethical imperative.

It is to help overcome that ethical forgetfulness, and to help us candidly face the population crisis and resolve it both adequately and humanely, that this book tries to speak.

PART I

THE POPULATION CRISIS:

AN ETHICAL APPRAISAL

CHAPTER ONE

TWO SCENARIOS

The year is 2025. Growing faster than predicted, human population exceeds nine billion people. And is headed much higher.

The United Nations is holding yet another world population conference. The cameras are clicking and rolling, CNN is reporting, much is being said, and again there is hope that — in ensuing years — much will be done.

It happened in Bucharest, Romania, in 1974, when world population was nearing four billion. It happened again in Mexico City in 1984, when the human family numbered between four and five billion persons. And it happened for yet another time in Cairo, Egypt, in September 1994, with world population at about 5.6 billion: the world's nations met for the ostensible purpose of confronting in earnest the human population explosion.

AS OF THE MID-1990s

Even today, conferences that supposedly confront the world population crisis in earnest are in danger of becoming an international tradition. But that does not make them useless. Governments and the media do focus upon the crisis during some of the sessions. And the conference even produces its own, or modifies a much neglected prior, "Program of Action."

Based on what we know thus far, what typically follows a world population conference? What I call "the Business as Usual Scenario." In most nations it could also be called the Drifting Along Scenario.

Business as usual? Governments and other people still talk about "the population explosion." They sometimes even seem alarmed by it. But, distracted by more immediate perils, not for long.

Demographers, of course, continue to study the data with appropriate scholarly composure. Public officials dutifully attend other population conferences and make the expected solemn pronouncements. But most governments still fail to act, except to a trivial degree.

Trivial degree? Consider today's developing nations, most of which are already poverty-stricken and where in most cases population ominously continues to explode. In recent years their governments have, in the aggregate, been spending roughly 40 times more on military might than they have been spending to support family planning.

And the rich nations? They have been helping, if at all, at merely token levels. As recently as fiscal year 1995, one rich nation, the United States of America, was limiting its annual aid to family planning programs in the developing nations to a grand total of about $600 million, which was less than one one-hundredth of one percent of its gross national product.

Much to its credit, the 1994 Cairo Conference inspired promises from at least some nations (including the United States) to do more. But what if the "more" they actually deliver continues to be much less than is needed?

RESULTS OF BUSINESS AS USUAL: THE YEAR 2100

What would be the demographic effect of continued casual resolve? What if most nations, rich and poor, keep failing to take nearly adequate steps for an early end to the population explosion? To see, we next visit the year 2100, when sons and daughters of today's children might, with enough luck, be celebrating their 80th or other well-seasoned birthday.

What do we find? For one thing, although the Business-as-Usual shortage of governmental support delayed and lessened the transition, this change has occurred: in 2100, people in most developing nations have for some time been having fewer children on average than did their predecessors in the 1990s. In other words, those nations have seen 21st century declines in what demographers call fertility and measure as children per woman.

Whatever had been the causes of declining fertility in the long-gone 20th century, most 21st century fertility decline was born of stark necessity. Stark indeed. Had fertility held constant at 1990 levels, thanks to continued high fertility in most developing nations the world's population in the year 2100 would, if death rates somehow allowed, be over 100 billion human beings.[1]

Granted, no one seriously believes that the year 2100 will greet anything like 100 billion people. But how many people will the year 2100 greet if, true to the Business as Usual Scenario, most governments, for much or most of the 21st century, continue to do little to help hasten the transition from high to low fertility?

Based in part on United Nations projections, a likely answer is this: unless disastrous death rates cruelly intervene, under the Business as Usual Scenario human population in the year 2100 will be somewhere between 12 and 17 billion persons, and could be headed much higher.[2]

Given the havoc that today's less than six billion human beings wreak upon the planet and upon each other, a doubling or tripling of our numbers in the next century is, to put it mildly, a troubling prospect. It tells us at least to consider a different scenario.

SCENARIO TWO

Starting in the 1990s, humankind gets serious about an idea whose time has come: end the population explosion soon enough to avoid massively tragic overpopulation. Equally important, the world's nations carry through with that idea without assaulting individual reproductive freedom or otherwise denying human dignity. Nations support a variety of efforts (described in this book) that include, among others, adequately funded family planning programs, improved educational and economic opportunities for women, and direct incentives for smaller families.

Call such an approach "the Serious Strategy Scenario." Though later chapters will look at its varied endeavors with a cautious eye, its potential effect upon population growth should be noticed now.

To take note quickly, we again visit your very-grown-up grand-children's birthday parties in the year 2100. Under the Serious Strategy

---

1. United Nations Department of International Economic and Social Affairs, *Long-range World Population Projections: Two Centuries of Population Growth, 1950-2150* (New York: United Nations, 1992), p. 22. Though the point is academic, the UN's precise figure exceeds 109 billion human beings.

2. Why not the UN's "medium" projection for 2100 of 11.2 billion persons (ibid., 14)? That projection has credibility only if one assumes that most nations will soon place much greater emphasis upon reducing high fertility than is now the case.

Scenario, how many human beings could they invite to share the celebration? The likeliest answer is somewhere between eight and ten billion persons.

Why not a year 2100 population of less than eight billion? Thanks to past and present procrastination, that is no longer a very likely goal. The main reason, which pervades most developing nations, is "demographic momentum." A nation with a high birth rate also has a high proportion of young people; even as eventual parents of only two children, they would keep population growing for decades. Moral: unless humanity wishes to forfeit any good chance of humanely limiting itself to eight or nine billion persons, the time for nations to act in earnest is now.

A WORLD OF DIFFERENCE?

Using the above figures, compare the likely demographic outcomes of our two scenarios. If death rates allow, the Business as Usual Scenario yields in the year 2100 a human population somewhere between 12 and 17 billion persons, which, if close to the 17 billion figure, would probably be headed much higher. The Serious Strategy Scenario yields a humankind in 2100 that is somewhere between eight and ten billion persons — and whose numbers have already substantially stopped growing.

Should we care? Note that the range of likely *difference* between each scenario's resulting world population is, for the year 2100, as few as two billion persons and as many as nine billion.

Looking first at the lowest likely difference, how many are two billion persons? They are enough to equal the world's entire human population of 1930. Viewed from that not so ancient benchmark, humanity's choice between the two scenarios is apt at least to make "a world of difference" in population size.

As suggested above, the highest likely population difference between the two scenarios as of the year 2100 (which would portend even higher differences later) is no less than nine billion persons. That possible difference in population outcome itself exceeds today's entire human population by over three billion persons. Numerically at least, that is a very modern world of difference — with even that difference multiplied by more than 150 percent.

How soon and how well the Serious Strategy Scenario was attempted would also matter greatly. There is a potential world of difference between an eight-billion and a ten-billion human population.

But numbers can only begin to tell the story. We must look behind the numbers to see the poignant world of difference between the two scenarios' likely outcomes.

Hence the next chapter.

CHAPTER TWO

QUESTIONS, CHANCES, AND ETHICS

We are still in the year 2100. Chapter 1 carried us there on two different scenarios.

The Business as Usual Scenario sped us to a human population of somewhere between 12 and 17 billion, perhaps headed higher. The Serious Strategy Scenario brought us to a probably fairly stationary human population of somewhere between eight and ten billion persons.

If ours were only a one-way ticket to 2100, which scenario would we hope had come true? Because the future is an unpredictable place, the best way for us to answer that question prior to actual arrival is to ask a series of telling questions.

But we must not let those questions be lifeless abstractions. Instead, when we ask each one, let us try to imagine some of the joy, the beauty, and the pathos that is at stake.

TEN QUESTIONS

First, recall any of those sorrowful scenes of emaciated, starving children you have already seen too often on television. Which population path, the one headed toward 12 to 17 billion people in 2100, or the one headed toward eight to ten billion persons, poses the greater risk of massive food shortages on an unprecedented scale?

Second, picture a schoolyard with children laughing and romping in the breeze. Which population growth scenario makes it likelier that the world's future children will have the safe drinking water, the adequate diet, and the health care to allow them to run and sing and shout with joy?

Third, you are walking in a rain-soaked forest in Asia, Africa, or Central or South America, your senses filled with its shady splendor.

Which of the two population scenarios is likelier to destroy most or all of the world's remaining rainforests?

Fourth, revisit a windy wetland, a rolling scrubland, a cool dry forest, or wherever is your favorite place of natural beauty. Which of the two scenarios would allow more of such places to remain and be better conserved?

Fifth, while you are by yourself in some lonely outdoor place, see and hear your companions — from whistling birds to shining buttercups to dancing moths and butterflies. And try to picture some of the millions of yet unknown but endangered species, any one of which might be the cure for your future grandchild's cancer. Which population scenario threatens the more massive rates of species extinction?

Sixth, say a special prayer for the world's many children who (especially in the developing nations) already suffer brain damage, lung damage, or other permanent disability from breathing poisonous air. Under which scenario are soaring fuel and other needs likelier to cause a magnitude of pollution that would kill and maim on a scale far beyond anything yet seen?

Seventh, feel some of the hurt of ethnic, racial, or religious hatred — using whatever may be the latest sorry example. Does a world population of 12 to 17 billion, or one of eight to ten billion, offer the greater hope of somehow ending humankind's most self-condemning malady?

Eighth, without ever forgetting the victims of genocide, please also remember the victims of humanity's other worst curse, war. Remember the dead, the bereaved, the dispossessed, and all the others whose bodies or lives war has broken or shattered. Whether future wars might be desperate fights over scarce resources or the bitter brew of simmering hatreds, more wars are the likelier outcome under which population growth scenario?

Ninth, take a relative breather. Just glance at two imaginary people. One, driving by too fast for you to see his face, is so rich he could not enjoy all his money if he lived a thousand lives. The other, who walks with hostile steps, is so poor he has nothing to eat, nowhere to go, and not much to lose. Given that massive unemployment and underemployment already plague most population-exploding nations, which population growth scenario locks the human race more tightly in the dismal, dangerous prison of extreme economic inequality?

Tenth, picture two strangers each waiting for a bus. One of them (you can easily tell which) is the picture of happy purpose, at one with the universe and with herself. The other (you can easily tell) is the perfect opposite: her face shows the pain of lost purpose; she is wholly at odds with self and world. Though feast and famine of the soul may both be found under either scenario, we still ought to ask: under which population scenario is the human spirit likelier to flourish?

CHANCES

Although none of the above questions are answerable with scientific proof, you rightly answered all ten with confidence. For every one of them, and for others that could have been asked, the message is the same. It is the Serious Strategy Scenario and its likely eventual population of eight to ten billion persons that offers the better chance for a humane future. It is the Business as Usual Scenario, headed toward a year 2100 population of 12 to 17 billion, that is likelier to destroy that precious chance.

During the more than 20 years I have studied the prospects for global well-being, I have become less and less able to deny an increasingly urgent truth: Humankind's ability or inability to limit sufficiently its own fertility is apt to be the most critical determinant between finding and losing a humane future.

If that statement is even half as true as I and numerous other observers believe it to be, here is a question for everyone else. Why, despite all the written and spoken words that have addressed the matter, is there still so little interest in seriously confronting the threat of massively tragic overpopulation?

Uncertainty. Looking at the possible reasons for most people's and most governments' lack of profound concern could keep someone busy another 20 years. But let me suggest one reason. It is simply that the future is so uncertain.

Though some prophets have done so anyhow, no one can certify that a further doubling or tripling of human population would be a sure disaster. Nor, though other seers have presumed to do so, can anyone assure us that such growth would allow a happy or even a tolerable outcome.

Thus your answers to the ten telling questions were not predictions of future events. Rather, they were probability judgments, judgments comparing the two scenarios' chances for good and bad outcomes. What those ten questions told us (vividly, I hope) was that a smaller increase in today's human population is apt to allow a much more humane future than would a greater increase.

ETHICS

So should we yawn and go back to sleep? And, if we are parents, should we not bother to teach our children to look both ways before they cross the street? After all, a child may fail to look and make it across anyhow. Or she may look both ways and then be killed by a drunken driver.

Despite such uncertainties, caring parents will still teach their children to "look both ways." Just as caring people and governments should confront the world population crisis in earnest. In both such cases, there is a duty to act despite the slings and arrows of unpredictable fortune.

Doing the right thing — morality — is seldom about acting in the face of certainty. Doing the right thing is usually about decreasing the risks of harm and improving the chances for good. "Look both ways . . . ."

Distance. Permit me to mention a second reason we usually yawn at the population explosion. Forgetting how fast time flies, we think the future is far away. We have to. There are already too many slings and arrows pointed at us in the present. "Protect me from terrorists and other criminals, killer viruses and other diseases, headaches and other pains *now*. I'll worry later about tomorrow."

Dreams. But here is the other half of that truth. As preoccupied as we are with the present, we are hungry, even starving, to care about the future. "What is the use of living," asked Winston Churchill, "if it is not to make the world a better place for those who will live after we are gone?" We yearn for a credible dream of the future that will give meaning and substance to our present existence.

In today's small world, that dream must be big. Without a believable dream of a peaceful and just world for all peoples, human society will continue to do what it has already started to do: to fall apart.

Incredibility. Why can we not believe the global dream we need to have? Seeing what five to six billion of us are already doing to the planet and to each other, I cannot believe the dream of a peaceful and just future for all peoples *unless* humankind decides to bring its population explosion to an early and humane end. Nor, if you are honest about your dreams, can you.

That is not to say that untenable population growth is the only impediment to a viable future. The prospect of such growth is killing the global dream in a less direct way. It threatens to intensify and enlarge humankind's other immensely difficult problems to an extent that would make solving them impossible.

Responsibility. Morality is about caring for the future. Here are two sets of tasks that such caring now requires every concerned citizen of the world to do. Set one is to honestly confront and to understand the world population crisis. Set two is to decide upon and then advocate solutions that are apt to be both adequate and humane.

The next few chapters seek to offer help toward the first set of tasks. The rest of the book then endeavors to help in the harder enterprise: resolving humanity's population crisis in an effective and decent way.

CHAPTER THREE

FROM THE PAST TO THE PRESENT TO — ?

No one likes the term "population explosion." Use it with respect to human beings and you could be deemed an alarmist, an insensitive oaf, or, more likely, both.

Some say that, when applied to humans, population explosion is an ideological or manipulative concept rather than a descriptive one. It is, we are told, used to further one's agenda, meaning to control other people's behavior, rather than to report reality.

The charge that population explosion is being used nondescriptively can be put to the test. Does the concept misdescribe the facts? To answer that question, some background, both historical and prehistorical, is essential.

THE PAST

For untold thousands of years, human population growth was an exercise in slowness. For no one knows how many years, Earth's human population at any given time could have been numbered in the mere thousands. Only after millennia upon millennia were there surely as many as one million people on earth at any one time.

Even when they started farming and herding instead of only hunting, scavenging, and gathering, there were probably no more than several or so million humans then living on this planet.

> But once our ancestors learned to till and sow,
> Human population would grow, grow, grow.

Though it may be dreadful poetry, the above two-liner is no exaggeration. Only about ten thousand years ago were there maybe *several* million human beings living on earth. Just eight thousand years later, about two thousand years prior to now, Earth's human population numbered in the range of 300 million persons.

Yet, even during that period of fast growth, it was taking on average more than a thousand years for humankind to double. Indeed, as late as the 17th century, the human species numbered only about 500 million — less than half today's China.

But subsequently, in just two more centuries, by about 1830, humanity had again doubled and thus reached the one billion mark. And then the pace got even faster. Though it took us all of prior human history and prehistory to reach our first billion, we humans reached our second billion in only a century, by about 1930. Then, in only 30 more years, by 1960, humankind had added its third billion.

In about 15 more years, by 1974–75, we reached our fourth billion. By 1987, just 12 or 13 years later, billion five had indeed arrived. Billion six appears to be on its way with comparable speed.

There is therefore only one reason to call what has been and still is happening a human population explosion. No milder term would nearly suffice to describe.

THE PRESENT

Explosions do not last forever. Is it today more telling to say that the human population explosion is ending or that it is continuing? The answer depends on where on earth you are looking.

In nearly all affluent and highly industrialized nations, fertility has fallen to about or below two children per woman. Unfortunately, however, most of those same nations act as if there is no tomorrow when they (we) use fuel and other scarce resources.

In most developing nations the decline in fertility has been much more modest. Though fertility in Latin America now averages slightly above three children per woman, some nations therein have a fertility rate of roughly four or five children.[1]

In South Central and Western Asia, fertility averages 3.8 and 4.3 children, respectively, in some nations exceeding six children per woman.

1. The above and ensuing recent fertility data are from Population Reference Bureau (PRB), *1995 World Population Data Sheet* (Washington, D.C.). This chapter's prehistorical and historical population chronology draws mainly upon Ansley J. Coale, "The History of the Human Population," *Scientific American*, Vol. 231, No. 3 (September 1974), pp. 41–51, and Edward S. Deevey Jr., "The Human Population," *Scientific American*, Vol. 203, No. 3 (September 1960), pp. 195–204.

In Africa, fertility averages almost six children per woman, with many African nations exceeding that rate by a fraction or more.

Most ominously, in many nations with high fertility, little or no progress is being made toward smaller family size. Hence, absent an early onset of much greater progress, the prospect of a 12- to 17-billion human population by the end of next century is all too real.

> Unless major changes happen and soon,
> Earth's overflow of people
> Could need a bountiful moon.

Given that bountiful moons are hard to find, one need not be an alarmist or a neurotic in order to be worried.

IGNORERS AND DEBATERS

But "worried" hardly describes most people's day-to-day sentiments toward the continuing population explosion. Though its dimensions and potential effects are of earth-shaking proportions, we earthlings seem most of the time, at least in our conscious minds, to be ignoring it.

Ignoring the ongoing human explosion is even the usual conscious stance of press, pundits, academics, and other seers upon whom (God help us) we rely for greater awareness. But no stance is constant. When our heads are not in the sand, we so-called intellectuals love to debate demographic issues. Year after year.[2]

We even debate whether human population growth is a problem. Like many normal people, some seers deny the problem by assuming that science will always rush to humanity's rescue. They imagine that no matter what the human race does or neglects to do today, tomorrow's technology will fix the future.

Those who cannot quite see science as an all-powerful savior can pretend in other ways. According to some, exploding population

---

2. In our defensive defense, it should be said that the debates and discussions are often of very high quality. See, for examples, Robert Cassen and contributors, *Population and Development: Old Debates, New Conclusions* (New Brunswick, N.J.: Transaction Publishers and Overseas Development Council, 1994); Laurie Ann Mazur, ed., *Beyond the Numbers* (Covelo, Calif.: Island Press, 1994); Godfrey Roberts, ed., *Population Policy: Contemporary Issues* (New York: Praeger, 1990).

is a nonproblem because *the real problem* is overconsumption by affluent nations.

The truth in those seers' half-true viewpoint is one that rich nations and other nations must soon take seriously. Overuse and misuse of Earth's resources is *a* critical problem, whose solution will need the participation of every nation.

The above viewpoint falls into a half-truth when it forgets that overconsumption is not our only critical problem. Anyone who notices a fraction of the damage humans are already doing to planet Earth ought to realize: humanity hardly has the luxury of deciding which problem — overconsumption or potential overpopulation — it would prefer to address. If we care about the future, we must deal with both.

Not convinced? Imagine what sacrifices would be required in both developing and developed nations to cut humanity's per capita resource use, per capita pollution, and other per capita harm-doing in half. Even were (despite developing nations' need to use more resources!) that herculean feat somehow accomplished, with a doubled population humankind would still be wrecking the earth just as much *in toto* as before. With greater population growth, or with less per capita earth-caring progress, total harm-doing would exceed today's reckless levels. With both greater population growth *and* (as is likely) less than herculean per capita improvement, the future looks doubly disastrous.

LIBERTARIANS AND DOWNPLAYERS

A most endearing voice in the population debates comes from doctrinaire libertarians. They well know what everyone else also knows: too much government is, by definition, a menace. Thus, for anything as sensitive as population policy, their advice is as simple as it is unsurprising: "Keep government out of it."

It is also supremely attractive advice, unless one notices some complicating and unattractive truths. Most nations whose fertility remains high are already experiencing massive unemployment; unsafe water and waste disposal systems; extensive undernutrition or malnutrition; high infant and child mortality; serious to severe agricultural, environmental, and ecological deterioration; and widespread deprivations in basic health care, housing, and education. Yet at today's growth rates, population in most of those nations would double in, depending on the nation, 20 to 40 years.

For such nations the realistic question is not *whether* their governments will act in earnest to help end their population explosion. The reality questions are rather about *when* they will so act and about *how they will act when they do.*

Here, then, as if we needed it, is another reason to be worried. Along with the need for governments to act comes a fearsome potential for abuse.

In population policy, as in so many other matters, the potential for abuse has been well demonstrated. Examples: episodes of coerced sterilization in parts of India in the mid-1970s; episodes of same, plus of coerced abortions, in parts of China.

The danger of governmental abuse has caused many recent commentators to downplay the urgency and the imperative of stabilizing human population. Unfortunately, that well-intentioned but tragically misguided response often dominated the UN's Cairo Conference in the fall of 1994.

Why tragically misguided? Unless the dire risk of massive over-population is faced forthrightly, governments are sure to do what they are supremely skilled at doing: postponing sufficient action until it is too late.

The longer governments postpone a serious and adequate response to the world population crisis, the more massively is population apt to grow — and the worse the plight of the people is apt to become. Every day that governments delay, they increase the risk that they will resort to inhumane measures. The best way to insure that horrendous means of population control *will* be used is for governments to postpone adequate action until the need for it becomes undeniably desperate.

CHAPTER FOUR

ROUND ONE OF A "SENATE" DEBATE

How many earthling human beings should there be? That is one of the most important ethical questions that has been given to humankind. It is also one of the most difficult.

Even God declined to answer it for us. "Be fruitful, multiply, and fill the earth" does not tell us the difference between filling and overfilling. (Or was there a strong hint? Since the world's nonhuman creatures were also to "be fruitful and multiply," ample room would be needed for them as well.)

For help with the above and other population questions, perhaps we should bring in the Senate. If not the U.S. or other actual senate, let it be a simulated senate from somewhere on earth.

We are invited to sit in the gallery to observe today's session, whose topic is, by chance, population growth. Senator Superlove is the first to speak:

"Fellow Senators, I am convinced that *any* desire to limit the number of human beings is an inherently evil notion. If human beings are as precious and as wonderful as we purport to believe, how can it ever be anything but wrong to try to limit their — our — numbers?

"Religious belief in eternal life in heaven gives further impetus [especially if we ignore the unhappy possibility of eternity in hell] to this moral imperative: the number of human souls should always be maximized."

Senator Sense, if she exists, might respond somewhat like this:

"One thing wrong with the trip toward higher and higher human numbers is that it could yield an effect totally opposite to the desire of good Senator Superlove. The Limits-to-Growth folks call it 'overshoot and collapse.' The worst case scenario, whose possibility no one can prove or disprove beforehand, is perhaps this: human population grows so rapidly and massively as to cause some extensive ecological breakdown that results in the death of most or even all of the human race. Such is not a very good way to maximize the number of human beings to be on earth or in heaven.

"But one need not dwell upon worst case scenarios to sense that there is something wrong with wanting human population to grow as large as it can as fast as it can. If we but remember that unexpected crop failures from pests, disease, unforeseen weather conditions, and other disruptions are a normal occurrence in human history, we are sufficiently forewarned. Continued rapid and massive population growth is almost sure to preclude the attainment of what is sorely needed: an adequate agricultural margin of safety. That preclusion will mean a needlessly high incidence of famine-caused death and deprivation."

THOUGHTS FROM THE GALLERY

In listening first to Senator Superlove and then to Senator Sense, we can hear a difference between them that is more basic than their competing words. Much like Descartes, Senator Superlove sees human beings essentially as souls abstracted from their physical bodies. Senator Sense sees us as being both spirit and flesh, even inseparably so.

Senator Sense thus sees human beings as connected to the rest of nature. Without at all denying our spirituality, she sees us as a member, albeit the dominant member, of the earth's total ecology. Unlike Senator Superlove, she would not have human population grow so large as to crowd out myriad other species of life.

Does that mean Senator Sense values human life less than does Senator Superlove? Proponents of ever higher population growth have been known to hint that they love people more than do those who sense the need for limits.

Unfortunately, however, Senator Superlove and those of his pro-growth persuasion do not quite merit that subtle, self-awarded accolade. It is Senator Superlove, not Senator Sense, who is willing to invite a higher incidence of premature death and other human tragedy for the sake of attaining greater numbers. It is Senator Sense who finds such willingness to accept a higher rate of casualties objectionable. It is she who sees each individual person as being too valuable for that kind of sacrifice.

As must be obvious, I cannot hide my preference for Senator Sense's position. Her views point us to a future worth dreaming about and thus worth living for.

What should that future be like? For one thing, *this planet's biological diversity — nature's festival of life — will have been conserved for all to enjoy.* For another, *every human being will have a real chance for physical, mental, and spiritual self-fulfillment.*

Is that too idealistic a dream? I should say yes if I thought that any lesser dream could fill our, everyone's, aching moral need.

It is the dream's twofold imperative, to protect nature's diverse splendor and to honor each person's human dignity (which also means honoring cultural diversity), that tells the world's nations, "Prevent massively tragic overpopulation." And it is that same reverence for life that also requires that efforts to encourage low fertility respect the human person.

Hence the need for as difficult an ethical "balancing act" as the world has even seen. The means to achieve low fertility must be adequate to the task. The duty to protect the planet and its people requires no less. But if those means assault human dignity, "victory" could taste as bitter as defeat.

CHAPTER FIVE

THE "SENATE" DEBATE CONTINUES

As we rejoin the debate, Senator Sunny rises to speak.

"Senators, I have great news. Because most of the world's future population growth is projected to occur in the less developed nations, and because people in those nations use so little energy and other resources and cause so little pollution, there is no need to worry."

Hearing those words, Senator Somber has to respond:

"Senator Sunny, one thing wrong with your great news is that it tends to assign most Africans, Asians, and Latin Americans, and their children, to a future at or near the level of bare subsistence. Would the peoples concerned accept that condescending assignment? Should — remember economic justice — they be asked to?

"Another thing wrong with your news is what it forgets. Even at the level of subsistence each human being makes significant demands upon the earth. Everyone needs food, potable water, fuel, shelter, climate-compatible clothing, hygiene, and, at least sometime, transportation and medical care. And virtually everyone seems to want (need?) some 'nonessential' goods as well.

"So here is some news for you. Even though less developed nations currently use far less of the world's resources, and usually pollute far less, *per capita*, than do affluent industrialized nations, large population increases in the less developed world have immense environmental consequences. We are thus already seeing massive destruction of forests and other natural vegetation in the developing nations from increased farming, herding, logging, and fuelwood-gathering. And the pollution in such developing world cities as Bombay, Lagos, and Mexico City is already starting to set world records."

At those words, Senator Strict breaks his vow of silence:

"But if all human beings would restrict themselves to bare necessities, population could just keep on growing."

"But [says Senator Somber] saving the planet is apt to require plenty of asceticism even if population levels off at a 'mere' eight to ten billion. If we zoom toward even higher numbers, the needed degree of sainthood would probably be an impossible one — with or without an Orwellian tyranny to enforce it. Population policy that expects the whole human race to outsaint St. Francis is immoral simply because of its unrealism."

HAPPIER TIMES?

"I can't stand your sad songs any more." Senator Slaphappy has begun to speak. "We humans are smart enough to solve whatever problems more and more billions of us create. There is no limit to human ingenuity. And the more people there are, the more ingenuity there will be."

"And the more ingenuity there will need to be," Senator Somber rejoins. "What makes you so sure, Senator Slaphappy, that a doubled or tripled human population won't be far better at creating problems than at solving them?"

"I can answer that!" It is Senator Strangescience who now speaks. "Most things have gotten better, not worse, as population has grown in the past. Therefore I scientifically conclude that most things will continue to get better as population grows higher and higher in the future."

Senator Somber: "That's like saying, 'If you feel good in a 70-degree room, you'll feel twice as good in one that's 140 degrees.' A strange science indeed!"

Then Senator Sense speaks her mind. "Senators Slaphappy and Strangescience, you both are making the same mistake. You are abstracting the human mind from its physical and social setting. You forget that the world already has a bad habit of wasting many more human minds than it nurtures and utilizes. If human population doubles or triples in the next century, is the waste of human talent likelier to decrease or to soar?

"But just ask today's tough question. With massive unemployment and underemployment already plaguing the world, is it people who are in short supply? Or are the shortages rather to be found in the natural and social resources needed for each person's talent to be utilized?"

"To all such questions," says Senator Similar, "I have the answer. Make the market free enough, and all the needed resources will materialize. Then population and prosperity will grow, grow, grow together."

"I see why," says Senator Somber, "they call you Senator Similar. You sound just like Chairman Mao sounded when he thought *his* economic system would make population limits unnecessary."

THE SHARING OF PLENTY?

At that point Senator Share speaks up. "Despite his faults, Chairman Mao was right about one thing. With a lot more sharing, there could be a lot more people. Studies show that, with proper management and fair distribution, agriculture has the potential to feed many more billions of people."

Enter Senator Sober. "What such 'studies' show is that it's easy to feed added billions of folks 'on paper.' Especially if you forget the added demands on arable land (and the greater ecological risks) posed by the massively increased *non*food needs and greeds of a far larger human population. It also helps to forget what human enterprises so often become: a tragedy of errors."

"And," adds Senator Somber, "because the task of feeding a much higher population will be so much larger, future agricultural 'errors' (e.g., overuse of pesticides, lack of crop diversity) are likely to be far greater, and far more tragic, in scale."

"But," counters Senator Share, "remember the potential power of sharing."

"Yes," nods Senator Sober, "much more sharing will be needed under *any* plausible population scenario. But also remember that people are least willing to share when they sense either of two things: that the unmet need is hopelessly enormous or that the sharing may cause more tragedy in the long run.

"So I ask you, Senator Share, are people going to be proportionately more or less willing to share if they see no credible effort to end the population explosion soon?"

CHAPTER SIX

THE "SENATE" DEBATE CONCLUDES

Seeing that the hour is late, venerable Senator Fencestraddler attempts to forge a compromise:

"Who knows who is right? We cannot possibly know the future consequences of adding several or many billions to human population.

"Though most scientists seem to be at least somewhat worried, there are scientists and other self-proclaimed experts on all sides of the question. Perhaps, as the most manic among them say, our new genie-god, Science and Technology, will let humankind soar to ever higher numbers without overshooting or destroying the earth's web of life. Or perhaps the outcome will be worse than even the worst worriers fear.

"Given that range of uncertainty, my experience and my inclinations tell me that we should just keep doing what we already do: give a small proportion of aid to population programs so we seem neither foolish nor unhelpful. But keep it low priority."

"In other words," says an unhappy Senator Sense, "let us virtually ignore all the warning signs of both overpopulation and resource misuse. Let us keep failing to heed everything from deforestation to wetland and shrubland destruction; to wholesale species extinction; to desertification; to massive soil erosion; to ground-water depletion; to carbon dioxide buildup; to ozone layer depletion; to massive pollution; to high infant, child, and maternal mortality; to widespread undernutrition, malnutrition, and other tragic scarcities.

"How can we see those already ominous signs, hear that humankind is now growing by almost a billion persons a decade, and yet pretend there is no urgent need for low fertility in nations where population is still exploding?"

"I'll tell you how," says Senator Sober. "We can recklessly pretend because the limits to human population on this planet cannot be proved in the scientist's laboratory or in the economist's computer. Similar uncertainties allow us to pretend with respect to all the reckless ways we abuse the planet."

"But Senators," argues Senator Fencestraddler, "not even your warning signs tell us what the planet's resource limits are."

"That's right," says a thus far silent Senator Sane. "Concerning today's topic, population, there is but one way to *know* how many people the earth is able to support on a sustainable basis. Have population grow so far beyond the planet's support limits that massive tragedy and pervasive misery will then tell everyone what those limits were. Not are. Were. As in too late.

"Today's warning signs, whose combined magnitude is historically unprecedented, are telling us that the above experiment may have already begun. Such an experiment seems sane because lack of expert unanimity remains the perfect excuse for most governments to vacillate and to procrastinate.

"But governments' business-as-usual drifting is not sane. With respect to the increasing threat of massive overpopulation, the only sane course would be a credible effort at enabling the population explosion to end *before* Too Late becomes Homo sapiens' last name."

SENATORS SEE AND STRAIGHT

Senator See now breaks her silence. "Senators Sane, Sense, and Somber, you are the white man's version of sense and sanity. I can easily see why you object to 'the population explosion': the populations that are still growing so fast are those of people of color. What some of your ilk call 'zero population growth' is but one more example of Western white racism and neocolonialism."[1]

An upset Senator Sane responds. "Senator See, the sense and sanity I value are woven from all colors. The population explosion would be no less alarming to me were it wholly composed of folks with white skin and pink elbows. But I fear there is no way I can convince you of that, given

---

1. The charge of neocolonialism or Western imperialism is addressed in chapter 23.

my race's shameful record of racism. Perhaps we whites of the North countries should say nothing about population growth in Africa, Asia, and Latin America."

"But," begins Senator Straight, "such cowardly silence would place not *seeming* to be racist ahead of not being racist. One of the most condescending things, and thus one of the most racist things, that can be done to the nations of the South is this: ask of them something less than their critical share of responsibility for building a humane global future."

"Nothing you say," says Senator See, "denies my prior point. It is the nations of the South, thus it is people of color, whose fertility is said to be 'too high.' "

"That," says Senator Straight, "is a truth with at least two sides. It is people of color who would bear the greatest share, by far, of the indescribable tragedy that massive overpopulation would bring. Glimpses of that future can already be seen.

"Thus more and more governments of the developing nations are attempting to lower birth rates. Their requests for family planning aid already exceed what the United States and other rich nations are thus far willing to give. And please know that the people in the developing world are increasingly concerned about their demographic future."

"The rich of the North countries are also at risk," answers Senator See. "Massive overpopulation would mean plenty of pain for everyone."

"Indeed it would," agrees Senator Straight, "which brings me to my main point. There are some issues so vital to the future of all humankind that we dare not deal with them except — at long, long last — simply as fellow human beings. If we are still unable to see beyond racial, religious, and ethnic differences in looking at those vital issues, there really is no hope for humankind."

PART II

RESOLVING THE CRISIS:

AN ETHICAL ENTERPRISE

CHAPTER SEVEN

AVOID A FANCIFUL STRATEGY

Must there be a "strategy" at all? Consider these happy words:

> If overpopulation is so great a threat, each individual couple,
> acting entirely on their own, will sufficiently alter their own
> reproductive behavior.

Why is that assertion not nearly as true as it is appealing? One reason is the contextual picture it paints. It portrays the individual couple as two equally empowered partners who mutually make their reproductive decisions in basic autonomy from the rest of society.

The problem with that picture is that it hides more reality than it shows. In much of the world, a woman has little if any effective veto power over a man's desire for more offspring. And even where she does, the couple is far from being autonomous. Instead, an abundance of social pressure — extended family, religious, cultural, economic, and/or other — has much to say about how many children the man or woman should, or must, have.

Does the reality of social pressure mean that there is no actual sphere of individual reproductive choice? Of course not. Nor does it mean that preserving that sphere is ethically unimportant! What it does say is that reproductive decision-making is an often mysterious combination of both social and individual choice.

What are patriarchs, mothers-in-law, neighbors, unspoken tradition, and household economics still telling couples in much of the world? Fertility remains high in most developing nations mainly because the sum of social forces within each of those nations is, despite the threat of over-population, still decidedly pronatalist — meaning that, on balance, those forces still encourage large rather than small families.

View strong pronatalist pressure through the lens of projected population growth in already poverty-stricken nations and a clear truth emerges: in nations where fertility remains high, the urgent need to counter the pronatalist bias of social forces is a need for governmental action.

As was noted near the end of chapter 3, the real questions are what kind or kinds of state action and when. Given the importance of honoring individual freedom and dignity, such questions cannot be easy ones.

A FAVORITE FANCIFUL STRATEGY

One bad thing about tough ethical questions is that they tend to attract ethically easy answers. The favorite fanciful solution to the population crisis has long been, and in some quarters may still be, something like this:

> Industrialization and its resultant affluence and modernization were what eventually caused fertility rates to decline so greatly in the now developed nations. Thus the most effective and humane way to achieve sufficiently low fertility in today's developing nations is to try to mimic the "demographic transition" that occurred in the Western world. First raise living standards with the help of general economic development aid, foreign investment, and/or favorable trade. Then watch birth rates fall more or less "naturally" to the extent needed.

The above approach and its perfect slogan, "Development is the best contraceptive," dominated Third World thinking at the 1974 World Population Conference in Bucharest, Romania. Unsurprisingly, both its longstanding appeal to many Western liberals and its new appeal to some Western conservatives cheerfully survive its decreasing credibility in the Third World itself. Which proves that being there is sometimes the best reality therapy.

The "development first" solution might have been a viable one for today's developing nations in, say, 1900, when the world's population was roughly a third what it is now. Reliance upon it today would soon set a world's record for Too Little Too Late,[1] for at least two reasons.

First, in most of today's "developing nations" the speed and magnitude of population growth is doing its part to prevent anything approaching the general economic development that could much affect fertility. With population continuing to grow greatly, there is no realistic general development aid, trade, and investment scenario that would generate the prosperity that might yield widespread low fertility within any nondistant future. For most population-exploding nations, the road to general economic development has thus become a demographic dead-end street. Untenably high fertility is itself impeding what was once its most touted cure.

Second, even were the developing world's economic horizons sunny bright for the next few decades, it would be folly to rely upon the first-raise-living-standards route toward low fertility in those critical years. At least for the generation in which they occur (if they finally do occur), higher income levels are a highly unreliable contraceptive. They may not be followed by substantial decreases in fertility anytime soon thereafter or remotely so.

Thus, though it has long enjoyed per capita incomes in excess of three times that of India, Syria still has a fertility rate of nearly six children per woman. Even Saudi Arabia's per capita income of almost $8,000 (about 25 times India's) accompanies a 5.5-children fertility rate.

In addition, economic progress and its accompanying optimism often encourage a high birth rate for quite some time. The post-World-War-II U.S. baby boom thrived, in affluent suburbia and elsewhere, amidst rising per capita income. Citing similar occurrences in a variety of cultural settings, anthropologist Virginia Abernethy argues that this "euphoria effect" (higher fertility from actual or expected economic gains) is the usual rule, not the exception.[2]

Whether or not one fully accepts Dr. Abernethy's thesis, this truth is clear enough: general economic development is *not* a necessary condition for major reductions in fertility. Fertility began to decline over a century

---

1. Is improving the status of women, the strategy most emphasized at the 1994 Cairo Conference, also a too-little-too-late fanciful approach? Chapters 14, 15, and 16 attempt an honestly balanced answer.

2. See Virginia D. Abernethy, *Population Politics: The Choices That Shape Our Future* (New York: Plenum Press, 1993).

ago even in parts of Europe where people were poor, rural, and illiterate. Likewise, recent evidence from Sri Lanka (though literacy is high, annual per capita income is still only about $600; fertility is now 2.3 children per woman) and from rural Thailand confirms what we should intuitively expect: modest economic circumstances need not prevent peoples from choosing to have markedly fewer children than did their parents.

AN EXCUSE FOR NOT SHARING?

The above comments do not say that development has become an unimportant goal. Nor, by the way, is development irrelevant to fertility. A number of endeavors recommended later in this book include or involve particular aspects of economic development that are or may be conducive to fertility decline.

What the prior section was saying with respect to most high-fertility nations is this: if their governments attempt general economic development in lieu of developing an adequate set of policies and programs for attaining low fertility, they will most probably reach neither goal.

Do rich nations have a moral duty to help low-income nations move toward sustainable economic well-being? As will be seen in later chapters, this book's answer is yes.

Though outside aid can and should play only a minor and subordinate role, the need for foreign economic aid is not going to vanish anytime soon. If such aid respects both the ecology and indigenous culture, if it is directed more toward ordinary people than to privileged elites, and if it avoids raising false hopes and stifling local initiative, it can do genuine good.

But here is an unhappy if. If a population-exploding nation lacks an adequate strategy for attaining low fertility, economic aid is good at making a bad situation worse. By supporting the recipient government's dangerously false complacency, the aid is apt to cause far more tragedy than it alleviates.

Thus there is little sense or morality in the current U.S. practice of devoting only about three to five percent of its aidgiving to family planning and related efforts. Recommendation: helping to enable fertility decline should be a primary emphasis in every donor nation's aidgiving.

The positive reason for that recommendation ought to be obvious. In fast-growing, poverty-stricken nations, early attainment of low fertility is a key to maximizing the chances for success of all other efforts toward sustainable well-being.

As if that were not reason enough, there is another benefit whose indirectness is exceeded only by its potential importance. The more expeditiously the world's needy nations progress to low fertility, the less excuse the world's rich nations will have for avoiding the question of international economic justice.

CHAPTER EIGHT

IS THE
URGENCY REAL?

You are head of state of a nation where poverty is widespread and fertility is high. How do you and your government choose an adequate strategy for enabling an end to your nation's population explosion?

You cannot begin to judge the adequacy of a proposed strategy unless you have some idea of the urgency of the problem. Hence this time-conscious question: to what extent is the need for low fertility an urgent one?

Though urgency varies from nation to nation, there is some "timely" demographic data that ought to be known by any present nation whose fertility remains high. To see the data with an understanding eye, we must first endure a couple of strange-sounding concepts that demographers use.

The first one is "replacement fertility" or "replacement rate." It is the number of living children per woman that every generation of women would bear if a population (with an unchanging death rate and zero migration) is perpetually to "replace itself." In possibly plainer English, it is the number of children per woman that, if adhered to long enough, would eventually yield long-term "static equilibrium" — eventual "zero population growth (ZPG)."

Even as pure theory, replacement fertility does not imply that each woman would or should bear the same number of children. It serves, instead, as a valuable benchmark concerning the average number of children born to women in their lifetime.

In a society without high mortality and with replacement fertility, the average number of children per woman would be a small fraction above two. The precise requisite fraction, which takes into account male-female birth ratios and premenopause female mortality, varies from nation to nation and from time to time. No one, of course, expects any society's actual fertility to equal that society's replacement fertility with exactitude.

DEMOGRAPHIC MOMENTUM

You met the other strange concept, "demographic momentum," in chapter 1. Or is it so strange? If you drive a car, you feel your car's momentum every time you apply the brakes. Even if you hit the brake pedal with all your might to spare a pedestrian, momentum carries the car forward for a possibly tragic distance.

But how is a fast-growing population like a speeding car? Unsurprisingly, a society where couples generally have more than two children will have a high proportion of young people. As suggested in chapter 1, that extra supply of future parents is a population explosion's "momentum."

How does demographic momentum work? If high fertility falls to replacement rate, a society has thereby "fully applied the brakes" to its population explosion. As with a braking car, however, momentum impedes the brakes' effect. Though women would then be bearing children at rates yielding a lifetime average of only about two per woman, there are so many youngsters slated for future parenthood (and so many young people just starting to have children) that the population explosion would "skid forward" for some time — despite the replacement fertility brakes.

But there is a momentous difference. Unlike a car, whose momentum after braking lasts for just seconds, the momentum of a high proportion of young people will cause population to keep growing for decades after fertility has declined to about two children per woman.

How great is that "population momentum" in nations where fertility now averages three or more children per woman? With the help of some demographers at the World Bank, we can get an answer by assuming a demographic miracle.

Pretend that all the world's high-fertility nations had suddenly achieved replacement rate in 1990. Despite that superhuman event, the population of each such nation would, thanks to demographic momentum, in most cases continue to grow for 50 to 70 years. And before each such nation's population stabilized at zero growth, it would have increased by, depending upon the nation, roughly 20 to 80 percent.[1]

---

1. See Eduard Bos, My T. Vu, Ernest Massiah, and Rodolfo A. Bulatao, *World Population Projections, 1994-95 Edition* (Baltimore: The Johns Hopkins University Press, published for the World Bank, 1994), pp. 38–41.

For example, Tanzania's 1990 population of about 25 million would keep growing until it eventually reaches about 38 million. For another, India's 1990 population of about 850 million persons would keep growing until it eventually reaches almost 1.2 billion. Even if replacement fertility had been permanently attained in 1990.[2]

URGENCY?

Large as they are, the projected population increases yielded by the replacement-rate-by-1990 fictional scenario are dwarfed by their counterparts from a more real-world scenario of future fertility. How much greater are realistically projected increases likely to be? The abstract answer is this: *the longer high-fertility nations delay in reaching replacement rate, the more their projected populations will exceed those of the replacement-rate-by-1990 scenario.*

Does so abstract an answer spell genuine urgency? The 1994 World Bank standard population projections provide the concreteness to help us tell. Without purporting to predict, those projections reflect the Bank's assumptions concerning how soon each nation will approximate replacement fertility. For Tanzania (present fertility about six children), the assumed year that replacement rate is reached is 2035; for the Philippines, it is the year 2020. For India and Bangladesh, it is 2010. And so forth.[3]

Were those and similarly serene assumptions of fertility decline to come true, how much would various nations' recent populations increase before they eventually stopped growing? Brace yourself for the following examples, which we can call "Exhibit A."

Egypt, Malaysia, and Mexico would more than double their 1990 populations. India's 1990 population would also more than double to almost 1.9 billion persons, while Nicaragua's would be tripling. Bangladesh and the Philippines would increase to, respectively, 2.4 and 2.8 times their 1990 numbers. Pakistan, when it numbered about 400 million persons, would be 3.6 times as populous as in 1990. Nigeria would

---

2. How nations might prevent some of their momentum-caused population growth is looked at in chapter 25.
3. For the assumed year of reaching replacement rate for each of the world's nations, see Bos et al., *Projections,* pp. 38–41.

grow to four times, and Iraq and Sudan would each grow to about 4.3 times, 1990 figures. Tanzania's population would be about 4.8 times, and Zaire's would be 5.5 times, that of 1990. Somalia's and Côte d'Ivoire's would be about six times 1990 numbers. A few African nations, Uganda and Ethiopia among them, are projected either to reach or to exceed seven times their 1990 populations.[4]

The above and most other nations expecting comparable population gains are, both ecologically and economically, already living on terribly precarious ground. Whether their projected population multiples are two, three, four, or higher, absent faster fertility decline the likely future facing the people of most such nations can only be characterized as indescribably grim.

That future is not far away. Over half of the population growth projected by the World Bank is expected to occur within the next four decades. Much of the increase will happen within the next two.

The World Bank's projections are hostage to a critical negative assumption. They assume the nonoccurrence of "overshoot and collapse." The projections assume that the coming decades of explosive population growth will not cause or contribute to some massive agricultural, environmental, or other catastrophe that would brutally end the population explosion by inflicting a deluge of death.

Clearly, that assumption could prove to be tragically false. Worldwatch Institute's Lester Brown has called projected population gains like those in Exhibit A "unrealistic for the simple reason that life-support systems will begin to collapse long before the additional numbers materialize." Where those systems are already disintegrating, such projections, says Brown, "can only be described as projections of disaster."

URGENCY INTENSIFIED

Unfortunately, there is more bad news. Astonishing though they be, Exhibit A's examples of projected population gains are part of a complete set of country-by-country projections from the World Bank

---

4. For a full by-country listing of projected growth multiples, see ibid.

that add up to an eventual world population of only about 11.5 billion.[5]

Why would I say "only" and "11.5 billion" in the same breath? Because, absent disastrous death rates, even as high a figure as 12 billion is, in my judgment, at the *low* end of the range of likely future world population if most of the world's nations continue what chapter 1 called the Business as Usual Scenario.

If most of the world's nations keep doing as little as most are now doing about the world population crisis, absent soaring mortality world population in 2100 or so is as likely to number about 17 billion as about 11.5 billion. In other words, unless the Business as Usual Scenario soon moves much closer to the Serious Strategy Scenario, the Bank's assumed pace of fertility decline most probably errs on the optimistic, meaning the early, side.[6]

Thus we must look — please do look — at the prior section's Exhibit A examples of the Bank's projected population gains (e.g., from 1990 India will more than double, Pakistan will more than triple) in an even more somber light. Though soaring mortality could cruelly prevent their fruition, those projected gains are most probably a gross understatement of the perilously steep population growth path facing the developing world if the Business as Usual Scenario prevails.

If the prior sentence does not spell urgency, the word has no place in our or in any language. The need for nations to act in earnest now — so as to greatly mitigate the enormity, and thus to reduce the consequent harms and risks, of future population growth — is not a mere policy preference. It is an ethical imperative.

It is by that imperative, and by the need to respect human dignity in choice of means as well, that present and proposed population policies must be judged. The recommendations in ensuing chapters are no exception.

---

5. The Bank projects that world population will almost reach 11 billion by 2100 and later stop growing at almost 11.5 billion. See ibid., 5 and 38.

6. However, under the Business as Usual Scenario, fertility could decline at the Bank's assumed pace for a reason that is anything but happy. With or without a great surge in death rates, conditions could become so inhumanly miserable that fertility would fall to replacement or subreplacement because of people's sheer despair. Though that fertility response is unlikely (misery has not brought Ethiopia's or Somalia's fertility to below six children per woman), it is — except for soaring mortality itself — the likeliest way that world population might not exceed 11.5 billion under the Business as Usual Scenario. Moral: humanity must avoid that scenario.

DIRECT MEANS:

FAMILY PLANNING AND POPULATION EDUCATION

CHAPTER NINE

ADEQUATE SUPPORT OF FAMILY PLANNING: NEEDED NONPANACEA

"When you come back, don't forget to bring *toötimarau*," Chomoshico called to me. I was leaving [a] Shipibo Indian village . . . in the Peruvian Amazon, where I had been doing medical research. Chomoshico . . . already had seven living children. Neither she nor her husband wants more. . . .

Toötimarau means "medicine to keep from being pregnant" . . . . I could informally provide other kinds of medical care, [but] I could not arrange to bring her birth control without risking reprisals from politicians who are against it. The Shipibo have been asking me for *toötimarau* for more than twenty-five years, but I haven't been able to arrange any yet. I can only refer them to a Peruvian doctor in Pucallpa, many days away by canoe. Most can never get there. The men even pull me aside to ask if I know about an operation to "fix" men — vasectomy — and, again, I tell them the name of my medical colleague in Pucallpa.

In the same village, a few weeks before, a young girl had died on her thirteenth birthday trying to give birth to twins.

> — Warren M. Hern, M.D., "Family Planning, Amazon Style"[1]

What — besides being one more way for governments and private organizations to meddle and spend money — is a family planning program? More thoughtfully, what would be the right family planning program in a high-fertility nation in today's endangered world?

---

1. *Natural History*, Vol. 101, No. 12 (December 1992), p. 31.

Here is an honest answer that might seem to say nothing: an appropriate program would have several components (listed below) and would vary from family planning programs in other nations according to the culture, attitudes, practices, and needs of the people it sought to serve.[2] From that seeming nonanswer comes a cardinal principle. Although affluent nations should offer financial assistance and professional expertise, they must not try to encroach. The program and the managing of it are the province of each developing nation, subject to a basic imperative: international norms of human rights must be observed — thus reproductive coercion must be avoided.

Diversity should also exist well below the national level. A nation's family planning program (or programs) needs to train and employ local people and be as decentralized and unbureaucratic as possible. It should and can even be nonarrogant, people-friendly, open to goal-consistent opportunities to share tasks with private groups, and solicitous of and responsive to popular local input.

COMPONENTS

Despite the need for national and local variation, some further guidelines are possible. An adequate family planning program in a high-fertility nation in the years ahead would almost surely do the following:[3]

1. Make available a reasonably diverse set of highly reliable contraceptive options, at readily affordable cost (or at no cost) to persons who wish to control their reproduction.

2. Provide, teach, and augment. Provide people with the basic facts (relative safety, effectiveness,

---

2. Concerning the political dimensions of family planning policies, see Jason L. Finkle and C. Alison McIntosh, eds., *The New Politics of Population: Conflict and Consensus in Family Planning* (New York: The Population Council, 1994) and sources cited therein.

3. For detailed consideration of the above and numerous other relevant matters, see the following indispensable resource: Robert J. Lapham and George B. Simmons, eds., *Organizing for Effective Family Planning Programs* (Washington, D.C.: National Academy Press, 1987). See also Bryant Robey, Phyllis Tilson Piotrow, and Cynthia Salter, "Family Planning Lessons and Challenges: Making Programs Work," *Population Reports*, Series J, No. 40 (Baltimore: Population Information Program, The Johns Hopkins University, August 1994). And see Chapter VII in the 1994 Cairo Conference's *Programme of Action of the International Conference on Population and Development* (New York: United Nations, 1994).

reversibility or nonreversibility) regarding each available option. If a chosen option is to be administered by the user, teach its proper use. Where a birth control method may yield side effects or poses any health risk, augment user education with appropriate medical backup as needed.[4]

3. Appropriate to the user's chosen method, renew supportive contact with her or him on a sufficiently frequent basis.

4. Educate the citizenry concerning the health and other personal benefits of birth spacing and lower fertility.

5. Provide for reasonable accountability within the program and for ongoing general evaluation by qualified persons independent of the program's management.[5]

6. See that women are fully and fairly represented at all levels of policy formulation and application.

UNMET NEED

Are family planning programs in the developing nations adequate for present needs? The situation varies from those nations who have very good programs to those that have no program at all. Though the

---

4. Competent family planning programs offer no method of birth control that subjects the typical user to a risk of injury or of death whose chances approach the corresponding risk posed to a woman by childbirth itself. But some birth control methods are medically inadvisable for some individuals, thus necessitating the availability of alternative choices. Further cautions apply postpartum and during lactation.

Given the acute shortage of medical services in much of the Third World, the task of medical backup is not an easy one. With prudent use of well-trained paramedics (which has proved highly successful) and with increased international assistance, the task need not be an impossible one. The same is true of sorely needed efforts to end high maternal and child mortality.

5. See pp. 694–96 and, among others, chapters 7–11, 13, and 14 in Lapham and Simmons, *Organizing*. And see Pamela Lynam, Leslie McNeil Rabinovitz, and Mofoluke Shobowale, "Using Self-Assessment to Improve the Quality of Family Planning Clinic Services," *Studies in Family Planning*, Vol. 24, No. 4 (July/August 1993), pp. 252–60, and Judith Bruce, "Fundamental Elements of the Quality of Care: A Simple Framework," *Studies in Family Planning*, Vol. 21, No. 2 (March/April 1990), pp. 61–91.

picture has been improving in many developing nations, most have programs that, even for today's populations, are severely underfunded.[6]

In most developing nations, a substantial proportion of couples (and in some countries a large majority) still lack access to, or cannot afford, reasonably safe and effective means of birth control.[7] In 14 of 38 surveyed nations, less than half the current need for family planning services was being met.[8] For the developing nations as a whole, excluding China, a middle-of-the-road estimate is that roughly one in five married women of reproductive age are not using birth control even though they do not currently wish to become pregnant.[9]

LOOKING AHEAD

Unless they are enabled to grow greatly, most family planning programs will fall much farther short of meeting tomorrow's need than they now fall short of meeting today's. From 1995 to 2010 the number of reproductive-age women in the developing world will increase by more than 350 million. Within that time an additional 125 million married or cohabiting couples in developing nations will need contraception — even if current rates of use remain unchanged.[10]

6. See John A. Ross, W. Parker Mauldin, Steven R. Green, and E. Romana Cooke, *Family Planning and Child Survival Programs as Assessed in 1991* (New York: The Population Council, 1992).

7. For a country-by-country assessment, see John A. Ross, W. Parker Mauldin, and Vincent C. Miller, *Family Planning and Population: A Compendium of Statistics* (New York: The Population Council, 1993), pp. 79–82, and Population Crisis Committee (now Population Action International), "Access to Affordable Contraception," *1991 Report on World Progress Towards Population Stabilization* (Washington, D.C.: 1991).

In many countries the greatest lack of access may well be people's lack of knowledge about family planning services. See John Bongaarts and Judith Bruce, "The Causes of Unmet Need for Contraception and the Social Content of Services," *Studies in Family Planning*, Vol. 26, No. 2 (March/April 1995), pp. 57–75. In some nations fewer than 40 percent of surveyed married women could even supply the name of any modern family planning method. In Nigeria, only 44 percent of married women were able to recognize any method, modern or traditional, even after hearing its popular name. Bryant Robey, Shea O. Rutstein, Leo Morris, and Richard Blackburn, "The Reproductive Revolution: New Survey Findings," *Population Reports*, Series M, Number 11 (Baltimore: Population Information Program, The Johns Hopkins University, December 1992), p. 15, citing Demographic and Health Surveys (DHS) reports.

8. Robey et al., "New Survey Findings," p. 24. See also Charles F. Westoff and Luis Hernando Ochoa, "Unmet Need and the Demand for Family Planning," *DHS Comparative Studies No. 5* (July 1991).

9. Compare John Bongaarts, "The KAP-Gap and the Unmet Need for Contraception," *Population and Development Review*, Vol.17, No. 2 (June 1991) (17 percent of reproductive-age married women for selected countries) with Robey et al., "New Survey Findings," p. 23 (extrapolating survey data to yield an estimated 120 million [or about 23 percent of probably about 520 million reproductive-age] married women). Different formulae for computing unmet need make up most of the disparity.

10. For estimated 1995-2010 populations of reproductive-age women and proportions married or otherwise in union, I am indebted to Mary Beth Weinberger at the UN Population Division and W. Parker Mauldin at the Population Council. For contraceptive usage and other data, see *Contraceptive Use and Commodity Costs in Developing Countries, 1994-2005*, Technical Report No. 18 (New York: United Nations Population Fund, 1994).

But, because population and the desire for contraception are both growing, *an unchanged proportion of contraceptive users would mean a large increase in the absolute number of persons who want contraception but are denied access to it. It would also mean seeing the population explosion continue full blast — toward, if such madness were to continue and death rates were somehow to allow, numbers far higher than even chapter 1's Business as Usual Scenario.*

In order for world population to stop growing at about nine billion people, it is probable that by the early 21st century 70 to 75 percent of all sexually active persons would need to be using birth control. That may well require a more than 300 million increase in family planning users in developing nations, from perhaps 470 million couples and other users in 1995 to perhaps 800 million within about the next 15 years.[11]

Achieving those goals would almost surely require other endeavors (see later chapters of this book) in addition to family planning programs. But one must assume the sufficient occurrence of such other endeavors in order to estimate family planning's part of the cost of a serious effort at preventing massive overpopulation.

DOLLARS AND SENSE

Family planning in the developing world currently costs about $5 to $6 billion, which averages about $12 to $13 per user, per year. Probably $3.5 to $4 billion of that estimated annual cost is paid for by developing-country governments for programs in their own countries, the largest expenditures being by the two giant nations, China and India.

Users themselves likely pay one-half to one billion dollars per year in fees and contraceptive purchases. The balance, which probably exceeds a billion dollars per year, represents the combined contributions of the world's affluent-nation governments and private international donors.

Recall this chapter's earlier listed components of an adequate family

---

11. No wonder that "both the developed and the developing countries need to reorder their priorities. Dramatic increases in population assistance by the donor countries must be accompanied by significantly increased political and financial commitments by the developing countries. A quantum increase in population funding by the world community is essential to achieve both universal access to voluntary family planning and early population stabilization." Quoted words from Shanti R. Conly and J. Joseph Speidel, *Global Population Assistance: A Report Card on the Major Donor Countries* (Washington, D.C.: Population Action International, 1993), p. 40.

planning program. Were humankind kind enough and sensible enough to do so, what would it cost in the year 2010 to provide up to 800 million users in the developing nations with family planning services of a quality that would pass fair-minded scrutiny?

Because no one knows for sure, I am suspicious of all cost estimates, including my own. But, with heavy reliance upon cost analyses by others, my own best guess is this: adequate family planning programs throughout the developing world would cost, in 1995 dollars, about $14.5 billion, or (if serving 800 million users) an average of about $18 per user, per year, by the year 2010 or soon thereafter.[12]

Reaching that spending level for family planning should mean a phased-in increase of roughly $9 billion above today's annual expenditure level. That recommended upward spending curve mainly reflects three imperatives: to meet today's large unmet need, to meet tomorrow's far greater need (a possible 70 percent increase in users), and to improve program quality.

Unless the world's affluent nations care nothing about the future or about justice, they should together contribute at least $7 billion of the likely needed $14 to $15 billion annual expenditure level. What would be a fair U.S. share? Would $2.5 billion be too much — or too little?

However the costs are divided, neither donor nations nor population-exploding nations should wait even one year to start a very brisk increase in their funding. Starting now is the way to address present needs and to be ready to offer quality services to the many more millions of people who will need family planning.[13] With sufficient will and focus, within three years those services could be available to all households wishing them.

---

12. For an extensive bibliography, survey of the prior literature, and discussion of the cost picture, see Robert E. Lande and Judith S. Geller, "Paying for Family Planning," *Population Reports*, Series J, Number 39 (Baltimore: Population Information Program, The Johns Hopkins University, November 1991). An essential update, prepared for the Cairo Conference, is *Background Note on the Resource Requirements for Population Programmes in the Years 2000-2015* (New York: United Nations Population Fund, July 13, 1994), which also notes other later sources. I thank Stan Bernstein at the UN Population Fund for his generous help in explaining aspects of the *Background Note*.

Partly because they include medical backup for contraceptive services, my cost guesstimates for family planning are higher than the family planning component of the Cairo proposals. Mainly because I did not include additional costs for other reproductive health efforts endorsed at Cairo, my dollar amounts for 2010 are lower than Cairo's total program package for that year. My figures omitted those vital endeavors only because I was trying to state the likely cost of quality family planning services themselves. That attempt is in no way meant to slight the importance of integrating family planning with other reproductive and general health services.

13. Another good reason for total funding to increase faster than expected gains in number of users is to enable the population education endeavors outlined in chapter 11.

EFFECTIVENESS

Considering how insufficient funding has usually been, how politically, ethically, and emotionally sensitive are their concerns, how much they have had to learn by trial and error, and how strong are cultural and other pressures to have large families, one might expect little or no fertility decline from family planning programs thus far. Instead, their degree of success, though highly variable and in most developing nations far from complete, has been remarkable — and should convince anyone of their actual and potential importance.[14]

Good programs can affect fertility even when conditions would seem to make that impossible. An example is Bangladesh. "It is one of the poorest countries in the world, with high illiteracy rates, low status for women, . . . high dependency on families — especially sons — for physical and economic security, and high infant and child mortality."[15] Yet with the help of a well-regarded family planning program, between 1970 and 1989 contraceptive use in Bangladesh increased from only 3 percent to over 30 percent, and fertility fell from almost seven to about five children per woman.[16]

But an already suggested caution bears repeating: family planning programs are not panaceas. In most cases, even the best possible program probably will not, by itself, cause a nation's high fertility rate to decline sufficiently.

Nonetheless, adequate support of family planning is an essential part of any feasible, credible strategy to end the population explosion before pandemic tragedy prevails. The sufficient supply of culturally attuned and human-dignity-respecting family planning programs would prevent many millions of unintended pregnancies each year (thereby also preventing millions of abortions each year).

---

14. The literature reporting, analyzing, and disputing the effects of family planning is extensive. For a very useful bibliography, a middle-of-the-road perspective, and a well-balanced summation of pertinent studies and views, see Robert J. Lapham and W. Parker Mauldin, "The Effects of Family Planning on Fertility: Research Findings," in Lapham and Simmons, *Organizing*, pp. 647–80. Among excellent later sources are John Bongaarts, W. Parker Mauldin, and James F. Phillips, "Demographic Impact of Family Planning Programs," *Studies in Family Planning*, Vol. 21, No. 6 (November/December 1990), pp. 299–310, and James F. Phillips and John A. Ross, eds., *Family Planning Programmes and Fertility* (Oxford: Clarendon Press, 1992).

15. Ronald Freedman and Ann K. Blanc, "Fertility Transition: An Update," *International Family Planning Perspectives*, Vol. 18, No. 2 (June 1992), pp. 44, 46.

16. Ibid. See also "Fertility Decline in Bangladesh: An Emerging Family Planning Success Story," *Asia-Pacific Population & Policy*, March 1992.

FUTURE FERTILITY EFFECTS

Widespread availability of family planning services can lower fertility substantially, sometimes even dramatically. Since the results would vary from nation to nation, let us look at the big picture.

Assume that for the developing world, excluding China, the average proportion of married women currently wishing to avoid pregnancy but not protected by birth control is about 20 percent (as noted earlier, a middle-of-the-road estimate). Were a good choice of options to be made sufficiently available and affordable, it is reasonable to believe that something like 60 to 65 percent of those current nonusers would become users of family planning.[17]

In other words, it is probable that in the non-China developing world an additional 12 to 13 percent of reproductive-age married (or otherwise cohabiting) women or their spouses would be using some means of contraception. Effect on total fertility? Demographers tell us that a 15 percent increase in "contraceptive prevalence" normally causes a fertility decline of about one child per woman.

Still with respect to the non-China developing world considered as a whole, the above range of increased contraception would mean a probable decrease from today's average fertility of about four children per woman to perhaps 3.1 to 3.3 children per woman. If China's fertility remained at its currently estimated rate of about two children per woman, fertility for the entire developing world would average almost or about three children per woman.[18]

But that is only part of the potential story. The above outcome does not depend upon a decrease in the number of children that couples would

---

17. Some would become users solely to delay becoming pregnant; others would do so with the intent not to have more children. There is no assumption that most of the latter group has made "definite, unambiguous decisions." Rather, most are apt to be "under cross-pressures between traditional values and institutions and new realities and ideas. A good family planning information and service program helps to crystallize latent demand for contraception by emphasizing the usefulness and legitimacy of family planning as a partial solution for the problems of families." Ronald Freedman, "Family Planning Programs in the Third World," in *The Annals of the American Academy of Political and Social Science*, Vol. 510 (July 1990), pp. 33, 41.

18. A somewhat similar scenario was offered in Steven W. Sinding, "Getting to Replacement: Bridging the Gap Between Individual Rights and Demographic Goals," paper presented at IPPF Family Planning Congress, October 23–25, 1992, Delhi, India.

hope to have.[19] Yet even under the status quo, desired family size has been declining somewhat.[20] Plus there are (see later chapters) various social reforms and other endeavors that, without reproductive coercion, could encourage smaller family-size preferences. In order for those preferences to result in actually lower fertility as soon and as fully as feasible, family planning services need to be widely available.[21]

Thus, if a high-fertility nation combines (1) a sufficient mix of means to encourage lower fertility preferences with (2) an ample supply of family planning services, what does that nation have? It has, by far, its best chance — in most cases, its only credible chance — of humanely reaching low fertility soon enough to avoid massive tragedy.

DIRECT LIFESAVING EFFECTS

Surely family planning services are best delivered along with reproductive and general health care. The Cairo Conference's *Programme of Action* rightly urges major commitments in both the latter areas, including greater efforts to prevent acquired immunodeficiency syndrome (AIDS). The vital importance of those commitments should not cause us to ignore the potential lifesaving effects from family planning services themselves.

A typical estimate is that about half a million women in developing nations die each year from complications of pregnancy, childbirth, and attempted abortion. Even larger numbers suffer nonfatal but serious complications, a travail that leaves many women with permanent disabilities that are painful, stigmatizing, or both.

Though only part of the answer, family planning would markedly reduce the number of women who are killed or injured from the above causes. Some authorities believe that as many as 200,000 maternal deaths

---

19. In his "Desired Fertility and the Impact of Population Policies," *Population and Development Review*, Vol. 20, No. 1 (March 1994), pp. 1–55, Lant H. Pritchett argues that increased contraceptive prevalence will not result in substantial fertility decline unless family-size preferences also fall substantially. For criticisms of Pritchett's article and his reply, see "The Impact of Population Policies: An Exchange," *Population and Development Review*, Vol. 20, No. 3 (September 1994), pp. 611–30.

20. See Charles F. Westoff, "Reproductive Preferences: A Comparative View," *DHS Comparative Studies No. 3* (February 1991).

21. Widespread availability of quality family planning services may itself strengthen couples' desire to plan small families.

in the developing world could be prevented each year with widely available and well-promoted family planning programs.[22]

Those same efforts would also save the lives and improve the health of infants and young children — and would do so on an even larger scale. A major contributor to that happy outcome is the encouragement and enabling of adequate child spacing.

For example, in many developing nations children born less than 18 months after the birth of a sibling are about twice as likely to die as those born after a two-year or longer interval.[23] The probable main reason, a cruelty to both mother and child, is "maternal depletion": a temporary weakening of the mother's ability to nurture the fetus and, in due course, the newborn child. By helping parents adequately space their next pregnancy, and by helping young women defer their first pregnancy until the much safer post-teen years, widespread use of family planning in the developing world would be saving the lives or enhancing the health of millions of young people each year.[24]

For the above and other good reasons, the United Nations Children's Fund (UNICEF), whose business is protecting children, has said this: "Family planning could bring more benefits to more people at less cost than any other single 'technology' now available to the human race."[25]

Given the benefits and low cost of family planning, to deny it sufficient funding would be ethically hard to defend even were there no threat of massively tragic overpopulation. With that threat being all too real, the paucity of funding must be called just what it is: evil madness.

But no enterprise is so beneficial as to be free of ethical issues. Hence the next two chapters.

---

22. See Ward Rinehart, Adrienne Kols, and Sidney H. Moore, "Healthier Mothers and Children Through Family Planning," *Population Reports*, Series I, Number 27 (Baltimore: Population Information Program, The Johns Hopkins University, May-June 1984). See also United Nations Population Fund, *The State of World Population, 1992*, p. 13.

23. See John Hobcraft, "Child Spacing and Child Mortality," in *DHS World Conference Proceedings*, Vol. 2, 1991, p. 1159.

24. Another vital help, if modernity does not abolish all past wisdom, is for babies to receive at least several months of breastfeeding.

As was also recognized at the Cairo Conference, family planning services can play a worthy role in helping to prevent AIDS and other sexually transmitted diseases.

25. UNICEF, *The State of the World's Children, 1992* (Oxford University Press), p. 58.

CHAPTER TEN

FAMILY PLANNING PROGRAMS: NEEDED FOR FREEDOM?

[B]irth control most often came up when women asked if I knew how some people managed to have only one or two children. Every woman I spoke to, with one exception, wanted reliable information about how to control their own fertility. The fact that most women had been forced to have more children than they wanted was the most damning evidence of the suffering and loss of human rights experienced by peasant women under the rule both of their husbands and the political factors controlling their lives.

— Audrey Bronstein, *The Triple Struggle: Latin American Peasant Women*[1]

There isn't much understanding in some marriages. My sister has six, and another one has eight. And I said to one of them that she shouldn't have any more. And she said, "What can I do? When my husband comes home drunk, he forces me to sleep with him." And that is what happens to a lot of women.

— Words of René, a Peruvian woman, in Audrey Bronstein's interview notes[2]

Even prior to the onset of modern contraceptive technology, there were times of subreplacement fertility in much or most of Europe and North America. And virtually every known society has kept its fertility

---

1. London: WOW Campaigns Ltd., 1982, p. 260.
2. Quoted in Betsy Hartmann, *Reproductive Rights and Wrongs: The Global Politics of Population Control*, Rev. Ed. (Boston: South End Press, 1995), p. 41.

below whatever maximum number of children the average woman was biologically able to produce.

Those facts lead, we are sometimes told, to the following conclusion: "If people want to badly enough, they can and will limit their childbearing to whatever number they wish without need of modern contraception."

Notice the phrase, "want to badly enough." It should give us pause in at least two respects. First, a person's desire to have no more than x number of children may be extremely weak, extremely strong, or anywhere in between. Are persons who feel that desire with the very strongest intensity the *only* ones entitled to fulfill their wish — and to do so in a not unduly sad way?

ALTERNATIVES

"In a not unduly sad way" recalls the second and more solemn side of "If people want to badly enough." Anthropologists, historians, and other observers have noted numerous practices that societies have used or still use, which — whether or not so intended — tend to limit fertility.[3] Consider the following:

1. Delaying marriage until, say, one's late 20s, with commensurate delay of sexual intercourse.[4]

2. Lifelong or premenopausal celibacy, with commensurate sexual abstinence. (Celibacy for life or throughout their reproductive years was the fate of an estimated 60 to 65 percent of European women in parts of the 19th century.)

---

3. See Abernethy, *Population Politics*, to which my ensuing description in the main text is especially indebted. See also Norman E. Hines, *Medical History of Contraception* (New York: Schocken Books, 1970), first published in 1936; Angus McLaren, *A History of Contraception: From Antiquity to the Present Day* (Oxford: Basil Blackwell, 1990); John M. Riddle, *Contraception and Abortion from the Ancient World to the Renaissance* (Cambridge, Mass.: Harvard University Press, 1992).

4. Despite their custom of early marriage for women, some societies attempt to deter premarital sex by sewing together the sides of the vulva when or before a girl reaches puberty. That and other forms of genital mutilation in more than 20 developing nations are a tragic assault upon the sexual well-being, and often upon the health, of millions of women. See Raqiya Haji Dualeh Abdalla, *Sisters in Affliction: Circumcision and Infibulation of Women in Africa* (London: Zed Press, 1982).

3. Making wealth or income-earning success a prereq-
    uisite for marrying, thus delaying or even prohibiting
    wedlock and parenthood for those who lack the
    Midas touch. (If, in addition, custom allowed only
    one offspring to inherit the family's land, the Midas
    touch — and marriage and children — could more
    easily be denied to the others.)

4. Polyandry, practiced in Tibet, which "depresses
    fertility because many women cannot find a husband
    when several brothers share one [wife]."[5]

5. Prohibiting the remarriage, or requiring the death, of
    widows.

6. Lengthy postpartum sexual abstinence, but with the
    husband's sexual desires often met either by polygyny
    or by other authorized or tolerated encounters with
    one or more other women. (Beware of AIDS and
    other epidemic sexually transmitted diseases, espe-
    cially but not only when prostitutes are used.)

7. Periodic abstinence: "natural," though now often
    technology-aided, family planning, which tries to
    avoid intercourse on days too close to ovulation
    (which are also the days when many women
    have a greater capacity for sexual pleasure).

8. Other regimes of abstinence, including various
    tribal taboos against sex during some festive, ritual,
    or other occasions.

9. Coitus interruptus, meaning withdrawal prior to
    ejaculation; other modes of noncoital climax.

10. Breastfeeding (a happy means, but whose contracep-
    tive reliability is short-lived; see chapter 13).

---

5. Abernethy, *Population Politics*, p. 50.

11. Crude condoms and cervical plugs, homemade douches, ointments, pastes, potions, and such. *Comment:* whatever may have been their sometime successes in ye olden days, one can hardly depend upon the general availability of pre-modern or homemade methods that are relatively safe, highly reliable, not unpleasant, and affordable.

12. Failure to treat sterility.

13. Infanticide, especially female infanticide; plus a slower-acting version — failure to allow girls their fair share of food or other necessities.

14. Last, but hardly least: induced abortion.

To say that many of the above practices pose serious ethical problems would be to understate the obvious. And few of the above fourteen are likely to thrive in — for better or for worse — an increasingly modern world.

IMAGINE YOU ARE —

Whatever your reaction to part or all of the above list, I hope you will do this: imagine you are a married or otherwise cohabiting woman who is able to have children and who lacks access to modern contraception. Imagine also that you wish to have no more children, or wish never to have children, or wish to wait a few or several years before conceiving your first or next child.

Assuming that an extended or permanent absence from your husband is an unacceptable or impossible choice, what are your birth control options? Even if your husband is compulsively dedicated to honoring your wish not to conceive, you and he probably have no choice that most people would think good.

Granted, many couples find periodic abstinence (natural family planning) satisfactory. But for many others it imposes a super-Draconian discipline that harms the marriage relationship. In the mid-1960s,

Patty Crowley and her husband served on the papal study commission that, unsuccessfully, recommended change in the Catholic Church's teaching on contraception. Now an 80-year-old widow, she still recalls letters from couples "trying to do what the church said" that were "just heartbreaking."[6]

Or should you and your husband practice another method that many couples find satisfactory, coitus interruptus (pre-ejaculation withdrawal)? You must totally depend upon his absolute resolve and his flawless male timing without, of course, feeling too anxious. All that is required of him is meticulous control at the very time eros most strongly invites mental abandon and physical-spiritual union.

COSTLY CHOICES

Despite each's possible psychological costs, neither periodic abstinence nor coitus interruptus can promise most couples the reliability of the more effective modern types of contraception.[7] Nor can any other likely option that most people would deem morally and otherwise acceptable.

Alas, then, the best that likely alternatives to modern contraception offer most couples is a combination of inferior reliability and unnaturally constrained sexual relations. For most couples wishing temporarily or permanently to prevent conception, the lack of modern contraceptive options thus would mean, or does mean, profoundly less freedom.

For couples who are sure they wish no more children, lack of

---

6. Peter Steinfels, "Papal Birth-Control Letter Retains Its Grip," *New York Times*, August 1, 1993, pp. 1 and 13. See also Michael Novak, ed., *The Experience of Marriage: The Testimony of Catholic Laymen* (New York: Macmillan, 1964). For a superb study of Catholic teaching on contraception, see John T. Noonan, Jr., *Contraception: A History of Its Treatment by the Catholic Theologians and Canonists* (Cambridge, Mass.: Belknap Press, 1986).

7. "Most" is not all. Supremely motivated couples using technology-aided natural family planning may be able to achieve results approximating those of oral contraceptives. But users' need for scientifically sound training (and the frequent added need for science-based though simple paraphernalia) makes technology-aided natural family planning a modern form of birth control. More importantly, such needs also make it an approach that requires adequate funding — to which it *too* is entitled. Because different people need or want different methods of pregnancy prevention, family planning programs need to offer a wide variety of options.

Concerning coitus interruptus: though finding that "in terms of efficiency [it] cannot compete with the pill or the IUD," one survey found it "closer to the condom" and "more effective than either rhythm or the diaphragm." See Gigi Santow, "Coitus Interruptus in the Twentieth Century," *Population and Development Review*, Vol. 19, No. 4 (December 1993), pp. 767, 772, citing Michael Bracher and Gigi Santow, "Premature Discontinuation of Contraception in Australia," *Family Planning Perspectives*, Vol. 24 (1992), pp. 58–65, and also discussing and citing other studies.

access to voluntary sterilization or to an equally reliable and safe alternative exacts an immense loss of peace of mind and freedom. *No woman should have to wait until menopause to escape the likelihood and thus the fear of becoming pregnant against her wishes.* Given the medical risks of childbirth, which are very high in most developing nations, lack of affordable access to sterilization or to other highly reliable contraceptive options can rob a woman of her life or health, as well as her freedom.

COERCION ASSURED

Back to pretending (though, for many, the facts are real). You are still a married and fecund woman who lacks access to modern contraception and who wants to prevent, or to defer, conceiving your first or next child. But your husband refuses to honor or, thanks to alcohol or some other cause, cannot always be relied upon to honor your wishes. And you are unwilling or unable to leave him.

What then are your reliable and otherwise acceptable contraceptive options? Unfortunately, you probably have none.

When we worry about family planning programs' potential for coercion (as we must and will), let us not forget this: the lack of affordable access to family planning services virtually assures coercion. Today's continuing scarcity of family planning services makes sure that millions of married or cohabiting women in developing nations are denied even minimal control over their own lives. In any given year, millions of those women will experience what is, in effect, a coerced pregnancy.

TOWARD FREEDOM?

A shortage of family planning services is not nearly the only cause of women's oppression, there or here. But in most developing nations, widespread availability and affordability of those services would be a critical step in women's achieving basic rights. Not a sufficient step, but an essential one.[8]

---

8. See generally Ann P. McCauley, Bryant Robey, Ann K. Blanc, and Judith S. Geller, "Opportunities for

What, then, are nations and individuals doing when they oppose adequate funding of family planning programs? What are we doing when we thereby deny contraceptive services to great numbers of women? Intentionally or not, we are voting for reproductive coercion — and making sure such coercion continues.

MEN, AND SINGLES

In focusing upon the needs of women, I do not mean to imply that men have no desire to limit family size. Likewise as to men's shared responsibility in the matter. As one writer reminded us, perhaps futilely, over a decade ago:

> Men are the forgotten sexual partner. Nearly a half billion men have little or no access to birth control services and few contraceptive options. Despite the fact that conceiving a child always involves two people, society often ignores the interest men have in planning their families. Male contraceptives are treated as second-class birth control methods: stores persist in hiding them under counters and in many countries their advertisement is banned. Until recently, there has been little research into new male methods of birth control. With sex education usually oriented toward women, men often have a poor understanding of anatomy and contraception. And few organized family planning programs have targeted men as clients.[9]

Having myself emphasized the special poignancy of women's contraceptive needs, I seemed, even in doing that, to speak only or mostly of women who are married or otherwise cohabiting. But what of women, and men, who are single and who live outside an ongoing and mutually devoted sexual relationship? Have they little or no right to contraceptive protection if (as many naïve people, me included, still believe) sexual intercourse outside such a relationship is wrong?

Unless holier-than-thou self-righteousness is more blessed than

Women Through Reproductive Choice," *Population Reports*, Series M, No. 12 (Baltimore: Population Information Program, The Johns Hopkins University, July 1994).

9. Bruce Stokes, "Men and Family Planning," *Worldwatch Paper No. 41* (December 1980), p. 5.

compassion, no society should deny single persons access to contraception. Even apart from compassion to fellow sinners, in a very imperfect world the most ethical social policy is usually that of choosing the lesser evil.

A very imperfect world? Though it is hardly a historical first, the contemporary decline of sexual morality in the West is almost as hard to ignore as is its parade of accompanying diseases and other (fatherless families, etc.) sorrowful consequences. Unfortunately, that decline is also occurring in much of the developing world,[10] with similarly sad results.

Choosing the lesser evil? With or without a life-threatening population explosion, this has to be true: "casual" sexual intercourse protected against pregnancy is a much lesser evil than "casual" sexual intercourse unprotected against pregnancy. In fewer if stranger words, a potential child has a right not to be "casually" conceived.

AND YOUTH?

Though they know the prior statement is true, some folks fear that availability of contraception to young people is itself the culprit, or a major culprit, in the modern decline of sexual morality. The erroneousness of that fear is, however, strongly suggested by how often contraceptive use lags well behind an increased incidence of sexual activity among the young in the United States and in various other nations.[11]

(Want some likelier culprits? Start with youth-targeted and wider-audience mass media entertainment and advertising whose prevalent culture of instant gratification, sexual materialism, and frequent violence is — while continuing to brainwash us here in the West — also polluting more and more minds in the non-Western world.)

Even though contraception should not be blamed for the increased incidence of sexual activity among youth, any society has difficult and important choices to make. How early in life should persons have access to contraceptive services? And, if access is to be afforded to persons below

---

10. See, for example, Bamikale Feyisetan and Anne R. Pebley, "Premarital Sexuality in Urban Nigeria," *Studies in Family Planning*, Vol. 20, No. 6 (November/December 1989), pp. 343–54.

11. See, for example (concerning urban Nigeria), ibid., 350–52. "It is clear . . . that only a relatively small proportion of women, even in the youngest cohorts, who were sexually active before marriage reported using any means to avoid becoming pregnant." Ibid., 352.

or well below a society's age of majority, what should be the context (moral, educational, etc.) of such access?

Foolishly liberal answers to such questions could adversely affect the moral well-being of young people and of the society in general. Foolishly conservative answers would in effect ignore the abnormally high risks that teenage pregnancy poses to the life and health of mother, fetus, and child. And foolish answers from the right or the left would condemn yet more youngsters to AIDS and other sexually transmitted diseases.

So difficult is the required decision-making, and so dependent upon social and cultural conditions is the wisdom or unwisdom of any set of answers, that this is surely true: each society needs to work out its own solution to the conundrum of precocious sexual activity. Each society needs to work out its own answers to the questions of youthful access to contraception.[12]

---

12. Perhaps we in the West — who often seem not to have a clue about teaching responsible sexuality to young people — will learn from the evolving wisdom of other societies.

CHAPTER ELEVEN

POPULATION EDUCATION: FOE OF FREEDOM? AND AN INTERIM SUMMARY

In Nigeria a music video by two well-known singers asks fellow Nigerians to choose the best time to have their children. In Mexico . . . a hit television soap opera [confronts family planning issues]. In Turkey a TV spot shows a popular comedian portraying a farmer dividing the family farm among his seven children: each gets only a pot of dirt. In Zimbabwe a feature film tells the story of Rita, whose life as a student falls apart when she becomes pregnant.

— Cathleen A. Church and Judith S. Geller[1]

If the components listed in chapter 9 are any guide, the life and breath of a family planning program is education. Any good family planning program will give people the basic facts on available birth control methods. And in every appropriate instance it will teach the person how to use the method she or he chooses; what side effects, if any, to watch for; what to do if they occur; and when to seek follow-up care.

A good program will also inform people of the life-and-health risks that high fertility and inadequate spacing of pregnancies pose to mothers and children. Plus, whether or not the family planning program is given the task, the citizenry deserves to be well informed about society's need to end the population explosion.

---

1. "Lights! Camera! Action! Promoting Family Planning with TV, Video, and Film," *Population Reports,* Series J, No. 38 (Baltimore: Population Information Program, The Johns Hopkins University, December 1989), pp. 1, 11.

WHO, HOW, WHY

Population education needs to reach husbands (and other men) as well as wives (and other women) for at least two reasons. First, men's as well as women's interests are clearly at stake. Second, it is often the husband who has the dominant voice in deciding how many children the couple will plan.[2]

How can more people be reached? Even in low-income nations, both radio and television (a community TV set may serve a whole village or neighborhood) can be vital educational aids to family planning.[3] Some "visual electronic media" examples:

— In Brazil the first vasectomy promotion ever on television helped increase vasectomies at the advertised clinics by nearly 80%.

— In Turkey a multimedia campaign involving humorous spots, dramas, motivational and documentary programs on television appears to have encouraged an estimated 240,000 women to start or switch to modern contraceptives.

— In Ibadan, Nigeria, nearly one-quarter of new clients at family planning clinics cited as their source of referral TV shows that broadcast clinic addresses.

— In the Philippines calls jammed the switchboard of a hotline promoted in TV spots that accompanied music videos encouraging sexual responsibility. Some

---

2. See, for example, Alex Chika Ezeh, "The Influence of Spouses Over Each Other's Contraceptive Attitudes in Ghana," *Studies in Family Planning*, Vol. 24, No. 3 (May/June 1993).

3. Concerning television, see Church and Geller, "Video." Concerning radio, see Richard H. Gilluly and Sidney H. Moore, "Radio — Spreading the Word on Family Planning," *Population Reports*, Series J, No. 32 (September-October 1986). See also Phyllis Tilson Piotrow et al., "Mass Media Family Planning Promotion in Three Nigerian Cities," *Studies in Family Planning*, Vol. 21, No. 5 (September/October 1990), pp. 265–74, and Charles F. Westoff and Germán Rodríguez, "The Mass Media and Family Planning in Kenya," *DHS Working Papers*, No. 4 (August 1993).

150,000 young people may have called in a period of
less than six months.[4]

Though it can be a cost-effective adjunct, media communication is
of course no substitute for personal encounter. The imperative is to
shortchange neither. Indeed, the critical importance of family planning
education in encouraging as well as enabling people to plan smaller
families is itself a key reason that increases in funding need to move
well ahead of projected increases in the number of contraceptive users.

The need for family planning education is made all the greater by the
mischief of misinformation. Thanks to a varying array of ideological and
other enemies, some leftist, some rightist, some religious, some secular, some
powerful, and some petty, modern contraceptive methods and family
planning programs are the incessant targets of false rumors (the pill will
make you barren, Norplant will kill you, etc.). No wonder that truth-
telling is an endless task.

MORE ABOUT TRUTH-TELLING

Though it is important to inform people fully about their society's need
to end its population explosion, that does *not* mean that the people are
intuitively unaware. One peasant woman's despairing words, "There is
never more land, only more children," said it far better than can I.

But education that motivates us to take sufficient action usually tells
us (and often tells us more about) what we already reluctantly know or
surmise. And it had better remind us of even an obvious truth if we are
being sent strong signals to the contrary. Given the steady supply of verbal
and other heavy messages urging them to have large families, persons in
most high-fertility societies need also to hear the other side.

SPEAK THE COMMON GOOD?

In suggesting that people need to be well informed about the threat
of overpopulation, I am embracing this idea: adequate demographic
education must go well beyond the immediate personal health concerns

---

4. Church and Geller, "Video," pp. 1–2.

of the individual and her or his family; it must also speak of the community's future well-being.

The just-stated view produces some fierce objection. A family planning program, say the objectors, must be *solely* to help couples achieve their own reproductive desires; it must not in any way try to influence those desires. For if it does try at all to influence, it is engaging in "population control." (The term is often meant to sound dreadful. It does.)

The above objection contains both truth and fallacy. Its fallacy is in presuming total moral separation — and absolute warfare — between the individual, or the couple, and society. That antisocial fallacy is a modern Western notion: that "You and Me Against the World" is how two persons should see themselves in relation to their society and, of course, in relation to their government.

YOU AND ME AND —

While purporting to recognize the moral connections that link closely related individuals in the society, the antisocial fallacy fails to see a larger moral bond. It fails to see the moral connection between the individual (or the individual couple) and the whole society.

The basis of that larger moral connection is that the individual's and the whole society's well-being are fundamentally intertwined. The lifeblood of that larger connection is moral dialogue between individual and society.

And bring in government? Unless a particular government has shown itself to be too evil to participate credibly, it should, as society's official spokesperson, be part of that moral dialogue.

Moral dialogue? Even though too many governments still deny it, the individual has every right to call upon his or her society (and to call upon society's government) to act responsibly. And the society (and its government, if morally credible) is entitled, even obliged, to ask the same of the individual.

Moreover, society and its government should participate without paranoia. Because the overwhelming majority of individuals want their lives and their important deeds to serve the common good. And they/we will gladly serve that good if (see chapter 17) the cost is not unduly high.

If, then, a society is facing a threat of massively tragic overpopulation, it *should* ask its members to assess their personal reproductive goals in light of that crisis. If society (and its legitimate government) does not ask that of them, it treats them as less than responsible human beings.

THE CRITICAL CAUTION

"Ask" is, of course, the essential verb. The truth in the wish to differentiate "family planning" from "population control" is an underlying imperative that ever deserves repeating. The need to prevent demographic tragedy must not become a warrant for reproductive coercion. Thus, in providing birth control services, family planning programs should scrupulously adhere to the medical model: the patient is free to decide whether or not to accept offered treatment.[5]

Because appeals to the individual's social duty could easily compromise a family planning program's adherence to the medical model, the following is a worthwhile safeguard. At least in the case of government family planning programs, and preferably always, the persons who provide birth control services should not also be communicating the society's need for lower fertility. The latter task is best left to persons who are organizationally and physically removed from those who are clinically advising and otherwise serving clients.

An even more important safeguard of freedom concerns how a family planning program and its individual workers and administrators are evaluated. Though the number of clients being served is obviously a legitimate concern, the question of numbers must always be secondary. The primary criterion for evaluation must always be client satisfaction and well-being.[6]

Though the risk of coerciveness can never be entirely eliminated, well-designed family planning programs can, and do, keep that risk to a minimum. That outcome is a happy contrast to the main point of

---

5. I cannot "prove" that reproductive coercion is wrong. I can only ask those who think it is right such questions as these: Does benevolent purpose *always* justify governmental power? Or are there some things that even with good purpose governments cannot decently do?

6. Thus, though it rightly acknowledges the need for nations to set demographic goals, the Cairo Conference's *Programme of Action* also rightly advises governments not to impose "targets or quotas" upon family planning programs. See also Sinding, "Getting to Replacement," pp. 12–13. If a program's staff feels at all obliged to bring about any specified increase in the number of contraceptive users, staff members may forget to honor fully each client's wishes.

chapter 10: any substantial lack of access to family planning services makes reproductive coercion a sure and frequent thing.

INTERIM SUMMARY: PART II'S STRATEGY

As suggested in chapter 9 with respect to the developing world outside of China, a sufficient supply of well-designed family planning programs would probably yield an average decline in fertility of fairly close to one child per woman. Were the societal and the personal-family advantages of low fertility both well portrayed, the foregoing average decline could be larger — or at least its strong probability would be enhanced.

With those educational and family planning efforts, and assuming no other endeavors were added to the strategy, fertility in the developing world exclusive of China would probably average somewhere between three and 3.2 children per woman. Compared with the non-China Third World's status quo fertility of about four, that would be vital progress toward demographic well-being.

But would it be almost enough progress? In nations where under-age-30 mortality is still as high as 30 percent, three live births per woman would approximate replacement fertility. But youthful mortality in most developing nations is already well below 30 percent. In all of those nations, a three-children-per-woman fertility rate would be clearly above replacement. And especially where youthful mortality is still very high (mainly in Africa), much can and must be done to help death rates dramatically decline. Consequent warning: the more success in ending high youthful death rates, the more explosive three-children fertility becomes. Indeed, three surviving offspring per woman will roughly double a nation's population in just two generations — even without today's demographic momentum.[7] Because, absent high mortality, it would keep population exploding, three-children-per-woman fertility is not low fertility.

There is another caution. An average fertility of three children per

---

7. Given the demographic momentum (recall chapter 8) that nations with above-three-children fertility now have in abundance, with "only" three-children fertility most of those nations' next population doubling would happen much sooner than that.

woman for the developing world would still find many developing nations decidedly above that figure. Here is a likely such scenario. In the Americas, fertility in Bolivia, Guatemala, Haiti, and Honduras would be near, at, or above four children per woman. In Asia, with Iran, Jordan, Pakistan, Saudi Arabia, and rural Uttar Pradesh (in India) then at about four or fractionally higher, Afghanistan, Cambodia, Iraq, Nepal, Syria, Yemen, and several smaller nations would be near, at, or above five children per woman.[8]

Likely scenario continued: in North Africa, Libya's and Sudan's fertility would be near, at, or above five. Though it too would vary by country, fertility for sub-Saharan Africa — 48 nations — would in the aggregate likely be fractionally above five children per woman.

Why not more progress? It would not be because the people were unable to see the demographic handwriting on the wall. Albeit with great reluctance, they would be seeing.

Nor would it be because the people were wanting their high fertility to be an exercise in tragic futility. No people ever wants that.

The lack of greater fertility decline would mainly be due to what might be called institutional or social rigidity. Too many women and too many couples would still be subjected to heavy economic and other traditional pressures (see chapter 17) to plan more children than is commensurate with the common good.

Hence the need for sufficient changes in the "You must have a large family" social signals that women and couples receive. Some of those changes, described in chapters 12 through 14, may best be called "indirect." Others, looked at in chapters 17 through 22, are quite direct.

Like adequate family planning programs, a sufficient mix of those changes is urgently needed. If humankind cares about the future.

---

8. Four-children or higher fertility would likely also describe parts of Oceania.

INDIRECT MEANS

CHAPTER TWELVE

POSSIBLE INDIRECT HELP TOWARD LOW FERTILITY — I: THE PRIME EXAMPLE

> Who in the world would reject an idea on the ground of its serving more than a single good?
>
> — Source unknown

Though they are possible means of aiding fertility decline, the measures recommended in this and the next two chapters are much more than that. Each proposed means is also an end in itself. Each is inherently good or is otherwise desirable.

Thus, that a proposed endeavor may also aid fertility decline is but one reason, and not nearly the most important reason, for governments to devote more attention to it. The help recommended in this chapter is the perfect example.

INCREASE EFFORTS TO END HIGH INFANT AND CHILD DEATH RATES

Efforts to reduce infant and child mortality rates go hand in hand with efforts to reduce fertility rates. Both sets of endeavors are part of the quest for a world where the quality and the preciousness of life are appreciated, protected, and enhanced. Both sets of endeavors deserve more help from the world's rich nations.

There being no accurate count, it is estimated that about 12.5 million of the world's infants and children below age five die each year.[1] Though death rates for the young have been falling in the developing world, under-age-five deaths probably still average well above 50 per 1,000 live births in North Africa and in parts of both the Middle East and Latin America. In sub-Saharan Africa and South Central Asia, under-age-five

---

1. See UNICEF, *The State of the World's Children, 1996* (Oxford University Press), p. 10.

deaths probably still average well above 100 (and in some African nations and in Afghanistan average above 200) per 1,000 live births.[2]

Most of the recent progress in lowering under-five mortality is the result of increased immunization. With vaccines already saving the lives of over three million developing-world infants and children each year, immunizing those who are still unprotected could mean another one to two million lives saved annually.[3]

A second great lifesaver is oral rehydration therapy (ORT), an inexpensive technique that parents themselves can easily learn. Having been taught to one-third to one-half of the developing world's families, ORT prevents over a million infant and child deaths per year from diarrhea-caused dehydration. Making ORT effectively available to all developing-world households could increase the number of young lives it saves to over three million per year.[4]

Many young lives could also be saved merely by educating more parents and parents-to-be as to (1) feasible food and water hygiene, (2) breast-feeding, and (3) prenatal, infant, and child nutrition that is geared to available low-cost food. As is true of immunizations and ORT, the high lifesaving potential and the low cost of those endeavors combine to make them undeniably imperative.

There are, of course, needed remedies that are more costly. One is increased availability of antibiotics and of the basic health services that they and other treatments require. Another would be greater efforts to increase the nutritional productivity of subsistence farming on an ecologically sound basis. And there would be huge gains for life and health from clean water systems for the roughly one billion people and safe sanitation for the roughly two billion people who are now denied same.

What If Fertility Stays High?

Though youthful death rates in the developing world can, should, and must be substantially reduced from today's high levels, here is news that no one, including me, wants to hear. In most developing nations where

---

2. For 1994 estimates by country, see ibid., Table 1, Basic Indicators, pp. 80–81.
3. See UNICEF, *State of the World's Children, 1992*, pp. 12, 14.
4. See ibid., 11 and 17 and UNICEF, *State of the World's Children, 1996*, p. 58.

fertility is also still high, it is extremely unlikely (even with more outside aid) that infant and child death rates can be lowered enough to resemble those of the West unless and until low fertility is achieved.

Why that unlikelihood? First recall that most developing nations fall far short of meeting the nutritional, medical, and public health needs of their present populations of youngsters. In assessing the chances of meeting those vast needs, bear in mind the distress and the precariousness of both the economy and the ecology of so many such nations. Then look ahead and see the economic challenge of continued high fertility: ever larger numbers of persons making ever greater total demands upon whatever increases in agricultural, medical, and other essential resources that the situation, with or without more aid, might allow.

Indeed, if population continues to soar, youthful death rates in much of the world are apt to stop declining before they are anywhere close to low. Worse than that, those (and other) death rates could easily start a hypertragic upward climb.

But let us also see the glass as half full. Today's high infant and child death rates in the developing world can be greatly reduced before low fertility is achieved. And with sufficient effort, low fertility can be reached soon enough to preserve the improved mortality picture and to enable further death-rate decline.

Would Lower Infant and Child Mortality Contribute to Lower Fertility?

It would, to whatever extent high infant and child mortality is causing fertility to be high. Unsurprisingly, societies with high fertility usually also have high youthful mortality, and societies with low youthful death rates are likelier to have low birth rates. But those outcomes could embody causation in either direction. They could also mean that both mortality and fertility are positively (or negatively) affected by one or more other variables. Unfortunately, demographers have not had great success in solving that complex puzzle.

It is clear, however, that infant mortality can have some upward effect upon fertility. In traditional societies with little or no modern contraception, an infant death may hasten the mother's next pregnancy because her breastfeeding, and/or her postpartum sexual abstinence, ceases.

Of much greater effect, infant and child mortality can be so high as to preclude any conscious attempt by couples to limit family size. Though "family building by fate"[5] once described most or all human societies, youthful mortality remains that high in few if any nations today.

Child replacement. But what about a society where infant and child mortality clearly exceeds that of the West but is below, say, about 10 percent of live births — and where many or most women have at least fair access to modern contraception? Those conditions, which prevail in most of Latin America and in parts of Asia and North Africa, are conducive to much "child replacement behavior." In other words, it will often happen that parents numerically "replace" a deceased child by causing a birth that they otherwise would not have planned.

But often is much less than always. Studies suggest that for every 100 infant and child deaths, there are no more than about (depending on the country) 30 to 60 consequent births. Thus, even where "child replacement behavior" is frequent, its upward effect upon fertility does not nearly equal the number of young lives lost.

Accordingly, as far as child replacement behavior is concerned, further reductions in youthful mortality would not have nearly enough downward effect upon fertility to offset the resulting increase in population. But reduced infant and child mortality could affect fertility for other reasons.[6]

Insurance. Probably the largest potential effect would be to spare couples the need for what demographers Cynthia Lloyd and Serguey Ivanov call "the insurance strategy." Parents who now use that strategy "insure" against the possible *future* death of one or more offspring

---

5. The phrase is from Cynthia B. Lloyd and Serguey Ivanov, "The Effects of Improved Child Survival on Family Planning Practice and Fertility," *Studies in Family Planning*, Vol. 19, No. 3 (May/June 1988). Though I bear sole responsibility for my own conclusions, this section is much indebted to Lloyd's and Ivanov's analysis. Among other helpful sources are David M. Heer, "Infant and Child Mortality and the Demand for Children," in Rodolfo A. Bulatao and Ronald D. Lee, eds., *Determinants of Fertility in Developing Countries*, Vol. 1 (New York: Academic Press, 1983) and Samuel H. Preston, ed., *The Effects of Infant and Child Mortality on Fertility* (New York: Academic Press, 1978).

6. One set of possible effects has to do with "parental demand" for children. But those effects are apt to be conflicting. Reduced chances of tragedy make having children more attractive and less costly, yet also make it likelier that parents will "invest more" in each of a smaller number of offspring. In great part because such factors are difficult to separate from other factors affecting desire for children, there is scant basis for expecting a large upward or downward net effect upon fertility from "the demand effects" of reduced mortality.

by going ahead and having one or more numerically "extra" children.

Why are many couples possibly using the "insurance" strategy rather than the "child replacement" approach? Under the latter, a couple would stop having children once the desired number was reached and would later plan another only if a present child dies. But if the couple lacks affordable access to reversible contraception, they cannot rely upon the child replacement approach to give them the number of children they wish. Thus, if youthful mortality is high, their only good chance of having at least their minimum desired number of surviving offspring is the "insurance" strategy — have at least one "extra" child just in case.

Continued insurance? Though adequate access to birth control would allow them to use the child replacement approach, couples might still practice an insurance strategy in lieu of, or in addition to, the replacement approach. The main reason is that the replacement approach cannot function after the mother is past her childbearing years. Thus Lloyd and Ivanov expect that the insurance strategy is still likely to be widely used in societies where two things are true: (1) the mortality of older children and young adults is not yet low and (2) parents have an economic stake in their children's surviving well into adulthood.

The above two conditions probably still exist today in most of sub-Saharan Africa, in much of South Central Asia, and in a few other developing nations. If so, then substantial further mortality reductions in those not-yet-low-mortality locales might, by lessening parents' need for the above "insurance strategy," contribute to lower fertility — if contraception is sufficiently available.

But there is cause for doubt. Though the idea of parents having a numerically "extra" child as insurance makes intuitive sense, demographers have found only slight evidence of its occurrence. If it is not much of a factor in keeping fertility high, its demise promises little if any fertility decline.

Even if the insurance strategy is a substantial part of today's high fertility in some or many nations, couples may not feel safe in having no "extra" children until long after mortality rates fall. Thus, where having at least one surviving son is still deemed essential, the old adage, "One eye is no eyes, one son is no sons," may still be felt to apply.

Summary. The effect on fertility from further reductions in youthful death rates is mostly unpredictable. Though those reductions can be expected to foster some fertility decline, that resulting decline will probably not be enough to offset (and for many years will not nearly offset) the population increases from the lower death rates.

There would, however, be one sure *noneffect* on fertility. In societies where the desired number of surviving children is three, four, or more, lower infant and child mortality would not reduce that desired number to two.

Though the above conclusions are as unwelcome as they are sobering, they are hardly a case against increased efforts to reduce youthful death rates. The undebatably primary purpose of combating high infant and child mortality is to do it for its own sake: to save young lives. No added justification is needed.

Poignant Ethics?

Caring for children requires caring about the future. Because a continued population explosion threatens massive mortality, and because infants and children would, as now, be especially at risk, some observers have voiced a most solemn fear: that saving lives today dooms far greater numbers of young lives tomorrow.

Accordingly, some have suggested that extensive lifesaving efforts should be deferred until fertility decline ends the threat of massively tragic overpopulation. What should we say about such a suggestion? At least two things. One is this: given that the world's nations can afford to do both, trying to lower high fertility without also trying to lower today's youthful mortality would be immoral.

The second thing to be said is equally true, yet is not as readily seen. It is this: given that the world's nations can afford to do both, making extensive efforts to lower today's youthful mortality without also employing a credibly adequate strategy to achieve life-protecting low fertility is also immoral.

The choice is not between the two. The only ethical decision is — to every reasonably feasible extent — to do both. Full speed ahead on efforts to end today's high youthful mortality. And full speed ahead on a credible strategy to end high fertility rates before overpopulation shows it can slaughter infants, children, and others on an incredible scale.

CHAPTER THIRTEEN

POSSIBLE INDIRECT HELP — II: OTHER EXAMPLES

This chapter also is about doing more than one good at once. It looks at four other possible indirect aids to low fertility that offer other benefits as well.

A. WHERE APPROPRIATE AND NOT ALREADY THE CASE, INCREASE THE LEGAL AGE FOR MARRYING TO AGE TWENTY — OR AT LEAST TO AGE EIGHTEEN.

The proportion of women who are married before age 20 has been decreasing in most of the developing world. Even so, surveys suggest that in much of today's Asia, Latin America, and North Africa, at least 30 percent of females marry while in their teens. In sub-Saharan Africa and in some countries elsewhere, proportions of 50 percent or higher are probably still common.[1]

The happiest way for each nation to discourage early marriage is of course by according women their full educational, economic, and social rights. But until that slow, uphill train reaches the station, each nation's requiring that both bride and groom be past (or nearly past?) their teen years is a potentially effective albeit imperfect expedient. The probable desirability of such a requirement is not confined to developing nations.

Effect on Fertility?

In societies where contraceptive use is still uncommon, a minimum marrying age of 20 would not nearly produce low fertility. Without

---

1. See Arjun Adlakha, Mohamed Ayad, and Sushil Kumar, "The Role of Nuptiality in Fertility Decline: A Comparative Analysis," in *DHS World Conference Proceedings*, Vol. 2, 1991, pp. 947–64.

modern contraception, even women who marry after age 25 are likely to average four or more children.[2]

Nonetheless, until contraceptive use in a society does become prevalent, delayed marriage can be an important component of fertility's decline. Looking at ten developing nations where fertility was falling during at least some part of 1957–75, demographers Parker Mauldin and Bernard Berelson estimated that later marriage accounted for (with great variation by country) perhaps 35 to 40 percent of the aggregate fertility decline.[3]

No feasible and appropriate marriage age law would be a substitute for widespread access to family planning. But a minimum marrying age of or near 20 could do much to hasten fertility decline in today's nations where fertility is still very high, contraceptive use is still low, and teenage brides are still a frequent occurrence.

Coercion or Freedom?

To forbid marriage until the likes of age 20 — indeed to require any minimum age — is, superficially speaking, coercion. But it is procedural coercion that could accord young women a substantive freedom that, in many societies, they are still denied. It would, if enforced, increase young women's chances of having an effective say in how, and with whom, they will live their lives.

Enacting a minimum age of or close to 20 seeks, for example, to end the practice, still a nonrarity in "the Middle East, South Asia, and parts of Africa, [of] arrang[ing] marriages . . . between adolescent girls and considerably older men."[4] It seeks generally, by attempting to defer a person's marrying until surer maturity, to increase the likelihood that marriage is more the result of personal choice than of social subjection. And it is apt to protect many women and infants from the greater mortality and morbidity risks that accompany teenage motherhood.

---

2. See United Nations Department of International Economic and Social Affairs, *Fertility Behavior in the Context of Development: Evidence from the World Fertility Survey*, Population Studies No. 100 (New York, 1987), pp. 76 and 96.

3. W. Parker Mauldin and Bernard Berelson, "Conditions of Fertility Decline in Developing Countries, 1965–75," *Studies in Family Planning*, Vol. 9 (1978), pp. 90, 94, 98.

4. Population Crisis Committee, "Country Rankings of the Status of Women: Poor, Powerless, and Pregnant," *Population Briefing Paper*, No. 20 (Washington, D.C.: June 1988), p. 4.

Unwed Pregnancy

Against the above potential gains must be weighed the risk that a legal marrying age of or near 20 would mean many more unwed adolescent pregnancies. Though the likelihood of that risk is apt to vary greatly from one society to another, and though weighing it is the province of each individual nation, the following two truths could be helpful.

First, the premarital mores of young people are shaped by religious, cultural, and other social factors that have far greater impact than does the legal age of marriage. Second, even in times of moral chaos there are ethically better ways to discourage unwed pregnancy than to perpetuate any amount of forced or virtually forced wedlock, which in many societies is what a young marrying age allows.[5]

Enforcement

Laws are not magic. A legal marrying age that conflicts with custom may be difficult to enact — and is apt to be even harder to enforce. A total or partial lack of birth registrations (which provide good proof of actual age) can only add to the enforcement difficulty. In addition, in order to protect girls against nonconsensual arrangements, the legal marrying age would also need to apply to, and be enforced against, nonmarital unions.

Despite all impediments, a law to increase the marrying age could "take hold" if political and social leaders can do this: convince a good proportion of the people that the increase is an important step toward according women the right to self-determination, which all persons deserve. Thus an emerging women's rights movement could be a boon to the age law's enactment and enforcement. Even so, other measures (the topics of chapter 14) would be needed to help encourage delay of marriage past the teen years and otherwise foster gender justice.

B. ENCOURAGE BREASTFEEDING.

Although breastfeeding can be a natural contraceptive, a couple should not rely upon it to prevent pregnancy once any of the following occurs:

---

5. Those ethically better ways include both the unequivocal teaching of sexual morality and the adequate availability of contraception for youths who cannot or will not learn. The United States of America's frequent aversion to both of those endeavors is world-class folly that no other nation need or should emulate.

1. the cessation of day-and-night demand feeding;

2. the introduction of supplementary feeding;

3. any substantial reduction in frequent suckling;[6]

4. first postpartum menses;

5. the mere passage of several (usually meaning six)
   months' time since childbirth.[7]

Despite its frequent unreliability for contraception, in societies where modern family planning methods are seldom used breastfeeding is the usual major help (whether or not so intended) in spacing births and in limiting total fertility.[8] One study in a rural area of Senegal gave breastfeeding the main credit for keeping total fertility at about six births per woman rather than at a hypothetical twelve.[9]

Thus, though breastfeeding is no ticket to low fertility,[10] its absence impedes the journey. In a society where use of modern contraceptives is increasing, a concurrent decrease in breastfeeding can partly or sometimes

---

6. "The hormone prolactin, secreted as a result of an infant's sucking, stimulates the production of breast-milk and also is associated with the inhibition of ovulation. A woman's levels of prolactin are highest and the duration of amenorrhea and anovulation is longest when the infant suckles frequently day and night. As suckling frequency decreases, prolactin levels fall, and ovulation resumes." Margaret F. McCann et al., "Breast-Feeding, Fertility, and Family Planning," *Population Reports*, Series J, No. 24 (Baltimore: Population Information Program, The Johns Hopkins University, March 1984), p. J-542 (with citations). My discussion is heavily indebted to that source, which also contains an extensive bibliography. I am also indebted to Johanna Goldfarb, M.D., and Edith Tibbetts, *Breastfeeding Handbook* (Hillside, N.J.: Enslow Publishers, 1989), and Robert A. Hatcher, M.D., et al., *Contraceptive Technology*, 16th Rev. Ed. (New York: Irvington, 1994).

7. Not even the continuation of breastfeeding as the infant's only food would obviate the need for other contraception. "While intensive suckling seems to extend postpartum infecundity, it apparently does not do so indefinitely. Even among women who are fully breast-feeding, so that suckling provides their infants' only access to food, fecundity returns gradually with time. In Malaysian and Guatemalan surveys, about 20 percent of fully breast-feeding women were menstruating by 6 months postpartum; about 30 percent were menstruating by 12 months. Thus, although full breast-feeding clearly delays the return of fecundity for some time in many women, it is not a guarantee against pregnancy for all." McCann, "Breast-Feeding," p. J-542 (with citation).

Nor is waiting for first postpartum menses a prudent course: "In eight studies the percentage of breast-feeding women identified as ovulating before first menses ranged from 12 to 78 percent. In general, the longer the time since delivery, the more likely ovulation is to precede menstruation." Ibid., J-540 (with citations).

8. In some societies a fairly lengthy period of postpartum sexual abstinence has also helped to space births and limit fertility. That custom, which, like breastfeeding, does not nearly suffice for low fertility, is also believed to be declining.

9. See Howard I. Goldberg, Fara G. M'Bodji, and Jay S. Friedman, "Fertility and Family Planning in One Region of Senegal," *International Family Planning Perspectives*, Vol. 12, No. 4 (December 1986), pp. 116, 121.

10. See Shea Oscar Rutstein, "The Impact of Breastfeeding on Fertility," in *DHS World Conference Proceedings*, Vol 2, 1991.

entirely offset increased modern contraception's downward effect on high fertility. It is even possible that the continued or future decline of breast-feeding in nations where contraceptive use is not increasing much or at all will mean a substantial increase in already high fertility.

Other Vital Concerns

The decline of breastfeeding in developing nations bodes ill not only because of its probable upward effect upon fertility. Mother's milk is apt to be the best available source of infant nutrition during at least the first four to six months.[11] And, unlike other infant foods, colostrum (the "foremilk" of the first days postpartum) and mature breast milk both contain substances that help guard the infant against infection.[12]

In stark contrast are the frequent health risks of bottle-feeding, especially among both the rural and the urban poor. "Clean water for washing utensils and mixing with formula is often unavailable, as is fuel for boiling the water or sterilizing the bottles, and refrigeration for storage. Under these conditions bacterial contamination is inevitable."[13] Moreover, breastfeeding may well offer emotional benefits to mother and child that transcend the ken of science.

Recommendations

For the above reasons, the following advice makes sense in every nation — and makes special sense wherever safe food and water are lacking to any degree:

1. Women who plan, or whose husband plans, to use reliable birth control postpartum should generally be encouraged, for the sake of the infant's health, to breastfeed for no less than several months — absent, of course, medical con-traindications in individual cases.[14]

---

11. See Goldfarb and Tibbetts, *Breastfeeding Handbook*, pp. 61–63 and 36–44.

12. McCann, "Breast-Feeding," p. J-527 (with citations).

13. Ibid., J-530 (with citation).

14. The discussion in McCann, "Breast-Feeding," pp. J-539–47 and J-550–58, on matters affecting the choice and the timing of various contraceptives during lactation is, like the rest of that report, must reading for any maker or student of policy. Likewise as to Hatcher, *Contraceptive Technology*, pp. 438–44, on contraception postpartum and during lactation, and generally for its coverage of numerous other topics.

2. Recommendation 1 emphatically applies to
    women who lack access to, or who are unwilling
    to use, and whose spouse does not use, a highly
    reliable method of birth control. For those
    unprotected women, however, six months of
    breastfeeding is not a complete answer. Most
    will be resuming sexual intercourse soon enough
    to cause an insufficiently spaced (and thus more
    dangerous) pregnancy. Should they therefore try
    to avoid conceiving too soon by continuing to
    breastfeed for at least an additional year? Absent
    individual contraindications, and in accord with
    much tradition, the answer is most probably still
    yes — albeit with cautions. First, by no later
    than six months of age the infant will start
    needing supplemental food.[15] Second, sufficient
    suckling frequency, day and night, will still be
    needed in hope of postponing the complete loss
    of breastfeeding's (progressively more unreliable)
    contraceptive effect.[16] Third, with continued
    breastfeeding the mother is more at risk of
    losing bone mineral density to a potentially
    harmful degree.[17]

Given the net benefits of breastfeeding, what might nations do (as

---

15. "Techniques of supplementary feeding are important. Infants should always be breast-fed before getting solids or formula since breast milk is the more valuable food. The supplementary foods should be given with a cup and spoon, not a bottle. Cups and spoons are easier to clean than bottles and nipples and thus safer for the infant. Moreover, if bottles are used, infants may find them easier than breast-feeding and reject the mother's breast." McCann, "Breast-Feeding," p. J-530 (with citations).

16. If breastfeeding is still being relied upon for contraception after supplementary feeding begins, it is essential that the amount of supplementation not be great enough to cause a substantial reduction in suckling. As the infant matures, however, that admonition will become increasingly difficult and then impossible to heed.

17. See MaryFran Sowers et al., "Changes in Bone Density with Lactation," *JAMA*, Vol. 269, No. 24 (June 23/30, 1993), pp. 3130–35. Women who breastfeed for any duration are apt to need extra calcium (and to have other increased dietary needs) and, like all mothers, need adequate spacing, meaning at least two years, between births. A woman who for too long relies upon breastfeeding to prevent conception is forced to risk serious bone mineral depletion from prolonged lactation in hope of avoiding (for self and children) the risks of inadequate child spacing. Moral: timely use of appropriate reliable contraception is the most healthful option.

some developing nations are doing) to help prevent, delay, arrest, or mitigate a decline in the practice?

1. Make sure that the usual advantages of breast-feeding are known to women — through mass media, posters, and health workers who know the relevant facts. Health workers should also be well trained to advise when breastfeeding is contraindicated[18] and to provide supportive pre- and postnatal advice — how best to breastfeed, how to minimize and cope with problems, etc.[19] That advice can be given through the media, in public forums, in small group settings, and in individual patient care.

2. For reasons that far transcend the encouragement of breastfeeding, enable pregnant and lactating women to satisfy their increased dietary needs.

3. Require employers to grant maternity leaves (a humane idea anyhow) and/or require them to allow working mothers the time and a place to breastfeed at or near work.

4. Regulate the marketing of infant formula at least as strictly as recommended by the World Health Organization.

---

18. For examples of possible contraindications, such as when mothers test positive for human immunodeficiency virus (HIV) or have AIDS or other transmittable disease, see Goldfarb and Tibbetts, *Breastfeeding Handbook,* pp. 118–22, and Hatcher, *Contraceptive Technology,* pp. 445–46.

19. For example, "[a]ll health workers should be taught that frequent suckling — the pattern of breastfeeding in many traditional societies — is necessary to maintain a high level of milk production. Frequent suckling is especially critical in the first weeks after childbirth, when lactation is being established. If there are long intervals between feedings or rigid schedules, the reduced suckling causes shortages of milk." McCann, "Breast-Feeding," p. J-549. Thus, even if the couple uses other contraception (and surely if they do not), day-and-night feeding on demand is normally the best breastfeeding method.

Where food-and-water hygiene is problematic, serious consideration should be given to feeding the infant exclusively on breast milk (no other food or water) for at least the first four to six months of life. That would not, however, be a satisfactory option in all cases.

Mothers should of course be taught to recognize the signs of breastfeeding-related (and other) dehydration in their babies.

The ideal outcome could well be this: to encourage all mothers who prudently can, and would enjoy doing so, to breastfeed (and to help them do so most advantageously), but not to cause mothers who do not breast-feed to feel guilty or inadequate; to make safe and affordable formula available to those who need it, without thereby inducing others not to breastfeed. That is no small order.

Finally, in order to minimize the incidence of unspaced pregnancies, two additional things should certainly be done. First, new mothers who do not breastfeed should be encouraged to obtain effective contraceptive protection at the earliest medically appropriate time — well before they expect to resume sexual relations. Second, new mothers who do breastfeed should be similarly encouraged to obtain reliable contraception on a medically sound, nontardy basis.[20]

C. CONCERNING CHILD EMPLOYMENT AND EDUCATION

First, nations that have not already done so should prohibit the nonincidental use of child labor and should reasonably and effectively enforce that prohibition. Second, nations that have not already done so should — to the extent that school funding allows — require that both boys and girls attend school through at least age 16.

Like attempts to reduce youthful mortality, those are a pair of reforms whose rightness goes far beyond their possible effect upon population growth. But they are reforms that happen also to be "antinatalist," meaning that they tend to encourage low rather than high fertility. (Notice that — as both of this section's above two proposals attest — "antinatalist" is hardly a synonym for "antichildren." Where fertility is perilously high, a sufficient and humane package of antinatalist policies is decidedly prochildren.)

---

20. The timing should depend in part upon accessibility of birth control options and the type of protection chosen. For example, women wanting no more children can often prudently opt for a minilaparotomy type of sterilization the day of childbirth. Again, see McCann, "Breast-Feeding," pp. J-539–47 and J-550–58, and Hatcher, *Contraceptive Technology*, pp. 433–49 and 392–94, concerning those and related questions. See also "Increasing Sterilization Services for Postpartum Women" in Cathleen A. Church and Judith S. Geller, "Voluntary Female Sterilization: Number One and Growing," *Population Reports*, Series C, Number 10 (Baltimore: Population Information Program, The Johns Hopkins University, November 1990), p. 16.

Like a minimum age for marriage, child labor prohibitions and school attendance requirements both use state coercion. But the coercion is hardly of a kind that assaults reproductive freedom. It is coercion used to offer young people much greater substantive freedom for the rest of their lives.

Early Effects on the Parents' Fertility

Child labor laws and school attendance laws can affect fertility in part because those sets of laws can change the economics of having children. In societies where parents expect their children to work on the farm or to do other substantial work, abolishing or greatly restricting child labor will, if enforced, end or reduce parents' short-run economic gain from having more children. (Thus child labor reform may need to be implemented gradually in order to avoid serious hardship to poor households. Relevant maxim: laws that mandate too much too soon often become a charade through nonenforcement anyhow.)

Because it would restrict their availability for nonschool work, requiring that youngsters attend school also tends to reduce the parents' aforementioned short-run economic gain. And, given that sending one's children to school usually involves some parental out-of-pocket costs (whether or not the school is "free"), required school attendance makes having children at least somewhat more expensive in that sense also.[21] Beyond that, as demographer John Caldwell has argued, parents may "regard the school child as a new and different type of child" who deserves better clothing and other extras in order "to participate equally with other school children."[22]

Schooling: Summary and Preview

School attendance laws are one small part of an adequate educational agenda. Again for reasons that transcend possible fertility effects, developing nations are right to make adequate education for all their

---

21. Required education could make each child more valuable to its parents in the long run. But any pronatalist effect of that long-term possibility is apt to be less than the combined antinatalist effect of the more certain short-run factors mentioned in the text.

22. John C. Caldwell, "Mass Education as a Determinant of the Timing of Fertility Decline," *Population and Development Review*, Vol. 6, No. 2 (June 1980), pp. 225, 227.

young people a high priority. That is also true of efforts to increase literacy in their adult populations.

Besides their intellectual benefits, increased schooling and literacy may also help reduce fertility rates in ways well beyond the examples in the prior section (which dealt only with the students' parents in the short run). The hope for further antinatalist effects points us especially to increased educational opportunities for women — the topic that begins the next chapter.

CHAPTER FOURTEEN

POSSIBLE INDIRECT HELP TOWARD LOW FERTILITY — III: TOWARD GENDER JUSTICE

Fertility transition occurs where, when, and to the extent that women have been empowered to pursue goals independently of their childbearing capacity.

— W. Penn Handwerker[1]

This is the last chapter on indirect means for enabling low fertility. But by no means is it the least important. Progress toward low fertility and progress toward justice for women are each other's devoted friend.

A. ACCORD WOMEN EQUAL EDUCATIONAL OPPORTUNITY.

Since education influences a woman's chances of paid employment, her earning power, her age at marriage, her control over childbearing, her exercise of legal and political rights, and even her ability to care for herself and her children, increased access to education is often the forerunner to a host of expanded opportunities for women.[2]

Like previous chapters' recommendations, increased educational opportunity for women is good policy with or without a population crisis. Like

---

1. "Women's Power and Fertility Transition: The Cases of Africa and the West Indies," *Population and Environment,* Vol. 13, No. 1 (Fall 1991), pp. 55–78, quoted words on p. 61. Some researchers take a much more cautious view. "Ideas concerning the status of women have been put forward as another potentially powerful agent of reproductive change. However, the available evidence does not support this thesis." John Cleland and Christopher Wilson, "Demand Theories of the Fertility Transition: An Iconoclastic View," *Population Studies,* Vol. 41, No. 1 (1987), pp. 5, 28.

For a useful bibliography and superb survey of various ways that women's status may affect fertility, see Karen Oppenheim Mason, "The Impact of Women's Social Position on Fertility in Developing Countries," *Sociological Forum,* Vol. 2, No. 4 (Fall 1987), pp. 718–45.

2. Population Crisis Committee, *Briefing Paper,* No. 20, p. 5.

social justice in general, women's fair access to schooling is crucial to both men's and women's future well-being. For example, women's educational attainment appears to be a critical factor in reducing child mortality in developing nations.[3]

Although in many nations women's educational gains have been impressive, they are far from complete. In much of the developing world boys are still much likelier to receive more years of primary school, and boys are much more apt to receive *any* secondary schooling, than are girls.[4]

In many developing nations less than two-thirds of the girls of primary school age are attending school. In some nations said proportions are not even 50 percent. The corresponding proportions for secondary school are generally much lower than for primary. In some nations fewer than 15 percent of girls over age 12 attend secondary school.[5]

Moreover, continued progress may prove exceedingly difficult. "Because of high birthrates and faltering economies, many of the poorest countries cannot keep up with their rapidly expanding school age population. Where places in school are limited, girls are at a particular disadvantage, especially as the grade level increases."[6]

Education and Fertility

But what if, with the help of international aid or other good fortune, a high-fertility nation can continue to increase educational opportunities for women? What effect would its doing so have upon women's reproductive choices?[7]

As we might expect, increased education for women appears, more

---

3. See John Cleland and Jerome K. van Ginneken, "Maternal Education and Child Survival in Developing Countries: The Search for Pathways of Influence," *Social Science and Medicine*, Vol. 27, No. 12 (1988), pp. 1357–68, and sources cited therein. Likewise as to George T. Bicego and J. Ties Boerma, "Maternal Education and Child Survival: A Comparative Analysis of DHS Data," in *DHS World Conference Proceedings*, Vol 1, 1991, pp. 177–204.

4. See UNICEF, *State of the World's Children, 1996*, Table 4, Education, pp. 86–87.

5. Ibid.

6. Population Crisis Committee, *Briefing Paper*, No. 20, pp. 5–6.

7. The possible relationships between educational attainment and fertility have been studied prodigiously. For their own analyses and for other excellent sources cited therein, see Susan H. Cochrane, "Effects of Education and Urbanization on Fertility," in Rodolfo A. Bulatao and Ronald D. Lee, eds., *Determinants of Fertility in Developing Countries*, Vol. 2 (New York: Academic Press, 1983), pp. 587–626; United Nations, *Fertility Behavior*, pp. 214–54; John Cleland and Germán Rodríguez, "The Effect of Parental Education on Marital Fertility in Developing Countries," *Population Studies*, Vol. 42 (1988), pp. 419–42.

often than not, to encourage lower fertility. As we might also expect, that result probably occurs more often in the case of increased women's education than men's.

There is a similar difference in the degree of effect. Female schooling may have as much as three times the downward influence upon fertility as does male schooling.[8]

Education — especially women's education — works against high fertility in two unsurprising main ways. It tends to delay marriage. Of greater potential effect, in most circumstances educated couples are likelier to plan smaller families than are uneducated couples and to use modern methods in doing so.[9]

But of course there are cautions. One is that a few years or so of primary school — which may be the most a poor nation can offer many of its young people — sometimes results in modest fertility increases.[10] A second caution is that in order for more schooling to have nearly its best chance of yielding substantial fertility decline, the added schooling needs to reach into the secondary school years.[11]

---

8. See Cochrane, "Effects," pp. 602–03.

9. Although most published research focuses upon amount of education, content can also matter. Age-appropriate courses on population issues could play an important role in encouraging responsible personal decision-making. See Paik Hyun Ki, *A Field Try-Out of Population Education Curriculum Materials for Teacher Education Programmes — An Experimental Study: A Case of the Philippines* (Bangkok: Asia Regional Office of the United Nations Educational, Scientific and Cultural Organization, 1973) (perception of ideal family size is significantly lower among an experimental group receiving a course in population education when compared with the control group).

John Caldwell suggests that "the main message of the school is not spelled out in textbooks." It is, he contends, one of replacing the traditional family's pronatalist duty-to-parents morality and economic structure with a new duty-to-self-and-children family morality and economics that is antinatalist. See "Mass Education," cited in the prior chapter.

10. The fertility increases are attributed mainly to a tendency of women with schooling to wean their babies sooner. The more usual outcome (at least eventually) — whose likelihood grows with additional years of schooling — is that greater use of contraception and/or higher marrying ages will more than offset the fertility-increasing effect of reduced breastfeeding. Strong family planning programs (and, primarily for health's sake, efforts to encourage breastfeeding) are musts to enhance the likelihood and the probable magnitude of fertility's net decline.

11. See Cochrane, "Effects," and Germán Rodríguez and Ricardo Aravena, "Socio-economic Factors and the Transition to Low Fertility in Less Developed Countries: A Comparative Analysis," in *DHS World Conference Proceedings,* Vol. 1, 1991, pp. 39–72.

In the latter source, Rodríguez and Aravena also report that in Latin American nations girls' completion of primary schooling does appear to have a strong downward influence upon fertility. But that does not appear to be the case in most other surveyed countries.

Rodríguez and Aravena further read the data to suggest that differences in fertility between more educated and less educated women in a society are mainly transitional: fertility decline first occurs among the more educated and through social diffusion later reaches the less educated. For today's nations where fertility is still high, the massively perilous urgency of the population crisis requires that "later" be translated as "probably too late."

Difficulties

The second stated caution is both important and unfortunate because many developing countries will have a hard enough time providing primary schooling to all of their girls and boys. For those nations, universal secondary schooling describes a very remote future.

The above constraint is similar to others faced by today's nonaffluent population-exploding nations. Here is a policy, "equal and adequate educational opportunity for women," that is both good in itself and apt to help reduce fertility. But continued high birth rates produce levels of human need that, even with more generous outside assistance, turn a needed educational goal into a distant hope.

What to do? One thing is for nations to move rapidly toward an essential interim destination: primary education for all girls and boys. It is a right thing to do — mainly for its own sake, but also for its antinatalist potential.[12]

B. INCREASE WOMEN'S EMPLOYMENT
OPPORTUNITIES.

As we might expect, the available data often show an inverse correlation between women's participation in paid employment and their fertility. But that negative relationship is less likely to exist, and if existent is apt to be weaker, in the poorer developing nations.[13] Some studies find a second qualification:

> [T]he negative employment-fertility relationship characterizes
> only certain sectors of the population or certain types of occu-
> pations. Women working in the urban market economy or in
> higher status occupations generally have lower than average
> fertility; but employment in agriculture, in the marginal urban
> market, or in the low status sales and service occupations . . .

12. Concerning the latter, John Caldwell argues that "the most potent force for change is the breadth of education (the proportion of the community receiving some schooling) rather than the depth (the average duration of schooling among those who have attended school)." Caldwell, "Mass Education," p. 249.

13. See United Nations, *Fertility Behavior,* pp. 255, 269–72.

is associated with higher fertility, occasionally higher than the fertility of women who have never worked [for pay].[14]

When they look beyond correlations and attempt to apprehend the complex and possibly reciprocal causal relationships among employment, fertility, and other relevant variables, most demographers are constrained to express further doubt. Concerning occupation-caused differentials in contraceptive use, one study concludes that "there is at present no basis for expecting that the size of differentials is very large or that occupation is very important in the sense of adding to explained variance [in contraceptive use] once statistical control is introduced for variables which are causally prior to occupation in most of the countries examined here."[15]

"Not very important" does not, however, necessarily equal "unimportant." To the extent that a society can credibly show women that motherhood is not their only worthy calling, their inclination to plan fewer children and their happiness in doing so are both apt to be enhanced.[16]

Accordingly, progress toward equal and adequate employment opportunity for women is a valid part of any effort to reach low fertility. It is also an essential part of the quest for social justice.

Obstacles

Once again, the problem is not the goodness of the goal. The problem is that "providing equal and adequate employment for women" is

---

14. Susheela Singh and John Casterline, "The Socio-Economic Determinants of Fertility" in John Cleland and John Hobcraft, *Reproductive Change in Developing Countries: Insights from the World Fertility Survey* (Oxford University Press, 1985), pp. 199, 216, summarizing a review of the literature in Arthur M. Conning and Albert M. Marckwardt, "Analysis of WFS Data in Colombia, Panama, Paraguay and Peru: Highlights from the CELADE Research and Training Seminar," *WFS Occasional Papers No. 25* (1982).

15. United Nations, *Variations in the Incidence of Knowledge and Use of Contraception: A Comparative Analysis of World Fertility Survey Results for Twenty Developing Countries,* ST/ESA/Series R/40 (New York: Department of International Economic and Social Affairs, 1981), p. 103.

16. See generally Christine Oppong, "Women's Roles, Opportunity Costs, and Fertility," in Bulatao and Lee, *Determinants of Fertility,* Vol. 1, pp. 547–89.

Past as well as present and prospective work can make a difference. It should be no surprise that young women's paid work experience can raise the age of marrying and the age of initial childbearing — or that wives who had done nondomestic work prior to marriage would have lower fertility than wives who had only worked at home. For those and other important concerns, see Guy Standing, "Women's Work Activity and Fertility," and sources cited therein, in ibid., 517–46.

infinitely easier to say than to do. In most high-fertility nations, there are at least two main obstacles. The first, which often also perpetuates educational discrimination, is the bias against women's moving into traditionally male roles. Such gender bias cannot be pronounced dead even in modern Western nations, though it continues to wane. In most of Africa, in much of Asia, and in parts of Latin America, gender bias is still very strong.[17]

The second major obstacle to an improved job picture for women in most developing nations owes most of its size to the population explosion itself. That huge impediment consists of a massive gap between the supply of job seekers and the supply of available jobs. Even if gender bias ended tomorrow, how would you meet women's and men's employment needs where double-digit unemployment already exists — and the number of persons needing jobs is headed far higher?[18]

Small-scale Strategies

Though the developing world has no short or easy road to meeting its enormous need for more jobs, sensible steps can make a big difference. One is for each nation to emphasize, to every feasible extent, ecologically sound modes of economic development that are labor-intensive. That means favoring environmentally and economically viable industries and practices that offer the most jobs per amount of capital investment. Foreign development aid needs to do the same.

The nurturing of labor-intensive development will often involve loans and other start-up help for individuals and other small-scale entrepreneurs. Unlike the "massive projects" emphasis of past development aid (which tended to ignore women), a more "human-sized" focus could better see and do what must be done: bring women into the development process as a full partner.

---

17. Despite our newfound disagreement with other countries' restrictions upon women's career choices, we in the West must fully respect the autonomy of traditional and other societies in all matters that do not genuinely threaten our own well-being. Our best aid to economic-political-social gender equality is to practice it ourselves and to prove that its problems are solvable.

18. "Taking into account the number of people unemployed or underemployed, the total requirement for the next decade is around one billion new jobs." United Nations Development Programme, *Human Development Report, 1993* (New York: Oxford University Press), p. 37.

Not Just Work

If household and other unpaid or underpaid work is taken into account, the prevailing injustice is hardly that most women in the developing world (and everywhere else) have too little work to do. Instead, the more typical unfairness to women, which is especially severe in high-fertility nations, is a life of too much work and too little power.

The foregoing truth could be as relevant to low fertility as it is to gender justice. In accord with other scholars, demographers Mary Kritz and Douglas Gurak are finding reason to believe that "it is not just work, or type of work that affects demographic behaviors, but whether a woman derives any control or autonomy from her work."[19] Noting that there has been far greater fertility decline in the West Indies than in Africa, anthropologist W. Penn Handwerker offers evidence to show that most of the difference is that "West Indian women have been empowered to pursue goals independently of their childbearing capacity, and African women generally have not."[20]

More power to women is, as Handwerker suggests, both a subtle and a (seemingly) simple goal. How to hasten its attainment? The following thoughts seek to help.

C. ATTEMPT VARIOUS OTHER REFORMS NEEDED TO ACCORD WOMEN FULL PARTNERSHIP IN BUILDING THE FUTURE.

There is a practical and an ethical harmony between (1) the goal of ending the population explosion and (2) the goal of women's becoming "full partners with men in the social, economic and political development

---

19. Mary M. Kritz and Douglas T. Gurak, "Women's Economic Independence and Fertility Among the Yoruba," in *DHS World Conference Proceedings,* Vol. 1, 1991, pp. 89–105, quoted words at 100. See that study's findings and analysis as well as other works cited therein.

Kritz and Gurak wisely advise that "researchers should not depend on single indicators of the status of women, nor expect that only 'modern' statuses can bring movement towards the increased control of fertility." Ibid., 103.

20. Handwerker, "Women's Power," p. 57. Most of the West Indies has been uncommonly fortunate. It has, besides some increased light industry, a vibrant tourist industry whose size in most nations has become large enough (in relation to small indigenous populations) to provide women with nontraditional employment opportunities. Even menial hotel jobs have been, for many Caribbean women, a ticket to more economic autonomy and less fertility.

of their countries."[21] Each of those two goals tends to enhance the other's feasibility and importance.

Society's recognition of women as equal partners would, for example, lessen the likelihood that parents would plan one or more additional children in the hope of having one or more sons. It would also curb the tendency of many parents to discriminate against girls as to schooling, chores, medical care, and, sometimes, even scarce food. And a family's having fewer children would itself likely mean less impoverishment of girls — and boys.

In pursuit of both low fertility and gender justice, the rest of this chapter will do little more than mention various measures to help women gain rights and freedoms equal with men. Many developing nations have accomplished much with respect to the matters to be listed. But many have not.

Preliminary Cautions

In any given society the specifics of how to offer women full partnership will be affected by religious and other cultural and institutional influences. Even so, any society can achieve genuine equality between women and men without destroying the integrity and the uniqueness of that society's religious and cultural heritage.

But, as the incomplete progress in "developed" nations attests, the path will not be short or easy. In much of the developing world the journey has barely begun. For example:

> In traditional African societies, women are required to be economically self-sufficient but remain legally and socially dependent on husbands and parents. Usually, African women are completely responsible for child care, cooking, cleaning, and food processing. They are responsible for at least half the effort needed to care for animals, repair homes, and market surplus products. They are almost entirely responsible for water and fuel supplies and food production . . . .

---

21. Quoted words from Population Crisis Committee, *Briefing Paper,* No. 20, p. 2.

Subsistence agriculture is the responsibility of African women, while landownership rights are [mainly] held by men.[22]

Some Steps a Developing Nation's Government Should Take

Compared with the profundity of the problem, some of the endeavors mentioned below may seem unduly modest. But where they have not yet been done they are apt to be worth doing.

1. Afford single and married women rights equal to men in the owning and managing of land and other property.

2. Prohibit gender discrimination in the granting and the terms of credit.

3. Abolish gender discrimination in the laws of inheritance.

4. Grant women and men equal legal status concerning the right to marry, the right to make decisions within the marriage, and the right to separate or divorce. Prohibit concubinage and other forms of unequal cohabitation.

5. Enact marriage dissolution laws covering property settlement, support, and child custody that, insofar as feasible, protect the interests of the weaker as well as the stronger, thereby serving the just interests of men, women, and children.

6. Make clear that marriage is not a license for violence. Indeed, make clear that all forms of gender violence, in and out of marriage, are unacceptable behavior.[23]

---

22. Jodi L. Jacobson, "Planning the Global Family," *Worldwatch Paper No. 80* (December 1987), p. 44, with citations.

23. And may all such clarity be far more efficacious than has generally happened in the "developed" world.

7. Require employers to provide "equal pay for equal work."

8. Where they still occur, prohibit or limit marriage payments — meaning in some societies "bride-price" or "bridewealth" (payment to the wife's family) and in others dowry (payment from her family) — allowing them, if at all, only in amounts that are essentially symbolic. Expectations concerning a substantial marriage payment diminish a woman's autonomy. In-laws' dissatisfaction with specific bargains has some-times even cost women their lives.

9. Make clear that women are entitled to full and equal participation in the political process.

10. Protect women's and girls' access to health care and other necessities on a basis equal to men's and boys'. In doing so, be sure that health care systems are suffi-ciently mindful of women's health needs.

Doubtless the list is incomplete.[24] But that is not its chief limitation. It is one thing to enact, as many developing nations have already done, laws that say the right words. It is something else to teach, promote, and enforce those laws gracefully enough and effectively enough to alter long-standing practices. Most governments are not apt to go that arduous and politically risky second mile unless the emerging political clout of women pushes them every step of the way.

Anyone involved in the marathon struggle for women's equality in the "developed" world can attest to the truth of the prior statement. Recall that it was only in 1920 that U.S. women finally won the right to vote — and that the struggle for full gender equity has had to continue for, thus far, nearly three generations thereafter.

---

24. For further proposals, see *Programme of Action of the International Conference on Population and Development* (United Nations, 1994), Chapter IV. See also the *Beijing Declaration* and the *Platform for Action* from the Fourth World Conference on Women held in Beijing, China, in September, 1995.

Accordingly, ethical realism requires the following almost paradoxical pair of conclusions. First, the realism. Even if the developing nations henceforth move toward gender equity much faster than have the "developed" nations, most of that progress will occur too late to help achieve a timely end to the population explosion. Second, the ethical. A nation's effort to achieve low fertility should nonetheless be graced by all economically and politically feasible steps toward recognizing women's full equality with men. Without further needless delay.

CHAPTER FIFTEEN

STRATEGY SUMMARY THUS FAR — AND SUFFICIENCY CRITERIA

This book's perusal of worthwhile ways to enable and encourage low fertility began with two *direct* means:

1. Family planning programs (chapters 9 and 10)

2. Population education (chapter 11)

Then came a variety of proposed *indirect* means:

1. Chapter 12 advocated enhancing efforts to reduce infant and child mortality.

2. Chapter 13 recommended increasing the legal age for marriage in some nations, encouraging breast-feeding, restricting the use of child labor, mandating school attendance, and otherwise increasing schooling and literacy.

3. Chapter 14 advocated improving women's educational and employment opportunities. It also favored attempting other reforms to hasten the day of full gender equity.

FORGOTTEN ESSENTIALS

Is the list of possible indirect means from the above three chapters an exhaustive one? Of course it is not.

A possibly critical omission involves "safety in numbers," which in many societies can have a fortress-like meaning. A large family or kinship group may seem the only way to protect both property and life from rival families or clans. Where that is so, the credible establishment of rule of law may itself be the most important indirect enabler of fertility decline.

"Safety in numbers" acquires its saddest dreadful meaning if racial, ethnic, or religious strife describes or threatens the scene. There too, the accomplishment of impartial societal governance — law that equally respects all races, religions, and ethnic ties — is the likely essential antidote to "competitive reproduction": groups' using high fertility as a power base for defense or potential offense against rival groups.

Differences. That the achievement of impartial public order could itself be a key enabler of lower fertility makes the point almost too well: the likely most needed indirect means of fertility decline in any society will vary with that society's political, economic, and cultural characteristics. So will the likely best emphases among whatever means are chosen. At least as to indirect means, there is no best antinatalist strategy for all high-fertility nations.

A common thread. Whatever its chosen mix of indirect means, a nation will need to combine that mix with adequate support of family planning. It makes incomplete sense to effect social changes that encourage low fertility without also making contraception sufficiently available and affordable. Indeed, to motivate people, even indirectly, to want smaller families without enabling them to achieve that goal gracefully would be unkind if not foolish.

SUFFICIENCY — I

Assume that, with judicious international aid if needed and wanted, each high-fertility nation acts in earnest. It well enables and promotes family planning, and it institutes its chosen mix of indirect means — indirect means at least somewhat like those favored in this book. Such a strategy would be similar to the antinatalist policies recommended by the UN's 1994 Cairo Conference. But that does not save it from this question: Would any such strategy be a sufficient response to the threat of massively tragic overpopulation?

To try to answer that question we must first try to define "sufficient." A sufficient decline in fertility would, I believe, meet at least two criteria. First, *in each nation where it exceeds replacement rate, fertility needs to fall to a level no greater than replacement.* Even a rate just fractionally above replacement will, if maintained, keep population perpetually soaring — until massive mortality brings it crashing to the ground. And the more its population keeps increasing, the more a nation risks that massively lethal crash.[1]

Opposing argument: Thanks mainly to oil revenues, some high-fertility nations are highly affluent — at least so far. And not all high-fertility nations seem dangerously close to exceeding the carrying capacity of their land and other resources. The need to reduce fertility to replacement should be said to apply only to nations where overpopulation is a fairly imminent threat.

My response: Waiting for a danger to seem imminent is a good way to wait till too late. (Demographic momentum, recall chapter 8, makes "too late" all the likelier.) Moreover, the risks of overpopulation viewed in Part I are global as well as local. All humankind is gravely imperiled.

Because all nations live on the same small and endangered planet, every nation has a vital interest in doing all it can to help bring about an early and humane end to the *world's* human population explosion. For some nations to exempt their own high fertility from that shared imperative, even "just temporarily" (all earthly things are temporary), is to promote failure through bad example.

High-fertility nations who exempt themselves from a serious present effort toward replacement rate risk inciting (or perpetuating?) "competitive reproduction" on an international scale. Both practicality and justice now require that all nations, rich and poor, North and South, East and West, see the road to zero population growth as a local as well as a global moral imperative.[2]

SUFFICIENCY — II

The second criterion of sufficiency cannot be stated with precision.

---

1. The above paragraph is hardly a call for demographic exactitude or for the excessive social control such exactitude would require. The goal of "no-greater-than-replacement fertility" is, in any nation, compatible with periods of above-replacement fertility if they are imprecisely but sufficiently preceded by periods of subreplacement fertility. Thanks also to the continuing ability of mortality rates to change, the goal of "zero population growth" is more a call for gentle waves than for a perfectly calm demographic sea.

2. That includes the United States as well. Though our fertility is at about replacement, we are in absolute numbers one of the fastest growing nations in the world. With our demographic momentum (from past high fertility) gradually winding down, our growth is increasingly a function of the heavy legal and illegal immigration we self-righteously still allow. Is continued heavy immigration a benevolent U.S. response to the world's population explosion? For a persuasive case that it is doing much more harm than good, see Abernethy, *Population Politics.*

It is that all nations with above-replacement fertility should reach a fertility rate no greater than replacement *as soon as is humanely possible.*

As was earlier noted in this book, "humanely" should be read as prohibiting reproductive coercion or other violations of human dignity. Why, then, must I use words like "as soon as," which recommend careful hurry (though, please, not careless haste)?

Because humankind has already waited long past the time for leisurely fertility decline. Thanks to past procrastination, the developing world's demographic momentum (projected further growth even if fertility suddenly fell to and stayed at replacement) is now between two and three billion people — and, where fertility remains high and actual population continues to explode, may still be growing larger.[3] Given that fertility's fall to replacement will not be sudden, the most probable question, then, is how many people *above* about eight billion will there be, or be trying to be, on this planet.

THE WAGES OF FURTHER DELAY

If humankind's fertility falls so as to reach replacement rate by the year 2030 rather than by the year 2010, world population is roughly projected to be an eventual ten and one-fourth billion people rather than to be less than 9.1 billion. That difference of slightly over one billion persons exceeds the entire world's population of 1830. The wages of reaching replacement by 2050 rather than by 2010 is a projected difference of well over two billion persons, meaning, in theory, an eventual population of over 11.5 billion instead of less than 9.1 billion.[4]

National differences. Global figures mask even sharper differences for nations whose people are specially at risk. Example: if Pakistan's fertility falls to replacement by 2030 rather than by 2010, its population (in 1995 about 130 million) projects for the year 2100 to well over 400 million

---

3. The possibility of mitigating some of momentum's effect is looked at in chapter 25.

4. That difference is thus about 2.5 billion persons. Notice that twice as much delay causes *more than* twice as much projected difference, meaning that each successive year of delay has a larger effect on projected eventual population.

The comparative global projections and the by-country examples that follow in the text were enabled by the Population Council's FIVBLD and FIVFIV computer programs and the United Nations Medium Variant Indicators 1992 tape. I am also indebted to the Council's Robert Sendek and Frederic C. Shorter, and to the Population Reference Bureau's Carl Haub, for each's kind advice.

The projections assume, for simplicity, that once replacement rate is reached, fertility stays constant.

rather than to well below 300 million. The roughly projected population difference in 2100 caused by that mere 20 years' time differential is over 125 million persons — a delay-caused difference that itself almost equals Pakistan's entire present population. Rhetorical question: which of those two national growth curves runs the far greater risk of plummeting into the abyss of catastrophic mortality?

Or what if Pakistan reaches replacement by 2050 rather than by 2010? The projected population difference for 2100 is over 300 million persons, meaning (were deaths rates somehow to allow) a population of nearly 600 million rather than one of not quite 290 million. That delay-caused difference is well above twice Pakistan's present population.

Nigeria. Its 1995 population is about 100 million persons. If its fertility falls to replacement by 2010, its projected 2100 population approximates 230 million; if Nigeria instead reaches replacement 20 years later in 2030, its projected population for the year 2100 exceeds 325 million people. The difference between those two projections almost equals that nation's current population. If replacement is not reached until 2050, Nigeria's projected population for 2100 is nearly 470 million — a delay-caused difference from the first scenario of (if death rates don't soar) roughly 240 million persons, well above twice Nigeria's current population.[5]

SEEING THE TRUTH IN TIME

How should such projected differences be viewed? Despite predictive uncertainty, nations need to see them (now, before it is too late) as differences between fair and poor and very poor chances for a humane future.

The above examples tell us what I have already suggested. At this very late date, the only ethically acceptable strategy for fertility decline is one that reduces fertility to no greater than replacement as soon as is humanely possible.

PREREQUISITES

To decide whether the strategy thus far presented in this book meets that ethical test of sufficiency, we must face a question that has

---

5. Like this chapter's comparative global projections, those for Pakistan and Nigeria assume that once replacement is reached, fertility stays constant.

been lurking between the lines of the last several chapters. That question is deceptively simple: What causes fertility to fall from high to low?

Demographer Ansley Coale set forth the basics of an answer in 1973 when he identified three (or, counting parts, at least eight) probable prerequisites for major decline in marital fertility.[6] The first consists of both choice and legitimacy:

> Fertility must be within the calculus of conscious choice. Potential parents must consider it an acceptable mode of thought and form of behavior to balance advantages and disadvantages before deciding to have another child . . . .

The second prerequisite is perceived personal benefit:

> Reduced fertility must be advantageous. Perceived social and economic circumstances must make reduced fertility seem an advantage to individual couples.

The third consists of no less than effectiveness, availability, knowledge, marital communication, and will:

> Effective techniques of fertility reduction must be available. Procedures that will in fact prevent births must be known, and there must be sufficient communication between spouses and sufficient sustained will, in both, to employ them successfully.

HOW TO SATISFY THE ABOVE PREREQUISITES?

Family planning programs and other efforts to inform people help engender both components of the first prerequisite. They surely can disseminate the idea of choosing family size. And, if graced by cultural sensitivity and palpable moral support from opinion leaders, they may also

---

6. Ansley J. Coale, "The Demographic Transition," in *International Population Conference 1973* (Liège: International Union for the Scientific Study of Population), pp. 53, 65. The three quoted passages that follow above are from p. 65.

do much to foster the legitimacy (the social acceptability) of that idea.

Skipping to the third prerequisite, we know that adequate family planning programs can both make "effective techniques of fertility reduction" available and provide knowledge thereof. Caring counselors may sometimes be able to encourage marital communication and bolster the couple's will to use birth control successfully to meet family goals.

Net personal advantage. Saving perhaps the most perplexing for last, what about prerequisite two, perceived personal advantage? Although family planning education can and should point out the advantages of small families, it cannot rebut what in many countries are strong social and economic pressures toward having several children. And though subsidized family planning can offer parents very-low-risk birth control at little or no monetary cost, it cannot revoke other perceived costs and benefits that may postpone the offer's acceptance until the family has grown large.

A pertinent question, then, is whether in any near future any economically and politically feasible set of indirect means would cause enough couples in high-fertility nations to conclude that having only two children would be to the family's net advantage. And would most parents who already had more than two deem it advantageous not to conceive another? Beware of easy answers.

CHAPTER SIXTEEN

ARE OTHER ANTINATALIST MEANS ALSO NEEDED?

Professor Coale's second prerequisite, perceived personal advantage, has us still asking, "What causes fertility to fall from high to low?" But we must now ask with special emphasis on a closely related and equally tough question: "Why do persons choose whatever number of children they in fact choose to have?"

It would hardly suffice to say that a couple chooses to have *x* number of children because the couple deems that number most advantageous. That would be more to rephrase than to answer the above added question.

TAKE A TRIP IN THEORY

Happily, there is a superb supply of demographers, economists, and other social scientists endeavoring to answer both of the above questions. Many of academia's best minds have labored mightily trying to solve part or all of the complex puzzle. They are still at it.[1]

To peruse just their published attempts is to take a theoretical road trip that would make Marco Polo and Ulysses seem like stay-at-homes. Were you to travel this long but scenic route, you would find yourself wandering through a theory lover's paradise.

On your right you would behold an array of theories about the economic costs and benefits of having children in different times and places.[2] Even the settings would catch your notice. You would see scenes of traditional societies, where the farms and other enterprises were the province of family

---

1. If bereft of cheerleaders, they are at least blessed with inside and outside critics of the first order. See, for examples, Simon Szreter, "The Idea of Demographic Transition and the Study of Fertility Change: A Critical Intellectual History," *Population and Development Review,* Vol. 19, No. 4 (December 1993), pp. 659–701, and works by Paul Demeny, Dennis Hodgson, and others, cited therein.

2. I mean to attach no political label to what would be "on your right" or to what would be "on your left." Such locations would, as usual, depend upon the direction in which you were going.

and larger kinship groups. You would there observe how children were needed as cheap labor, as support in their parents' old age, and as means of (further safety in numbers) political power and physical security.

Still on your right, but moving well forward in time, you would then view the complex urban and industrial scene that we call, with mixed emotions, modern economic life. There you would find that, thanks to such things as expensive formal education and state-provided social security, children (though ever a joy) have become an economic liability, rather than an economic necessity, to their parents.

You would encounter macroeconomic studies (big landscapes) and microeconomic analyses (intimate family closeups) of the rising costs and the diminishing economic benefits of children to their parents as societies moved from traditional to modern. Some of the microeconomic portraits of how couples rationally decide whether to have another child could make you think every parent is either a higher mathematician or a certified public accountant.

Keep looking. The most flexible economic theories you would meet are those that widen their picture of how couples decide (and of why fertility falls) by including biological and social factors such as mortality, marital practices, and cultural values. You would want, for example, to spend time with economist Richard Easterlin's and his colleagues' "supply-demand theory."[3] By considering both the "supply of" as well as the parental "demand for" children, plus the economic and psychological costs of fertility regulation, that theory can extend to both sides of almost any road.

Among other worthy theories you would surely want to visit is demographer John Caldwell's theory of "intergenerational wealth flows."[4] It contrasts traditional economic systems and morality (duty to revere, and to transfer goods and services to, one's parents) with modern Western economics and morality (duty of parents to provide each child with the best possible education and every other conceivable advantage). You would not come away wondering why fertility tends to be high in the former and low in the latter.

---

3. See, among other works, Richard A. Easterlin and Eileen M. Crimmons, *The Fertility Revolution: A Supply-Demand Analysis* (University of Chicago Press, 1985).
4. See, among other works, John C. Caldwell, *Theory of Fertility Decline* (London: Academic Press, 1982).

TAKE THE IDEA TRAIN

You would also not want to miss the left side of the road. There too the theories of why fertility falls will chronicle the passage from traditional to modern life. But these theories focus more on differences of ideas than on economic change itself.

Some such theories point us to what John Cleland and Christopher Wilson call a "psychological shift" wrought by "structural modernization of societies, in particular [by] the growth of formal education." That resulting mental transformation is, say Cleland and Wilson, "from, *inter alia*, fatalism to a sense of control of destiny, from passivity to the pursuit of achievement, from a religious, tradition-bound, and parochial view of the world to a more secular, rational, and cosmopolitan one."[5]

Other idea-focused theories point us to the social diffusion of technological and behavioral innovation (such as how family planning practices tend first to catch on among elites and then to spread to the rest of society). Notice that both this and the above group of idea-focused theories seek to know people's attitudes about and propensity to use modern family planning methods as much as they seek to know the couple's computation of desired family size.

Modern aspirations. Even as to the costs and benefits of having children, idea-focused theories are apt to look beyond mere objective change in the equation. Like sociologist-demographer Ronald Freedman, they may "think it is crucial [for fertility decline] that increasing numbers of people have become aware of alternatives to their traditional lifestyles and aspire to something different, even though these aspirations often are poorly defined."[6]

Modern communications are of course the frequent conveyer of "a different way of life transcending what is actually available," even including "new models of family and parent-child relations."[7] And, says Freedman,

---

5. That passage and both groups of quoted words preceding it are from John Cleland and Christopher Wilson, "Demand Theories of the Fertility Transition: An Iconoclastic View," *Population Studies,* Vol. 41, No. 1 (1987), pp. 5, 9. My abbreviated theoretical travelogue is indebted to that article and to other works cited therein.

True to the spirit of its subject, the literature on modernity is already voluminous. See, for example, Alex Inkeles, *Exploring Individual Modernity* (New York: Columbia University Press, 1983) and its bibliography.

6. Ronald Freedman, "Theories of Fertility Decline: A Reappraisal," *Social Forces,* Vol. 58 (September 1979), pp. 1, 4.

7. Quoted words from ibid., 3 and 4.

aspirations for the new way of life may be tangibly validated by the influx of even such modest things as bicycles, motor scooters, sewing machines, and motorized pumps.[8]

Freedman has warned that, though massive economic development is not required, in many rural areas there may not be much perceptual change without "administrative, communication and transportation systems capable of reaching the village masses, either with the ideas of the outside world or with the minimal services and goods which make the new ideas and aspirations credible."[9] Note that (economists again get the last word) even ideas cost money.

"POST-TRIP" IMPRESSIONS

Had we had sufficient travel time, what conclusions would we have drawn from taking the above theoretical road trip? One is that, despite their diversity, all thoughtful theories of fertility decline and reproductive choice are true. All of them paint at least part of the panoramic picture of human reproductive reality.

Lest we be too pleased, the other conclusion to be drawn is not so exuberant. Though social scientists have learned and told much about reproductive choice and fertility decline (especially about decline once it has begun), such subjects are still as much matters of mystery as of scientific knowledge.

Scientists Cleland and Wilson report with unabashed candor: "[N]either the historical nor the contemporary data will permit a definitive appraisal of any single theory."[10] Though the theories and the data often illuminate, and though "[p]lausible *post factum* explanations for particular trends abound," the candid report rings true. "[A]n understanding of causal mechanisms, such as would allow confident prediction is out of reach."[11]

---

8. Ibid., 4.
9. Ibid., 5.
10. Cleland and Wilson, "Demand Theories," p. 11.
11. Both quoted clauses from ibid., 9. Thus Easterlin and Crimmons rightly suggest that at different times

IMPORTANCE OF THE UNPREDICTABILITY FACTOR

People's propensity to be unpredictable is a truth no policymaker can afford to forget. That propensity cautions against expecting sure success from any set of policies and programs, whatever the goal. It should make nations extraordinarily cautious about relying mainly upon indirect means to achieve — at this eleventh hour — expeditious fertility decline.

Time. The high risk of relying upon indirect means stems in part from the time required for substantially instituting the more ambitious of them. Though infant and child immunization and oral rehydration therapy training efforts can be increased rather quickly, other needed endeavors, such as widely improved medical care and safe water and sanitation systems, would be much slower undertakings. Unfortunately, greatly increased schooling and sufficient employment opportunities for women (and for men) fall into the latter time frame, at best.

Money. Some of the inevitable time delays are a function of the scarcity of needed funds. Even with generous outside help, developing nations will not soon be financially able to do nearly all of the things recommended in prior chapters. (And remember Ronald Freedman's added indirect means for remote rural areas: communication and transportation systems to bring in the ideas and tangible goods that may be needed to encourage antinatalist social change.)

Choices. Scarcity of resources requires choices. Each developing nation will need to decide such issues as which indirect means of hastening fertility decline most need doing first and which deserve what share of available resources at each point in time.

Easy choices? Which, then, merits the greater early emphasis? Offering more schooling to women or extending mass communication to remote communities? Installing safe sanitation systems or building

---

and places the major causes of fertility decline may be quite different. *Supply-Demand Analysis*, p. 30.

Though it frustrates both the scientist and the policymaker in all of us, the inability to predict most human behavior with confidence may be more a reflection of the reality of finite free will than a result of scientific failure. If so, it is more a cause for celebration than for dismay.

more roads and rail tracks? Training more doctors or investing in labor-intensive manufacturing?[12]

UNCERTAINTIES

Our abbreviated theoretical road trip and our earlier look at various proposed indirect means tell the same true story. Selecting the mix of indirect means that would likely have the greatest and soonest antinatalist effects is still about as much a matter of hopeful guess as of scientific knowledge.

In selecting its mix of indirect means, a high-fertility nation can expect to face ethical conundrums as well as the finitude of social science. For example, most of the relevant research suggests that universal primary schooling and increased availability of secondary and higher education would yield much more fertility decline than would increased job opportunities. Does that mean that Nation X should give primary, secondary, and higher education a much higher priority than it gives to improving the job picture? Or is it both cruel and foolish to provide people with secondary or advanced schooling for jobs that are not about to materialize?

Nations facing such possible dilemmas would do well to remember a point that was apparent throughout chapters 12 through 14 and into chapter 15. The indirect antinatalist means advocated are much more a matter of doing their own essential good (nourishing children's minds and bodies, promoting gender equity) than they are a swift and sure formula for low fertility. Accordingly, a developing nation's choices of which indirect means to emphasize first and most are probably best made by trying to "consider the whole social good" rather than by merely considering each means' likely antinatalist potential. Given that either of those two approaches involves choosing among vital goods, either approach will require miraculous amounts of wisdom — and enough guesswork to bridge our huge gaps in predictive knowledge.

---

12. Though all such choices must and should be made by each high-fertility nation, it can hardly be helpful for international population conferences (or book authors) to urge "governments to tackle a virtually endless list of tasks, large and small, feasible or manifestly hopeless, eminently desirable or at best marginally appetizing." Quoted words from Paul Demeny, "Bucharest, Mexico City, and Beyond," *Population and Development Review,* Vol. 11, No. 1 (March 1985), pp. 99, 102.

PROSPECTS

So what should be expected from indirect antinatalist means? Progress in instituting most of them will be slow at best. And even after the more emphasized means are sufficiently in place, they may or may not be enough of an additive to family planning programs to achieve no-higher-than-replacement-rate fertility anytime soon.

For some nations, whose fertility is above replacement but is everywhere nearer to three than four children per woman, and whose economic and ecological health is at least fairly good, the bet seems sensible. For those nations, a strategy consisting of both strong family planning support and a good mix of indirect means probably would, *if* funds make it feasible, prove sufficient.[13]

But recall the more frequent and much tougher situation: imprecisely, nations, or large locales therein, with fertility near four children or higher — remembering that most of these nations are beset by immense poverty, overstressed agriculture, and ecological deterioration and peril. It is in the many nations where the population crisis is most urgent that implementation of the needed indirect means would be the most difficult, would take the longest, would probably be the most incomplete, and would offer the poorest chances of augmenting family planning support enough to yield an expeditious fertility decline to approximate replacement.

Hence a conclusion that is as unavoidable as it is apt to be unwelcome. In the great majority of cases, if a high-fertility nation relies *entirely* upon family planning support and indirect means to achieve low fertility, it runs an awesomely high risk of losing the race against massively tragic overpopulation.

WHAT TO DO AND WHY

Nonetheless, the time for adequate family planning support is now. Likewise as to endeavors that can save the greatest number of young lives soonest. And the other previously discussed indirect means should be instituted as promptly and fully as feasible, albeit primarily because of

13. By family planning support I mean population education (per chapter 11) as well as, of course, family planning programs.

their own intrinsic goodness. *But if there are supplemental antinatalist means that are likely to hasten the transition to low fertility, and if they do not involve reproductive coercion or other inhumanities, it is morally imperative that, if affordable, they be added to the strategy without needless delay.*

Why the last statement? For all the reasons stated in prior chapters, morality itself — basic respect for human and all life — requires that nations reduce their fertility to no greater than replacement as soon as is humanely possible. That ethical test of fertility-reducing sufficiency is violated if nations fail to add or needlessly delay adding other feasible and affordable humane means that would hasten fertility decline.

PREVIEW

Are there other feasible and affordable antinatalist means that, if designed and implemented with due care, (1) would hasten the transition to low fertility and (2) would not involve reproductive coercion or other loss of human dignity? My study of the matter convinces me that the answer is yes.

Those other antinatalist means are called "direct incentives and disincentives." Though those direct means will be explained and scrutinized in the chapters that follow, some preliminary points need noting now.

First, why should high-fertility nations not give the indirect means approach a fair try before adding something as awful-sounding as "direct incentives and/or disincentives" to the mix? Albeit in different words, that question has already been asked and answered in the present and prior chapters. The answer still is that, even with good family planning support, there is far too much risk the indirect approach will fail to yield sufficient fertility decline soon enough to prevent massively tragic overpopulation. By the time the indirect approach is given that kind of a "fair try," failure would spell "too late."

Second, as will be shown in ensuing chapters, nations would *not* need to choose between emphasizing indirect antinatalist means and utilizing direct incentives and/or disincentives. Indeed, direct incentives can often be combined with indirect antinatalist means so as to increase the latter's efficacy in saving lives, improving health, and enhancing women's and men's educational and employment opportunities.

Third, why, then, do so many proponents include only indirect means when they recommend antinatalist policies other than family planning support? One reason they and the rest of us prefer indirect to direct anti-natalist means is that everyone is still fundamentally uneasy at the idea of low fertility as a crucial societal goal. Given an almost instinctual aversion to that goal, the advocacy of indirect means to attain it makes everyone feel far less uncomfortable.

Our escape from discomfort is aided by the palpable goodness of such indirect means as reducing mortality, increasing literacy, enhancing other education, and pursuing gender justice. Unfortunately, however, our justified approval of those means may cause us to place unjustified reliance upon their antinatalist potential.

Fourth, an ethical hazard lurks throughout point three. Beware of "feel-good social ethics." Let us not rely upon policies because they make us feel virtuous. Thou shalt not bet the whole farm upon a virtuous but insufficient demographic strategy for helping to enable a humane future.

The main trouble with feel-good social ethics is that it is unethical. It puts our own feelings of goodness ahead of what we should do: advocate and support an affordable set of policies apt to offer the best chance of allowing a sustainable future in which all human beings and the rest of nature can flourish. Though that set of policies would certainly include dedicated use of indirect antinatalist means like those earlier recommended, it would in most nations with above-replacement fertility also include the judicious use of direct antinatalist incentives and/or disincentives.

FIFTH, AND FINALLY, AN ETHICAL AND CULTURAL PITFALL

Given that direct incentives and disincentives pose obvious ethical problems (to be faced in chapters 18 and 19), we might assume that a more indirect antinatalist strategy entails little or no risk of abuse. That assumption needs examining.

The method of the indirect approach is to affect reproductive choices obliquely. Change the general social setting enough to cause most people to have no more than two children. Does obliqueness guarantee harm-lessness? Though the specific indirect means favored in this book are benevolent ones, undue reliance upon the indirect route to low fertility could for some or many nations be a road to cultural ruin.

In nations where economic or other social pressures to have large families are strong, a successful indirect approach to making small families the popular choice may require much more than the span of indirect means favored in this book to augment family planning support. Such a nation's *un*willingness to add direct incentives and/or disincentives to its mix may require that, for any hope of sufficient success, its indirect antinatalist approach include sweeping attempts at pervasive "modernization," "Westernization," and "secularization" that destroy the nation's cultural heritage.

But let me be clear. I reject any notion that the goal of a low death rate and other affirmations of individual human worth are exclusively modern, uniquely Western, or primarily secular ideas. The ethical question I am asking is this: what about traditional societies who want a low death rate and other celebrations of human dignity, who reluctantly realize that (unless the earth has no limits) the sustainable attainment of those goals requires a low birth rate, who suspect that the time to save the future is now, but who do not wish to lose their cultural identity?

Stating the question more pointedly, what about nations whose leaders see the urgent need for low fertility but are unwilling to import a drastic dosage of Western modernity in order to get there? For those nations, the happiest course could be to use direct incentives and/or disincentives as a supplement both to family planning support and to beneficent indirect means (improved child health and education, gender equity, etc.). That course offers greater hope of soon reaching low fertility without resorting to an extreme modernity whose harmful side effects (unbridled materialism, disparagement of family and related moral values) are all too frequent. That course could both prevent tragic overpopulation and preserve each nation's cultural soul.[14]

---

14. Implicit in that conclusion is my belief, stated in chapter 14, that any society can achieve genuine equality between women and men without destroying the integrity and the uniqueness of that society's religious and cultural heritage.

FURTHER
DIRECT MEANS

CHAPTER SEVENTEEN

DIRECT INCENTIVES "AND" DISINCENTIVES

Incentives "and" disincentives? The "and" is in quotation marks because I doubt we are looking at two fundamentally different concepts. Yet we are often told: incentives are rewards to encourage favored behavior, whereas disincentives, or "negative incentives," are penalties to discourage disfavored behavior.

That distinction sounds simple until we ask, isn't being spared an unwelcome penalty itself a kind of reward? And isn't being denied a desired reward itself a penalty, and sometimes a sorrowful one?

Adding further confusion, is it always easy to tell a "denial of reward" from an "imposition of penalty" in the first place? One college student may deem his grade of C an outright punishment; his more philosophical classmate may simply think of her C as not being an A this time.

Still another student may, with a great sigh of relief, gladly accept his C grade as a merciful reward or escape from punishment. One's expectations count for much.[1]

Though the difference between a denied reward and an imposed penalty is often wholly or mainly a matter of psychology or mere form, such differences can be important. So I shall call some antinatalist incentives "rewards," and call others "penalties or fees," in fair accord with ordinary language. But when there is no need for that often tenuous distinction, I shall let the word "incentives" refer to the entire spectrum of antinatalist rewards and penalties or fees.

Generally speaking, the important ethical question is not whether a given incentive is a matter of reward "or" of penalty. The important ethical questions, which are confronted in chapters 18 and 19, concern

---

1. See Robert M. Veatch, "Governmental Population Incentives: Ethical Issues at Stake," *Studies in Family Planning*, Vol. 8, No. 4 (April 1977), pp. 100, 102.

coerciveness, fairness, and human dignity. Those questions are not answered merely by deciding, if one can, whether an incentive essentially involves penalty, or reward, or both.

OVERVIEW

Some antinatalist incentives are, except for brief mention, outside the scope of this book. Those are payments to medical and other family planning workers on the basis of actual work done, case load, number of new clients, or other indicia of effort or success.[2] I shall instead look at the most direct of all direct incentives: those that focus upon the family planning "consumer" rather than the service provider.

Even as to direct "consumer incentives" to low fertility, there are two basic types. The first, *personal or family incentives*, offers rewards to and/or imposes penalties or fees upon persons as individuals, as couples, or as parents. The second basic type, *community incentives*, dispenses its rewards and/or penalties to entities larger than the nuclear family — villages, towns, districts, or the like.

Community incentives will be examined in chapter 22. Until then, the main focus will be upon personal or family incentives. Even so, much of what is said should also apply to community incentives.

RATIONALE

Why are direct incentives to low fertility needed in nations where fertility markedly exceeds replacement? Previous chapters gave step one of the answer. The chances are unacceptably great that the fertility decline enabled by other feasible means will not be large enough, soon enough, to prevent massively tragic overpopulation.

Now to shorter step two. Why are family planning support and all affordable and otherwise feasible indirect means of fertility reduction apt to be insufficient? The major reason is that they probably would *not* cause

---

2. If such payments to workers are nothing more than efficient means of fair compensation and accountability, they may well be desirable. However, as India's experience during the 1975–77 Emergency demonstrated, great care must be taken. Family planning workers must not be constrained or enticed to "succeed" at the expense of anyone's informed and voluntary choice. As urged in chapter 11, the primary performance criterion should be the satisfaction and well-being of the people being served. All workers need to be thoroughly trained to see that voluntarism is not just a rule but is also the essence of their services.

enough timely change in this social reality: despite a population-exploding nation's need for low fertility, many or most couples in each such nation are still subjected to strong inducement and pressure to have a large family.

ECONOMICS

As the work of John Caldwell and others well shows, much of that pronatalist inducement and pressure is economic. In much or most of the developing world, most children are sooner or later of economic benefit to their parents, and often to their grandparents as well. Caldwell's account of the traditional extended family illustrates:

> As soon as the young bride enters the household, there is much interest in her reproduction. Her husband may be 25 years old, and his father will probably be between 50 and 75, depending on whether the husband was the first or last child. The old couple will urge the young couple to have many children as soon as possible: if young children mean work, that work will no longer fall upon the old people's shoulders . . . . In the traditional family, the young have little option but to be fertile. Even for them there are advantages. Only by bearing children can the young wife establish her position, work a little less hard, enjoy a somewhat larger share of food and other consumption items, and, ultimately, achieve a major breakthrough with regard to all these matters by becoming a mother-in-law. The young husband can have helpers in the field within 10 or 12 years and can shift some of the harder work off his shoulders by the time he is 40 years of age.[3]

The flow of goods and services from children to parents becomes more critical as the parents advance in age. In a traditional society, "those who live most comfortably will be the parents who have a continuing supply of children of both sexes growing up; to meet the need of having persons of different ages to do the age-specific tasks, to engender sibling competition in providing labour during their parents' maturity and comprehensive aid

---

3. Caldwell, *Theory of Fertility Decline*, p. 170.

during their decline, and to supply successive new daughters-in-law, who probably work harder than anyone else. Descendants are the most valued protection that a couple can have against destitution in old age."[4]

URBAN ALSO

As Caldwell's studies in Nigeria make unmistakably clear, the economic benefit of children to their parents is by no means confined to rural families. His team's 1974-75 data showed that "the return from investment in children is greater for urban than rural residents." And it was "greatest of all among the city white-collar and professional class."[5]

Like their rural counterparts, most urban parents in the developing nations must look to their children for much, most, or even all of their old-age security. The more children, the more apparent security. Despite high unemployment, the parents with several children still have, or still think they have, the greater chance of having one or more income-earning offspring. And those parents may also enjoy the greater likelihood of having one or more *prosperous* offspring — both because more children mean more chances and because several siblings often can pool their efforts to the family's advantage.

A prime example of pooling is the "sibling chain of educational assistance." Older, working children pay or help pay for the younger children's secondary or advanced schooling. Whether it means being able to buy an education, or simply getting and keeping a choice corner for the family's street vending business, the pooling game (which for many urban families is the only available game) is best played, and sometimes must be played, with at least several players on your team. There is family power and (no pun intended) relative safety in numbers — sometimes.

FUSION OF FORCES

As earlier suggested, the pressures and inducements to high fertility are not merely economic. They are also cultural, religious, and psychological,

---

4. Ibid.
5. Both quoted excerpts from ibid., 145.

both conscious and unconscious. In any traditional or semitraditional society they are powerful indeed.

The economic forces and the noneconomic forces favoring or dictating high birth rates are socially and psychologically intertwined. Thus do two already strong sets of forces further strengthen each other.

Kenya. A good example of the fusion and the combined pronatalist strength of economics and custom is Kenya's traditional social order. The following brief look is based on work by Odile Frank and Geoffrey McNicoll.[6] Though there are major differences both between and within nations, the prevalence of a social order somewhat like Kenya's still typifies most of sub-Saharan Africa.

Access to land is controlled mainly by men or by their lineages. Because the work of subsistence agriculture is largely assigned to women, wives are allowed "use rights" to the land they must farm to supply their family's food needs. Except for initial land clearing and plowing, women are responsible for "all elements in the chain from food production and the purchase of or trade for nonproduced foods, to meal preparation," which also includes "collection of water and fuel (mostly firewood)."[7] Besides childcare and other household duties, Kenyan women also do various income-earning activities in order to buy market food, clothing, etc. Unsurprisingly, in her many tasks the mother needs and normally receives whatever help her children can provide. Plus there is her future need. "Since a woman must in large measure assure her own livelihood, often with little or no claim on her husband's estate after his death, children offer a promise of old-age security that may in effect be indispensable."[8]

Whose children? Though her husband allows her the use of their labor, the children, like the land, belong to him or to his lineage. The husband's "entitlement" to all children borne by his wife is secured by the practice of "brideprice" or "bridewealth": the husband (and/or other members of his lineage) must make suitable payment to the bride's parents and lineage. So closely is brideprice tied to the expectation of and to the rights over

---

6. "An Interpretation of Fertility and Population Policy in Kenya," *Population and Development Review,* Vol. 13, No. 2 (June 1987), pp. 209–43.
    7. Ibid., 215.
    8. Ibid., 216.

children that the husband may well pay "in installments — for example, following the successful birth of a first, second, and third child" — or childlessness may be grounds for a refund of any earlier payment.[9]

PRESTIGE AND SURVIVAL

For a Kenyan man (and for his lineage), a large family means standing, prestige, and political and personal influence in the community. It confers, and it is, social power. His wife's or wives' continued childbearing tends to maximize and to perpetuate that power.

For a Kenyan woman, high fertility may well be necessary (or at least seem necessary) for both economic and social survival. Consider economic survival. "According to the terms of the marriage, it is the children she bears that guarantee her access to the land she needs in order to meet the family's subsistence."[10] Also consider her general social survival, including society's perception of her basic worth as a person:

> By continuing to bear children a woman confirms her status in the marriage (in part, in competition with existing or potential co-wives) . . . and serves the family and lineage interests of her husband (as well as ensuring that her own family can keep the brideprice that was given for her). That she also accumulates a very large family is a byproduct of this economically and culturally defined and socially enforced obligation.[11]

PROGNOSIS

What is surely most needed is what has been most fundamentally denied: equal rights and justice for women. But even were that long and hard road to be traveled with miraculous rapidity, other pronatalist pressures and inducements, such as needful reliance upon children for old-age support, and the manifold advantages of "pooling," would remain.

Is a social system like Kenya's an immutable bastion against all reduction in fertility? Of course it is not, as Kenya's own recent fertility decline to

---

9. Ibid., 214.
10. Ibid., 215.
11. Ibid., 217.

five or six children per woman readily attests.[12] If and as modernization increases (which, like fertility decline, seems to be happening more in Kenya than in most of sub-Saharan Africa), this too should occur: the above social system and similar ones will start or continue to gradually lose some degree of power. Some of the indirect antinatalist measures proposed in earlier chapters should facilitate that process.

But let such hope be realistic. With or without intentional increases in speed, modernization is an unsudden undertaking. And even when modernity arrives resplendent in neon signs, social systems like the one described above can be stubbornly slow to step aside. For the relevant future, then, the following prognosis still applies: without direct antinatalist incentives, in most of today's high-fertility nations the economic and other social forces (the "extrinsic" pressures and inducements) acting upon most individual couples will remain, on balance, decidedly pronatalist.

THE HAPPIEST FACTOR

Unsurprisingly, the factors favoring or dictating high fertility do and will vary both from nation to nation and within nations as to specifics and efficacy. But among all high-fertility nations, each nation's set of pronatalist factors has one crucial thing in common with the others besides each set's very considerable strength. The extrinsic pressures and inducements to having a large family are an addition to, not a substitute for, what exists in every society: the intrinsic joys of having children. It is only by bearing that truth in mind that one can perhaps appreciate the total impetus upon a couple or a woman in a high-fertility nation to have, despite the population crisis, more than two surviving children.

TRAGIC CONFLICT

Nations facing probable overpopulation from continued high fertility are caught in a conflict akin to biologist Garrett Hardin's "tragedy of the commons."[13] The perceived self-interest of the individual couple in having

---

12. Interestingly, much or most of Kenya's fertility decline has been attributed to the combined effects of family planning programs and worsening economic conditions. See, for example, William Brass and Carole L. Jolly, *Population Dynamics of Kenya* (Washington, D.C.: National Academy Press, 1993).

13. See Garrett Hardin, "The Tragedy of the Commons," *Science,* Vol. 162, No. 3859 (December 13, 1968), pp. 1243–48.

enough children to be survived by three, four, or more of them is poignantly at odds with the common good. By acting to maximize perceived private well-being, each high-fertility couple brings the whole society closer to catastrophe.

Are individuals depraved if they act against the common good? Not if acting for the common good specially subjects them and their loved ones to costs and risks that only the saintliest saints would willingly bear.

RESOLVING THE CONFLICT, IMPROVING THE EQUATION

To understand the problem is to approach its solution. In most high-fertility nations the problem is this: sufficiently changing the economic and other social structures that encourage or dictate high fertility will take much more time than the threat of massively tragic overpopulation is apt to allow.

Both prudence and ethics therefore require a more expeditious remedy. With the help of international aid if such aid is needed and wanted, high-fertility nations need to act soon to counter their society's pronatalist pressures and inducements that imperil the people's future. Every nation whose fertility markedly exceeds replacement should devise, and should phase in on a soon-as-practical basis, a credible set of direct antinatalist incentives. Those incentives should supplement ample support of family planning and a feasible mix of indirect endeavors and reforms, as earlier proposed.

What would an adequate set of incentives need to do? Would it have to offset fully the society's pronatalist pressures and inducements, so that an individual couple would incur *no* net economic or other social cost in having only two children? I doubt it would need to do that. I also question whether that strong a set of counterincentives would be economically and politically feasible. And I can think of no feasible, ethically acceptable set of antinatalist incentives that could nearly repay loving parents for the intrinsic joy that one or more additional children would have brought them.

What, then, could a feasible and ethical set of antinatalist incentives do? Although it could not make low fertility a cost-free option, it could make low fertility a very reasonable option. *It could enable the individual couple to serve the common good, to opt for a small family, without that family's likely suffering severe social or economic disadvantage vis-à-vis families who ignore or reject the need for low fertility.* Given most people's desire to uphold their society's common good if the cost is not too high, a total or virtual negation of low-fertility costs should not be needed.

COHERENCE

A substantial set of antinatalist incentives would also establish reasonable coherence between leaders' low-fertility preaching (which would still be needed!) and actual governmental policies. A developing nation's government would avoid the inconsistent and thus unconvincing stance of touting low fertility to the people yet doing little or nothing about the often heavy disadvantages placed upon small families by a pronatalist society.

If government acts to substantially counter those disadvantages by rewarding low fertility and/or by levying a fair cost upon high fertility, it speaks to the people with a credibility that words alone could not attain. It conveys something of the importance of soon ending the population explosion. Government shows that its own commitment to help the nation attain that goal is real and earnest. And although it cannot eliminate the sadness in having a smaller family than originally desired, the government's antinatalist incentives show its awareness of, and its concern to alleviate, that sadness. It tells the individual couple that their willingness to serve the common good is recognized and valued.

TWO PRACTICAL QUESTIONS

First, can low-income nations economically afford to make direct incentives a substantial part of their antinatalist strategy? Because we need to look at several ethical issues before dealing with economic affordability as such, an explained answer to that question will come later. But the short answer is yes.

Second, what about political feasibility? Given the dominance of large families in any high-fertility nation, how could antinatalist incentives gain sufficient elite and popular acceptance? Part of the answer is to make the incentives essentially prospective rather than retroactive. Today's large families — the fruition of high fertility prior to the incentives' introduction — need not be penalized in relation to their small-family peers. Thus today's large families could support antinatalist incentives without jeopardizing their own members' already vested interests.

Another part of the answer is population education. The great impetus to incentives' popular acceptance is the ever increasing seriousness of the population explosion. A government that first supplements people's intuitive awareness of their nation's demographic crisis with good information on its gravity and urgency multiplies the chances that needed incentives will gain public approval — or at least public tolerance. Those chances will be further enhanced if, also beforehand, the government explains the specific rationale and the fairness of each incentive it devises.

EFFECTIVENESS

There is a third practical question. Do antinatalist incentives work? That is a lot like asking, "Do medicines work?" To both of those questions, the probable answer is the same: some do, and some do not. Effectiveness much depends upon choosing the right medicine(s), or the right incentive(s), and on using the right dosage for the illness, or for the pronatalist social setting, at hand.

Certainly humanity has had far more experience trying different kinds of medicines than in trying different antinatalist incentives. But there has even been enough of the latter to show that devising effective incentives does not require infinite foreknowledge.[14]

Unfortunately, our ignorance is much closer to infinite than is our knowledge. Humankind knows precious little about what magnitudes of what types of antinatalist incentives are needed, under what societal conditions, to reduce the fertility rate by any given approximate amount.

A DIVERSITY STRATEGY

What, therefore, should high-fertility nations do? If they defer the widespread use of direct incentives until the ratio of ignorance to knowledge is much less daunting, they will have waited until far too late.[15]

---

14. See, for example, Ronald G. Ridker, "The No-Birth Bonus Scheme: The Use of Savings Accounts for Family Planning in South India," *Population and Development Review*, Vol. 6, No. 1 (March 1980), pp. 31–46. For a descriptive listing of incentive endeavors in developing nations and bibliography, see Patricia G. Barnett, *Incentives for Family Planning?* (Washington, D.C.: Population Crisis Committee, 1992).

15. Though population is exploding with dizzying rapidity, scientific knowledge about the specific efficacy

The imminent need for antinatalist incentives' widespread use and the paucity of scientific knowledge about them combine to recommend a "safety in diversity" strategy. Because no one knows how well or how poorly any specific incentive will work in a given society, this is what needs to happen and soon: to the fullest feasible extent (see chapter 20), each high-fertility nation should institute a wide variety of antinatalist incentives, varying the specifics from locale to locale.[16] Much of that diversity could be the result of different localities devising or helping to devise their own incentives.

Although the lack of leisurely, long-term controlled studies would peeve the scientific purist, the above scenario would yield much useful knowledge. If a nondogmatic attitude prevails, each nation will learn from other nations' and its own unique successes and failures. Each nation could prospectively modify its own mix of incentives from time to time — in the light of continuing experience.

FROM DOUBT TO DANGER

Any serious doubt that nations could fairly soon find an effective mix of antinatalist incentives is almost humorous. I must smile at any such doubt because, like most of the human race, I live in a society that relies upon economic incentive to get almost everything done. Though at home in such a society, I am still amazed at how profoundly that system of incentives affects how most people spend most of their waking hours and most of their physical and mental energies.

The real danger is not that antinatalist incentives will prove ineffective. The main danger is that such incentives could "work too well." In more direct words, would antinatalist incentives be destructive of freedom? Neither the claim of reproductive coercion nor other ethical objections to incentives deserve to be ignored. I am thus compelled to confront them in the next two chapters.

---

of various types of antinatalist incentives can only advance slowly. Even were there time for scientifically rigorous long-term studies in the most prevalent cultural settings sufficient to reveal half of what demographers would like to know, such controlled studies are apt to vary between difficult and almost impossible. But there is not nearly that much time anyhow.

16. As earlier suggested, essential prerequisites are (1) access to family planning services and (2) public education concerning the need for the incentives.

CHAPTER EIGHTEEN

ETHICAL OBJECTIONS AND THEIR ANSWERS — I

Are antinatalist incentives (rewards "and" penalties or fees) an ethically acceptable means of helping to reduce fertility? To decide, we must consider at least five ethical arguments against them.

OBJECTION ONE, COERCIVENESS. When applied to people in poverty, antinatalist incentives necessarily violate reproductive freedom.

Though it took just twelve words, Objection One is an immediately convincing argument. It can immediately convince us because we tend to assume that for persons in poverty any type and magnitude of antinatalist incentive is apt to resemble a desperation deal, the proverbial offer that one cannot refuse.

The falsity of that condescending assumption — and indeed the falsity of Objection One itself — can be seen if we remember two points from chapter 17. First, antinatalist incentives are needed to counteract (meaning to neutralize to some extent) an existing array of pronatalist incentives. Second, any high-fertility society's set of implicit pronatalist incentives is bound to be formidable, even, one might say, coercive. Given that situation, some antinatalist incentives can actually *increase* the individual couple's reproductive freedom.

Example one. A rural young couple is trying to make a living from small-scale farming and miscellaneous enterprises. Their only viable scenario: have several children, sufficiently spaced, and use that cheapest labor supply in various household, farming, and other economic tasks as each child's age allows. But add a second scenario: if the couple will defer conceiving a first child for five years and will plan no more than two children, thus losing much cheap labor, the couple qualifies for special agricultural assistance (discounts on seed purchases and other supplies, first priority on using shared animals or equipment, etc.). Result? Thanks to the incentive, with respect to having children the couple now has two plausible options rather than only one. What has thus been added is some genuine choice.[1]

Example two. Now consider an urban young couple. She is unemployed. He works at a low-wage job with no pension plan. And their nation can hardly afford a general social security system. So must the couple meet future needs by having several children? What if, through some modest taxation, a reduced military budget, and perhaps some outside aid, the government could start an old-age security fund for today's young people who are willing to have no more than two children? Would young couples have less, or more, reproductive freedom? Clearly they would have more.

But the foregoing examples are not meant to prove too much. They do not say that incentives present little or no danger to reproductive freedom. The sobering truth behind Objection One is that governments will need to be especially careful not to pose coercive reproductive choices to impoverished persons.

What Is Coercive?

The term "coercive" connotes a continuum of choices. At one extreme of the continuum are no-choice choices that are more than coercively posed; they are tantamount to being coerced outright. As in Mario Puzo's *The Godfather*, they involve "offers" that one cannot refuse — really threats that one dare not defy — because the cost of refusing or defying would be intolerably high. "Do as I say or I'll shoot you dead" would be a terminal example, perfect for prime-time viewing. At the other, much happier end of the continuum are choices that can be made at no or at trivial cost.

If we are living agreeable lives, we are used to finding most of our choices nearer the gentler end of that long continuum. What I think we

1. See Bernard Berelson and Jonathan Lieberson, "Government Efforts to Influence Fertility: The Ethical Issues," *Population and Development Review*, Vol. 5, No. 4 (December 1979), pp. 581, 591, and Veatch, "Incentives," p. 103. Edward Pohlman, in his *Incentives and Compensations in Birth Planning*, Monograph 11 (Chapel Hill, N.C.: Carolina Population Center, University of North Carolina, 1971), p. 114, rightly notes that added choices enabled by positive incentives can enhance the individual's freedom to benefit both self and society.

mean when we call a posed choice "coercive" is that it is closer to the dismal rather than to the happier end of the scale.

Let us apply that general definition of coercive to antinatalist economic incentives vis-à-vis reproductive freedom. The state withholds a subsidy from, "or" imposes a fee upon, individuals who later have more than x number of children. Whether we call that state action "coercive of reproductive choice" should depend upon our answer to this question: does the incentive require persons who go ahead and plan the added child(ren) to accept a deprivation that is closer to intolerable or closer to inconsequential?

Though the resulting deprivation may fall far short of intolerable, if it is closer thereto than to inconsequential, the antinatalist incentive deserves to be deemed coercive. Similarly, though the deprivation may be more than trivial, if it is closer to zero than to intolerably heavy, the incentive should — as to reproductive freedom — be deemed noncoercive.

Coerciveness as Nearly the Whole Continuum?

Some will argue that any but the most trivial possible deprivation makes an antinatalist incentive coercive. One thing wrong with that argument is that it applies a far different standard of coerciveness to reproductive choices than we apply to the rest of life's important decisions. For all important decisions involve substantial cost or risk. Were we to apply "the more-than-trivial-deprivation standard" to choices in general, all but the most trivial decisions in life would be deemed substantially coerced! If almost all choice-making situations are thusly deemed coercive, the word loses much useful meaning.

Imprecise Criteria

Like almost all choices, most antinatalist incentives are apt to fall somewhere between the extremes of the coercion-versus-perfect-freedom continuum. It will often be difficult to tell whether a specific incentive offers persons a reproductive choice-making situation that is, on balance, coercive or noncoercive.

Though that difficulty cannot be removed, the following criteria can help a government decide whether a given incentive is more apt to be coercive or noncoercive:

1. Will denial of the reward ("or" imposition of the penalty or fee) leave the person or household with no alternative plan for meeting affected needs or wants? And do people's likely alternative plans seem tolerably viable — given life's and a population-exploding society's inevitable risks?[2]

2. How valuable are the incentive payments (whether subsidies or fees, cash or noncash) in relation to the usual incomes of affected people? Caution: other listed criteria may be more important.

3. Does the incentive offer or withhold necessity or nonnecessity goods, and are any cash payments more apt to involve necessities or nonnecessities? Here too there is no clear line between two categories. But it is helpful to consider where on a necessity-nonnecessity continuum the incentive is apt to function vis-à-vis different groups of affected persons. Other things being equal, coerciveness is most apt to accompany incentives dealing with clear necessities.

4. Are the payments to be paid or received promptly or later? Other factors being equal, a deferred cost or reward poses much less danger of coerciveness. For one thing, present and imminent needs cannot dictate the person's decision. And whatever our short-term situation, we humans tend to discount the at-all-distant future. It is indeed "farther away." And it is uncertain. Other events may intervene that will lessen or even cancel the eventual reward or penalty's importance. A distant future subsidy is

---

2. Yes, the latter risks are much too high. Hence the poignant need to reach low fertility as soon as humanely possible.

unlikely to be coercive even if it would provide basic necessities someday.

Comment on 4. The distance and the uncertainty of the remote future also tend to make deferred rewards less effective than immediate ones of like magnitude. And yet, to take an earlier example, the offer of special old-age-support entitlements to today's young couples who forgo the traditional protection of several offspring is both noncoercive and fair. Those future entitlements may, however, lack even minimum present appeal unless individual-account funding occurs from the start on a regular, credible basis.[3] Even with credible funding of deferred rewards, effectiveness will probably also require *some* prompt or short-term incentive "or" disincentive (but which, lest immediacy yield coerciveness and be otherwise inhumane, should not cause people to lack necessities).

5. Like the first criterion, this one includes two questions. First, does the incentive consist of a definite benefit or deprivation or does it merely affect one's chances of receiving the benefit or deprivation? An example of a definite-benefit-or-deprivation incentive is a rent subsidy offered only to couples with two or fewer children. An example of an affects-one's-chances incentive is merely to offer the above couples first priority in obtaining subsidized housing that at least in theory is open to others also. The latter type of offer — call it a contingent incentive — is thus saying, "If a shortage of an item occurs or continues, low-fertility persons will have a better chance of getting that item than will high-fertility persons." Clearly, however, if there is and probably will be only enough subsidized

---

3. That was done in the South India tea estates example discussed in Ridker, "Bonus Scheme."

housing for couples with two or fewer children, there is little if any difference between the "contingent" and the "definite" incentives. Hence the criterion's second question: if the incentive is a contingent one, what is the apparent likelihood that the contingency (usually meaning the shortage) will occur?

Comment on 5. The second question is often crucial. If the relevant contingency is generally believed to be unlikely, even a contingent incentive involving basic necessities can, on balance, properly be called noncoercive.[4]

Criterion 5 would not always be important. If a definite-benefit-or-deprivation incentive does not involve otherwise unobtainable necessities, or if its reward or fee is to be substantially deferred, it is likely noncoercive anyhow.

Cautions

The above five criteria for recognizing coerciveness are hardly a magical or mechanical formula to resolve every close case. And though a given incentive may on balance properly be deemed noncoercive, governments should also consider the likely combined effect of several incentives that apply to the same person or household. Although I cannot prove it, I believe that combinations of incentives, present and future, definite and contingent, can be devised to mesh together in ways consistent with the

---

4. The following intentionally distressing example well illustrates:

Though Nation X has a high birth rate and a low per capita income, the people do not think famine a likely risk, at least for the foreseeable future. It is also widely believed that even if a food crisis did occur, the combination of outside relief assistance and domestic governmental commitment would (unlike some recent tragic failures) probably prove adequate. But Nation X's government is not so sure. Fearful of the sooner-or-later consequences of continued high fertility, it has instituted a variety of antinatalist incentives. Hoping that more people will accept the risks of having no more than two children, it also decides to offer young couples an additional hedge. "Should food shortages unavoidably occur in the future," it announces, "needy households with two or fewer children will be first to receive emergency relief."

Clearly the above contingent incentive deals with a possible life-and-death necessity. But if couples think it unlikely that a shortage of needed food relief will happen to them, they are hardly "coerced" to limit their fertility by a present offer of future food-relief priority. They are not nearly coerced even if accepting the offer is apt to be the safer option. For, as car drivers and passengers, affluent residents of earthquake-poised cities, and countless other wise or unwise voluntary risk-takers vividly prove, people routinely choose to take life-and-death risks if they think the harm unlikely and the benefits of doing what they want sufficiently great.

What makes the above example terribly distressing is not the (false) fear that the incentive is coercive. What causes us distress is our true perception that there would be no nongrievous way to distribute an inadequate food supply.

right goal: to make low fertility sufficiently appealing to enough individuals and households without subjecting them to choice-making situations that are coercive rather than genuine.[5]

Cost-free Choices?

Despite the difficulties of attaining it, the just stated goal will not satisfy all commentators' ethical sensitivities. Some commentators are apt to say or imply that any set of rewards and penalties strong enough to help engender an at-all-rapid transition to low fertility is coercive. In other words, incentives that actually induce most people to act in the common good are thereby shown to be coercive. Thus the only acceptable antinatalist incentives are substantially ineffective ones.

The problem with that hypersensitive view of coerciveness is that it confuses freedom of choice with "free choice." To have freedom of choice, meaning to have the freedom to choose from two or more thinkable options, is, I hope, a reasonable expectation.

But to have *free choice* is neither a realistic nor a reasonable expectation — for none but the most trivial type of choice is cost-free. (A possible example of a free choice would be my choosing which of two seemingly identical shirts to wear, but even that choice might have unforeseen consequences.)

All choices of any significance are choices between or among different costs, risks, and benefits. That is normally what the idea of choice means.

Thus it makes no sense to say that an incentive is coercive because the choices it poses are costly or risky. If one finds coerciveness that easily, she or he is saying that the terms of all meaningful choices are coercive. One can of course say that they are. But in doing so one has not found a useful way of determining which antinatalist incentives are acceptable — unless one has irrationally predetermined that all such incentives are unacceptable.

Consistency, Please

Let every kind heart who would call any apt-to-be-effective antinatalist incentive coercive please tell the rest of us: what should we call a high-fertility nation's strongly pronatalist status quo? Or what will we call the

---

5. Warning: if governments delay long enough for overpopulation to cause substantially increased economic and ecological distress, the above difficult goal is likely to become an impossible one.

desperate antinatalist measures that overpopulating nations will eventually employ if they wait much longer to act in earnest? And what will we call the conditions of indignity and unfreedom that will imprison immense numbers of people if the population explosion is not ended reasonably soon?

> **OBJECTION TWO, UNFAIRNESS. Even if they are not necessarily coercive, incentives that pay people money or other value are unjust. All such reward-oriented incentives are unjust because they are apt to attract disproportionately the economically poorest members of a society.**

Objection Two, like the other four, expresses an important concern. A nation's transition to low fertility should not create or perpetuate avoidable substantial differences in fertility rates among that nation's different economic classes. To state the most obvious example, the poor should not be induced to have smaller families, on average, than the rich.[6]

Happily, a nation's system of antinatalist incentives need not violate that principle of fertility fairness. In the first place, a combination of other social factors may well cause fertility among the poor to approximate that of the rest of society despite the government's reliance upon reward-oriented incentives. Thus it could easily happen that the new lower fertility rates would, for similar age groups, describe the rich, the poor, and the middle-income citizenry with substantial parity.[7]

Correctives

In the second place, if it appeared (or if it was suspected or feared) that a nation's transition to low fertility was occurring disproportionately among the poor, that nation's government could take corrective steps. The idea would be to increase sufficiently the cost of having children to nonpoor couples, so that their fertility-limiting motivation would be

---

6. The equation should take into account any substantial interclass differences in mortality from birth through the childbearing years. It should do so in order to protect the right of unprivileged economic groups to beget future generations on a parity with privileged groups.

7. Such equality could occur even though specific family planning or incentive programs were attracting a much greater proportion of low-income households. What satisfies the valid concern that fertility reduction not be economically discriminatory is that *actual* fertility rates among contemporaries not substantially vary according to economic status.

comparable to the poor's.[8]

For example, mandatory school fees for nonpoverty parents could be enacted or increased with respect to each of their subsequently conceived children. Though the fees should not be allowed to exceed a couple's ability to pay, the total cost to the couple of each additional child could properly become significantly greater than would have been the case without the new or higher fee.

Or a nation could enact an explicit "fertility tax" on nonpoverty parents with respect to each of their not-already-conceived children. (And it could repeal, as to the future children of nonpoverty parents, any existing child-based tax exemption or the like.) The tax could be scaled according to the couple's income and the number of living children conceived after the tax's effective date. Making the tax an annual obligation rather than a one-time levy would likely maximize effectiveness within the bounds of taxpayer affordability.[9]

High-fertility nations most probably should adopt some type of ability-to-pay fertility tax or fee for nonpoor income groups to complement reward-oriented incentives without waiting to see if the latter incentives cause disproportionately low fertility among the poor. If sufficiently explained beforehand, that would be good policy for at least four reasons:

1. It would reduce the risk that the poor would in fact contribute disproportionately to the nation's fertility decline.

2. It would communicate the government's concern that low fertility be equally the responsibility of all strata of society, rich, poor, and middle.

3. The tax or fee would raise revenues that could be used to finance or to help finance the necessary reward-oriented incentives.

---

8. Why not instead offer extra rewards to the nonpoor? First, doing so would probably be prohibitively expensive. Second, it would increase the income disparity between the economically poor and the rest of the society.

9. The annual tax would also likely have an effectiveness advantage over the school fees approach: the parents would begin making payments soon after each child's birth rather than being able to defer any payment until the school years.

4. Couples who procreate and are able to pay need
    suffer no substantial injustice; their tax or fee is
    apt to be far less than their fair share of the
    population explosion's probable costs and risks
    to society at large.

Penalties?

Reason 4 requires some comment. It is usual to speak of antinatalist
incentives as consisting of "rewards and penalties." Despite our tendency
to place those two terms in tandem, the penalty label is not an accurate
way to describe a fertility tax or fee or any other cost fairly imposed upon
procreation in order to help prevent or mitigate overpopulation.

Penalty is an inaccurate label because it suggests punishment. But
there is nothing punitive in expecting persons to reimburse society for the
probable net costs and the risks their behavior causes — just as there is
nothing punitive in asking anyone to pay his own way in matters generally.
Thus, considering the enormous costs and risks in continuing the
population explosion, fertility taxes and the like should be thought of
merely as fees, and indeed as very modest ones.

Fee is the right idea for another reason. As Robert Veatch has noted,
penalty connotes disapproval and blame.[10] It suggests wrongful conduct.
But having children is hardly wrongful conduct. Having children is
wonderful conduct. The problem, which defines overpopulation and
makes trying to prevent that poignant tragedy an ethical labyrinth, is a
truth we'd rather not know: there can be too much of wonderful. Fees are
an appropriate means of attempting to limit a most joyous goodness so
that it can remain as wonderful as ever.

Structural Problem

Part of the need for some kind of fertility fee would also be part of the
difficulty in making it work. That need-difficulty stems from a problem
continually noticed by those who study the determinants of fertility in
developing nations. The problem (which also has its manifestations in

---

10. Although I have here mixed it with my own similar views, I am most indebted to the discussion of
penalties and fees in Veatch, "Incentives," pp. 102–03.

developed nations) is that fathers are often unduly insulated from the economic costs of parenthood.

That insulation may occur because economic (like other) child-rearing costs are mostly placed upon women, and/or because such costs are diffused among extended family members, and/or because costs are transferred from the father or from both parents in other ways. The specifics of course vary greatly from society to society.

In the abstract, the solution is obvious: bring the biological father sufficiently into the cost-bearing picture. Unsurprisingly, however, the means of doing that (1) will be a matter of trial and error and (2) will depend upon the particular economic, social, and cultural setting.

OBJECTION THREE, INDIGNITY. Incentives to affect fertility degrade human dignity by "monetizing" children. Or, stating the argument in religious terms, procreation is too holy to be subjected to fee (tax) or to material reward.[11]

The vital concern behind this objection is the insistence that man must not live by bread alone. What the objection forgets, however, is that people must also live by bread — along with the spiritual.

Of course a child is far more than his or her economic and other social costs and benefits! But this is also true: couples in developed and in developing nations do consider, consciously or unconsciously, economic as well as other factors in deciding — if they do at all decide — how many children to have. And there is nothing necessarily wrong with parents and prospective parents' taking bread and other mundane matters into account.

Likewise, there is nothing necessarily wrong with society's affecting the economic cost benefit equation that confronts couples planning a family.

11. Parallel argument: government cannot tax fertility because there is an inalienable human right to have children. But is there an inalienable human right to have more children than society can humanely accommodate? Even if you answer yes, the parallel argument still does not prevail unless the tax or fee would be so heavy as to prevent people who devotedly want additional children from having them. I am not advocating a tax or fee that would have such an effect.

Concerning Objection Three itself, the claim is not that the necessarily small monetary value of a fiscally affordable reward offends human dignity. (If large rewards are coercive, and if small rewards are degrading, is there an affordably priced reward structure that the objectors would find unobjectionable?) As was already noted in chapter 17, the incentives cannot and should not purport to be repaying couples for the intangible personal loss of a future child forgone. The crux of Objection Three is rather that *any* antinatalist incentive, large or small, monetizes children and thereby degrades.

In fact, it would be impossible for society not to affect that equation. Societies have been controlling it and other factors for millennia, in a mostly pronatalist manner.[12]

But, one might say, it is antinatalist incentives that are evil. If so, school attendance laws are evil. So are laws that prohibit child labor. Both tend to be antinatalist. Both usually make children more costly and/or less economically beneficial to their parents, at least in the short run.

So should one say instead, "It is *intentional* antinatalist incentives that are evil and degrading"? Only if one enjoys making irrelevant distinctions. If it was ethically acceptable for societies to encourage high birth rates to offset high death rates, how can it be ethically unacceptable to encourage low birth rates amidst a life-and-freedom-threatening population explosion?

Taxing holiness? Of course procreation is holy. Procreation is holy because life is holy. But guess what every tax or fee that has ever been levied is a tax upon. Land? Property? Income? Sales? Wrong. Governments can only tax people. Every tax is a tax on people. Every tax is a tax upon human life.[13] Sadly for us when we pay, but happily for the common good, life, though holy, is not too holy to be taxed or to be charged reasonable fees.[14]

Heart. Though chapter 19 will deal with other objections, perhaps the ultimate ethical argument against antinatalist incentives is that they seem wrong to us at the level of the heart. Dare a heartfelt mind reply? If allowed to do so, a heartfelt mind might say this:

It is fine to let the heart guide our ethical choices except when following the heart's feelings is a trip to heartbreaking results. Failure to use sufficient, humane means to prevent massively tragic overpopulation is one of those exceptional times.

---

12. And there are the modern low-fertility nations (and a few high-fertility nations) that offer a variety of economic incentives purposely to encourage more procreation. The beneficence of those items (birth grants, educational subsidies, housing allowances, etc.) apparently exempts them from any "monetizing children" criticism. Such criticism is reserved for antinatalist incentives in the developing nations.

13. One of the oldest taxes, the *per capita* tax, literally a tax upon the human head, makes the point quite well.

14. But, the objectors will then argue, isn't procreation too *private* to be taxed or charged a fee? I agree that procreation as sexual intercourse and pregnancy is essentially private — and in those respects it should remain so. But the number of children that a couple adds to a society's population — at least in the context of threatened overpopulation and all its harm and risks — is undeniably public.

CHAPTER NINETEEN

ETHICAL OBJECTIONS AND THEIR ANSWERS — II

As was warned, this chapter must consider further ethical objections to direct antinatalist incentives.

OBJECTION FOUR, A TRAGIC OUTCOME. Even if noncoercive, antinatalist incentives would encourage abortion.

Though the concern behind it is totally valid and profoundly important, the just stated prediction is wrong. Noncoercive incentives are not going to change a pregnant woman's mind and heart concerning so emotionally agonizing a decision as whether to destroy her own child-to-be.[1] Likewise as to the father's and other family members' wishes.

Anyone who thinks that people would somehow allow noncoercive economic antinatalist incentives to tell them whether to resort to abortion needs to see the rest of the picture. High-fertility nations' rapid transition to low fertility enabled by good family planning programs, population education, antinatalist incentives, and other feasible social change would be the most effective antiabortion effort humankind has ever seen.

How so? Partly because there is a far greater risk of higher abortion rates from what a much-continued population explosion would do to the valuation of human life than there is from any and all means needed for sufficient fertility decline. Though we are facing a future that no one can prove or disprove beforehand, we should believe this: the actual incidence of abortion and of born infant and child deaths would be much lower with antinatalist incentives than will be the case if population-exploding, economically distressed nations further postpone their transition to low fertility.

---

1. Child, child-to-be, fetus — choose whatever label you prefer. She will not decide because of labels.

Prevention

And, as should be old news by now, with respect to sexually active persons the gentlest and the most efficacious means of preventing intentional abortions is an effective family planning program. For the sake of enabling low fertility, reducing the incidence of abortions, and protecting health needs of women (especially of older premenopausal women), family planning programs must not only provide short-term contraception. They also need to provide (or to continue providing) medically sound voluntary sterilization options, intrauterine devices (IUDs), and the new long-acting methods of hormonal contraception.

For most persons who have definitely decided against having more children, voluntary sterilization, if available, is at this writing probably still their best choice.[2] For the great majority of such women, a minilaparotomy or a laparoscopy, performed by competent personnel, offers a very high degree of safety.[3] And either of those operations — or, for men, vasectomy — provides more reliable pregnancy prevention than does the pill or IUD and much more than, with or without spermicide, the diaphragm or the condom.[4]

Thanks in part to the frequency of user error, many or most couples who rely upon self-administered contraceptives after they complete their desired childbearing will have at least one more pregnancy. If a man and woman have their desired family by age 30, with most short-term contraceptives their chances of eventually having at least one more pregnancy are substantially above 50 percent, and they could easily have two more.

Those probabilities are a significant additional obstacle to low fertility

---

2. Voluntary sterilization has become the most widely used birth control method among married women in the United States and in numerous other nations. With an estimated world total of 138 million couples protected by it as of 1990, female sterilization is the world's most used means of pregnancy prevention. Church and Geller, "Voluntary Female Sterilization," pp. 3, 7.

Worldwide, male sterilization was protecting an estimated 41 to 42 million couples by 1991. For helpful information and bibliography, see Laurie Liskin, Ellen Benoit, and Richard Blackburn, "Vasectomy: New Opportunities," *Population Reports,* Series D, No. 5 (Baltimore: The Johns Hopkins University, March 1992).

3. For a detailed examination and appraisal of minilaparotomy and laparoscopy, see Church and Geller, "Voluntary Female Sterilization." A still helpful earlier work is Laurie Liskin and Ward Rinehart, with others, "Minilaparotomy and Laparoscopy: Safe, Effective, and Widely Used," *Population Reports,* Series C, No. 9 (Baltimore: The Johns Hopkins University, May 1985). Because of the convenience of postpartum minilaparotomy and the desirability of an unstressed and well-considered decision concerning it, the discussion of that and other birth control options should be a routine aspect of prenatal care.

4. See James Trussell, Robert A. Hatcher, et al., "Contraceptive Failure in the United States: An Update," *Studies in Family Planning,* Vol. 21, No. 1 (January/February 1990).

in a high-fertility society, and they everywhere increase the likelihood of abortion. They show that despite our instinctual uneasiness about it, voluntary sterilization is, because of its high reliability and relative safety, a benevolent trend.

But uneasiness warrants caution. Despite impressive progress in reversal surgery, sterilization is apt to be, or at least may be, permanent. Family planning programs must take special care to prevent uninformed, unconsidered, or otherwise ill-advised decisions.

To the extent that it has not already happened, it may soon happen that Norplant, improved IUDs, and/or other new long-acting but reversible contraceptives will equal or even surpass sterilization in long-term safety, effectiveness, affordability, and availability.[5] Concerning all such developments, everyone should cheer.

OBJECTION FIVE, AFFECTED CHILDREN. Antinatalist incentives would be unfair to "third party innocents born in disregard" of the low-fertility goal.[6] In other words, they will unfairly penalize the future children of those couples who will opt for a large family despite the incentives.

That is both a plausible and a serious objection. Generally speaking, imposing costs upon or withholding benefits from the parents will also have at least some economic effect upon the children.[7] The likely magnitude and nature of that effect will vary, sometimes drastically, from one incentive to another.

Manifestly unfair and cruel (and extremely coercive) is an incentive

---

5. For a detailed survey of the more or less new hormonal methods, see Robert E. Lande, "New Era for Injectables," *Population Reports,* Series K, No. 5 (August 1995); Ann P. McCauley and Judith S. Geller, "Decisions for Norplant Programs," *Population Reports,* Series K, No. 4 (November 1992); and Laurie Liskin and Richard Blackburn, with Rula Ghani, "Hormonal Contraception: New Long-Acting Methods," *Population Reports,* Series K, No. 3 (March-April 1987). Concerning IUDs, see Katherine Treiman and Laurie Lisken, "IUDs — A New Look," *Population Reports,* Series B, No. 5 (March 1988). All four issues from Baltimore: Population Information Program, The Johns Hopkins University. See also Hatcher, *Contraceptive Technology,* pp. 285–326 and 347–77.

6. Quoted phrase from Berelson and Lieberson, "Ethical Issues," p. 592.

7. It has also been suggested that antinatalist incentives would harm children psychologically by engendering parental resentment or other negative feelings because of the added cost. That argument strikes me as far-fetched, even if we forget that the incentives are not to be excessive. An increase in the cost of a child does not cause parents to love him or her less. It may, if anything, cause them to love the child even more. Further, with adequate family planning services to enable people to control their own fertility, the persons having several children despite the incentives would be persons who clearly wanted them. By making procreation a more conscious choice, both family planning and antinatalist incentives tend to increase the wantedness of each child.

that would penalize the parents' high fertility by denying available necessities to their children. In welcome contrast to that unacceptable extreme, a fertility tax or a benefit reduction deferred to the parents' later years would impose negligible if any economic cost on their children while they were children.[8]

One wishes that all antinatalist incentives could have at least as small an effect upon large-family children as that in the latter, far happier case. Unfortunately, a point made earlier applies with special force: any feasible and acceptable set of incentives with payments confined to the parents' old age would probably not be a sufficient impetus to low fertility in nations where high fertility reigns. For one thing, it is too easy, especially in or near poverty, for a couple to doubt they will ever reach old age. For another, even optimists (or especially optimists?) greatly discount the seemingly distant future.

Quandary

Unhappily, if a sufficiently efficacious set of antinatalist incentives must have a significant early impact upon parental income, it likely will also have some impact upon children born in disregard of the entire scheme. Does that mean that any viable set of incentives will be unjust? The question deserves careful consideration.

Because refusing children available food, shelter, basic health care, and the like is intolerably unjust, incentives that would do that are (let us hope) still excluded from consideration, careful or otherwise. Let us instead consider two incentives that, though not malevolent in intent, would potentially disfavor, and could seriously affect, the future offspring of parents who hereafter exceed low-fertility norms.

I choose the following two examples — call them Incentives One and Two — mainly because they pose the unfairness issue so starkly. If such tough examples are found to be sufficiently just, then all easier ones should readily pass muster.

8. It could, however, eventually cause the adult children of a large family to provide more economic support to their aged parents (who spurned the incentive) than they would otherwise have felt obliged to do. But that outcome is not necessarily unfair. Without the antinatalist incentive involving the parents' later years, adult children of small families would have a decidedly heavier burden of supporting their elderly parents than would adult children with several siblings to share that burden.

Incentive One

The first incentive deals only with schooling beyond the level apt to be finally attained by the majority of the now-being-born generation in the society. It is schooling beyond what the society both deems essential for citizenship and is able to offer to all.

Thus, except perhaps in a very affluent high-fertility nation, Incentive One would pertain to university education. In many a nonaffluent developing nation it would, most regrettably, also pertain to some or even all secondary education. (Whatever be the situation, the incentive should not apply to primary education. No nation, no matter how destitute, can afford not to provide at least a primary education to every child.) Incentive One might read something like this:

> If the number of qualified applicants for a given college or university [and, if also applicable, "or secondary school"] exceeds the number of openings, among applicants of substantially equal qualifications the following priorities for admission shall apply: applicants who are both of their parents' only living child receive first priority; applicants whose parents have a total of two living children receive second priority; applicants of three-child parents receive third priority; and so forth.[9]

Sounds totally terrible. And yet some schools explicitly give preference to applicants who have, or who previously had, a brother or sister in that school. That unremarkable policy clearly discriminates against the only child and against firstborn children. And it tends generally to favor the children of large families over the children of small.

Plus remember the "sibling chain of educational assistance." Among the nonaffluent it can virtually restrict secondary and higher education to children of nonsmall families.

By countering to some extent the educational injustices of a pronatalist

---

9. For the sake of nonretroactivity, the incentive should only affect applicants conceived after its having been officially proposed and publicized. Likewise, brothers and sisters conceived prior to the incentive's official public proposal should normally not affect a sibling's priority. However, fairness and good sense warrant an exception to that latter rule of nonretroactivity. The rule should not be allowed to cause a child from an actually larger family to receive priority over a child from an actually smaller family.

society, seemingly unfair Incentive One would probably add much more justice than it would subtract. But that is not a full answer to the objection under discussion. Right now, however, let us also look at the second tough example.

Incentive Two

Though it too is meant to influence today's couples, this incentive involves the allocation of scarce employment in the next generation. Whenever there was more than one applicant for a given job opening, hiring among its applicants of substantially equal qualifications would come under a priorities scheme like that of Incentive One. Adult children of small families would thus often be first in line for scarce jobs.

Is Incentive Two evil? It is surely evil for there to be too few jobs or other means of earning a livelihood — just as it is evil for young people to be denied full educational opportunity. Neither of those evils should be perpetuated, much less should they be increased. Yet both of those scarcities will greatly increase if the population explosion is not soon ended.

But the question now is whether Incentive Two is on balance a fair or an unfair way to apportion scarce jobs. In deciding may we remember that, in a high-fertility society, persons from a small family are often at an income-earning disadvantage vis-à-vis their peers from a large family? They have less "pooling power." Even the lack of an older brother with established connections may lessen one's chances of finding work.[10]

Therefore, as in the case of scarce education, the antinatalist apportionment of scarce jobs can often diminish unfairness. It does so by countering disadvantages faced by small-family children in a pronatalist society.[11] However, that too does not settle the question of possible unfairness to at least some future children of large families.

---

10. There can also be economic factors in the other direction. For example, children with more siblings may eventually inherit a smaller share of any land or other family wealth. But that parentally caused potential disadvantage is not apt to become an actuality until much later in life. And it is likely to be greatly offset by this earlier and long-term advantage to large-family children: there are several siblings to share the often heavy burden of supporting aging parents.

11. Incentive One's protections against nonretroactivity should also apply. With both incentives, nonretroactivity involves justice to the parents. They, like their children, have a strong psychological interest in (and will often have an economic interest in) those children's economic opportunity.

Further Quandary

Hence a very fair question. Would it be better *not* to introduce any incentive that directly favors small-family children over large-family children? Specifically, shouldn't any antinatalist employment or school admission incentive speak to the parents' own educational or job opportunities rather than to those of their children, who have no say in the parents' fertility decisions?

Sometimes an incentive dealing with the educational or job opportunities of a person making fertility decisions would be both feasible and appropriate. A society unable to provide advanced education for all women wanting such education might decide to offer it preferentially to childless women who are willing to postpone having a family. And women with only one or two children might receive such a preference over women with more. Provided the shortage of educational resources was genuine and uncontrived, there would be some obvious justice in those allocations: women who were postponing or forgoing their traditional path to social esteem would be the ones most in need of increased educational opportunity.

But a much wider use of incentives like the prior paragraph's is problematic. *First, education.* Relating young men's educational opportunity to their own reproductive behavior would be administratively difficult at best; plus the endeavor could have but little effect in many traditional societies where most men already marry at somewhat older (postschooling) ages.

Second, jobs. With respect to men and women who are making reproductive decisions, an incentive by which their fertility affected their own eligibility for all or most jobs could — if they are family breadwinners — be very coercive. And because an increase in their fertility could move couples and single parents to a lower-priority hiring status, when applied to unemployed parents the incentive could deny jobs to households with the most mouths to feed. Job-getting incentives related to job seekers' own fertility should therefore be confined to a small portion of the jobs in each employment sector.[12]

---

12. The avoidance of coerciveness also requires that one's right to keep an already attained job should never be the subject of an antinatalist (or pronatalist) incentive.

A Gentler Verdict?

The above perils and problems should cause us to lessen our dislike of Incentives One and Two. By only affecting large-family children's more distant prospects rather than greatly affecting the parents' more immediate prospects, Incentives One and Two allow both society and the high-fertility household time to try to prevent or reduce any actual future harm. And because the children of high-fertility parents may well opt for low fertility, Incentives One and Two do not tend to disfavor the job-seeking breadwinners of large families.

Those two incentives also offer two added advantages that together seem paradoxical. *First,* because parents want their own kids to be first in line for everything (even if shortages are unlikely!), Incentives One and Two are apt to be an effective help in encouraging the parents to plan a small family. But, *second,* because the incentives' possible benefits or burdens upon the parents' offspring are confined to the somewhat remote future, and because the extent and even the existence of any substantial benefit or burden is highly contingent and at least somewhat unpredictable,[13] Incentives One and Two are unlikely to affect the parents' family planning in a way that deserves the damning label, "coercive."

In more than a few high-fertility nations, an affordable, noncoercive, and sufficiently effective set of antinatalist inducements may require something like Incentive One or Two or both of them as part of its mix. That is added reason to keep trying to decide if those incentives are truly unjust. To make the task harder, assume that Nation A has today added *both* Incentives One and Two to its repertoire.

Another Journey in Time

To monitor their fairness to any eventually affected children, we now take a magic-carpet trip to Nation A about 20 years in the future. We instantly arrive at a local college that has only enough room for one more student in its next entering class. Vying for that one remaining seat are three applicants, whose qualifications are, as best anyone can tell, essentially equal.

---

13. If wise demographic and other policies are pursued, tragic shortages are likely to wane. Crazy optimists say they'll wane anyhow.

One of the three hopefuls is an only child, one has a sister, and the third has two or more brothers or sisters. As required by Incentive One, the one remaining space in the class will be offered to the only-child applicant. If he or she fails to accept, it would then be offered to the applicant with only one sibling. Such is life in Nation A.

At the very same time, a local college in nearby Nation B is facing the above same fact situation, except that Nation B's government has never enacted anything like Incentive One. Because all three applicants appear equally able, the college in Nation B decides to award the remaining space purely by chance.

In comparing the two cases, assume that Nation A and Nation B have been equally serious in devoting resources to make college available to as many young people as feasible. But, to keep our task hard, let us also assume that both pairs of rejected applicants are unable to find another college with an unfilled space.

Were the Nation A applicants who were rejected under the contingent terms of Incentive One treated substantially more unfairly than the Nation B applicants who were "impartially" rejected by chance? I think the answer is no. Two applicants lost out because of their parents' fertility. Two lost out because of the toss of a coin. Neither pair, it seems to me, was the victim of invidious discrimination.

But our visit is not over. Nor are some young people's troubles. The two college-rejected applicants in Nation A are both looking for a job. There is only one opening, which happens to be at a nearby flour mill. Both are equally qualified for that job. Under the terms of Incentive Two, the applicant with only one sibling will be the person hired.

In Nation B, the two college-rejected applicants are faced with an exact replica of the above job shortage.[14] But if both individuals are equally qualified for it, the job in Nation B will go to whoever wins a coin toss. Again a justice question: was the person denied college and job in Nation A treated substantially more unfairly than the person who was

---

14. If, however, Nation B's failure to adopt Incentives One and Two means it has been doing little to end its high fertility, expect, absent a much more morbid catastrophe, the number of apt-to-be-rejected job applicants for any available job to be far higher than one.

"impartially" denied college and job in Nation B? Though the question has become sadder, the answer is still no.

Unjust scarcity. It is the shortage of schooling and jobs that is unfair. And *if* doors must be rudely closed to persons in the next generation because those shortages cannot or will not soon be ended, it is not an *additional* injustice that some faultless losers in that sad game are selected by their parents' fertility rather than by the toss of a coin or other happenchance. Nor, as to persons of essentially equal qualifications, can I think of any less unfair way to apportion the losses.

Justice to Parents?

Though we could argue endlessly about whether rejected applicants in antinatalist Nation A were treated more (or less) unfairly than rejected applicants in coin-tossing Nation B,[15] there should be little argument about this question: which approach promises more justice to the *present* generation, who are the parents of the future children we encountered (and who may look to said children for old-age or other support)? With respect to those parents' psychological and likely economic interest in the success of their children, Incentives One and Two or similar measures would be a much less unfair allocation of scarce education and jobs among the next generation than would any other feasible approach.

How so? Without such incentives in their children's favor, parents who plan only one or two children would have a much greater risk of having *no* child who gets a full education and a good job than will parents who allow themselves the safety-in-numbers of producing several children. Without the above incentives or some equivalent, the parents who will do the most toward ending the population explosion and its tragic shortages are thus apt to become their own generation's chief losers, psychologically and economically, from any continuation of school and job shortages into the next generation.

---

15. My guess: even the applicant who was denied both college and job by Nation A's incentive system is apt to suffer *less harm* than the person denied both of those opportunities by unlucky coin tosses in Nation B. Having more siblings (especially if they are older), the doubly rejected applicant in Nation A is apt to have more economic pooling power than would the doubly rejected applicant in Nation B if the latter person is an only child or has but one sibling. And, though a person with no or just one sibling *might* eventually inherit more land or whatever, he or she *most probably* will long bear a much heavier support-of-aging-parent duty than would someone having more siblings with whom to share that burden.

If there still must be school and job shortages in that next generation, with consequent psychological and economic losses among the future parents in today's generation, *among whom of said parents would such losses more unjustly fall?* Upon parents whose high-fertility decisions will increase the likelihood and potential severity of school, job, and even sadder shortages? Or upon parents whose low-fertility decisions will decrease those shortages' likelihood and potential severity?[16]

Justice to Children?

But justice to parents is no substitute for justice to their children. And it is no excuse for forgetting the fairness owed each individual child who will be born of high-fertility, poverty-stricken parents. For that precious and vulnerable person, is the best that can be said of Incentives One and Two that they are not more unjust than other ways of apportioning possible future shortages? And is "not more unjust" also the best that can be said of how fairly other antinatalist incentives affect those children?

To answer such questions I must try to put my overprivileged self in those underprivileged children's place.[17] I must, at least right now, believe in reincarnation. I must imagine that in my soon-to-begin next life I'll be one of at least several siblings who will be born over the next ten to fifteen years to our poverty-stricken new parents. My future brothers and sisters and I must be born in a nation that at least as far back as the 1990s appeared to need a strong set of antinatalist incentives to salvage its already slim chances for a humane future.

X versus Y. But I do have one choice. I can be born in overpopulating and impoverished Nation X that fails to take seemingly needed steps to end its population explosion expeditiously. Or I can be born in overpopulating and impoverished Nation Y that in the late 1990s adopts a credible low-fertility strategy whose diverse components even include the likes of Incentives One and Two. If I must be one or the

---

16. Such questions cannot be fairly asked with respect to parents who already have a large family. Thus, if enacted, Incentives One and Two should, as described earlier, be nonretroactive. A valid answer to the above questions also requires that population and family planning education and services be readily accessible to all couples. As to those basics of justice, there is no excuse for any further delay.

17. See John Rawls, *A Theory of Justice* (Cambridge, Mass.: Harvard University Press, 1971).

other, do I choose to be a child of high-fertility parents in laissez-faire Nation X or in activist Nation Y?

Please write me in care of Nation Y. I'd rather be a child, boy or girl, in Nation Y — whatever my new parents' fertility. I'd also rather be a teenager in Nation Y — whatever my then parents' fertility. And I'd rather be of college age, indeed an adult of any age, in Nation Y — whatever my then parents' fertility. And yes, I'd also rather be an infant or a fetus, of either gender, in Nation Y — whatever my new parents' fertility.

Why Y? It is not hard to imagine why I'll choose Nation Y. At every possible age shy of 105 I'd have both a better chance for survival and a better chance for a humane existence in Nation Y than in Nation X. And, given an unfair world, that is why, if they reasonably appear necessary, antinatalist incentives — even Incentives One and Two — are fair to me and to all other future children in high-fertility nations, whatever our own parents' fertility.[18] And that is also why nations' continued failure to take sufficient steps to end high fertility is so cruelly unfair to all of us.

An Imperfect Ethical Conclusion

Are carefully constructed antinatalist incentives certain to do no harm? Of course they are not. Unless they prove starkly different from schools, hospitals, and every other governmental or private human endeavor, some harm-doing must be sadly expected — though everything feasible should be done to prevent it.

Ethics seldom allows perfect choices. Whatever one may surmise are the harms and risks of direct incentives and other antinatalist endeavors, he or she should weigh them against the immensely greater evils and risks that would come with massive overpopulation.

There is a moral that applies to every unanswered or insufficiently answered ethical objection to antinatalist incentives or other measures proposed in this book. The moral is this: humanity must not fall prey to

---

18. Like all fairness in this unfair world, the above fairness is highly imperfect. For example, the discussion was forced by current realism to deal only with *intra*national justice, fairness among the members of a given nation. For some imperfect thoughts on international justice, see chapters 23, 25, and 26.

the self-indulgent fallacy of requiring an ethically flawless and ethically riskless solution to the world population crisis.

But what a temptation the perfect-or-nothing fallacy is! People who make their living or enhance their self-image by professing to be more righteous than the rest of us are not apt to resist it. Finding ethical fault in present and proposed efforts to reduce fertility — and publicizing one's moral outrage — can be heavenly sport to pious clerics, to secular scholars, to sanctimonious journalists, and, most of all, to demagogic politicians. And the game is so easy to play.

No matter how well-meaning the players may be, there is a grievous wrong in such self-indulgent ethical perfectionism. It tends to prevent any feasible, credible, humane scenario for ending the population explosion in time to salvage the future for all humankind. It risks imposing unimaginably tragic dimensions upon that already true French proverb: the perfect is the enemy of the good.

CHAPTER TWENTY

MAKING INCENTIVES AFFORDABLE

Though it may become even more obvious by the end of the next chapter, the point can be stated now: the world's rich nations should generously aid attempts by economically poor nations to finance and fiscally maintain an adequate set of noncoercive antinatalist incentives. Rich nations are morally obliged to offer that help. Their doing so is also vitally in their own self-interest, if they have any interest in world peace, human freedom, widespread prosperity, and ecological survival.

But let us assume that the world's rich nations are too wrongheaded to respond to what is both a moral imperative and a dictate of long-term self-interest. Were the rich nations to refuse to pay even some of the cost, could poverty-stricken high-fertility nations somehow afford sufficient, freedom-respecting antinatalist incentives on their own?

Though the lack of financial help would be a great hardship and an injustice upon the poor nations, the answer to the just posed question is yes. This chapter is about why and how even poor nations could afford needed antinatalist incentives without outside aid therefor. Some of the following whys and hows are also ideas for making incentive programs as inexpensive as feasible. In a world of scarce resources, that is an essential goal — with or without outside aid.

FIRST, NET SAVINGS

In any high-fertility nation, the cost to state and society of well-designed antinatalist incentives would be far less than the total of later governmental and societal costs the incentives would most probably prevent.[1] Failure to adopt an adequate set of incentives invites an escalating sum of

---

1. For a concise and valuable summary of the then-existing literature on the economics of antinatalist incentives, see Pohlman, *Incentives and Compensations,* pp. 89–97.

state expenditures and other societal costs from prolonged population-explosive fertility rates.

That escalating sum would likely include soaring school expenditures (and/or poorer or no education for more and more children and young people), soaring public health expenditures (and/or higher mortality and poorer health, especially, but not only, among infants and children), and soaring public relief expenditures (and/or much more hunger, malnutrition, and other inhumane living conditions).

In a Taiwanese township in the early 1970s, families were offered education savings accounts that rewarded low fertility.[2] "Annual deposits averaging about $15 were made for families with two children or fewer; smaller amounts were paid to three-child families. Savings accounts were cancelled after the fourth child. After 14 years, the account totalled nearly $400 for two-child families, enough to pay for three years of high school for two children."[3] According to the project planners, "A very rough cost analysis using present education costs and estimating that each enrolled and retained couple would prevent one birth yields a ratio of savings to investment, in education costs alone, in the neighborhood of seven to one."[4] Although it does not itself pay the bills, the adage clearly applies: low-income high-fertility nations cannot afford not to have a viable set of antinatalist incentives.[5]

SECOND, PROPORTIONALITY, AND THIRD, FUND SOURCES

The second and perhaps most important positive reason incentives would be affordable even to poor nations is this: the lower a nation's per

2. See Oliver D. Finnigan III, and T. H. Sun, "Planning, Starting, and Operating an Educational Incentives Project," *Studies in Family Planning,* Vol. 3, No. 1 (January 1972), pp. 1–7, and C. M. Wang and S. T. Chen, "Evaluation of the First Year of the Educational Savings Program in Taiwan," *Studies in Family Planning,* Vol. 4, No. 7 (July 1973), pp. 157–61.

3. Judith Jacobsen, "Promoting Population Stabilization: Incentives for Small Families," *Worldwatch Paper No. 54* (June 1983), p. 14.

4. Finnigan and Sun, "Educational Incentives Project," p. 6. The much larger question of the total probable net economic effects per avoided birth in a given society is one about which there is much expert disagreement. See Pohlman, *Incentives and Compensations,* pp. 89–91.

5. The above Taiwan experiment also points to a more modest fiscal consolation. Except for administrative costs (which should be small), with respect to couples who do not opt for lower fertility even a reward-oriented incentive scheme need cost the state nothing.

capita income, the smaller rewards could be and still likely be effective. In very-low-income nations effective rewards could be extremely small. Indeed, were they to be any larger a host of commentators would be sure to call them coercive.

But what about a poor nation's minority of citizens with enough income to make them impervious to small rewards? As earlier suggested, they are proper candidates for some kind of reasonable, nonretroactive fertility tax or fee. That possibility points to affordability reason number three: if poor nations accord antinatalist incentives an appropriately high priority, even those nations can find the minimally necessary funds, despite the undeniable difficulties. The funds can often be found in excessive military and/or other questionable current government expenditures. And the nonpoor segment of the citizenry, often including a substantial underground economy, is apt to be an undertapped source for general income and wealth taxation.[6] Semi-easy solutions? Of course not. Impossible ones? Not if they are necessary.

FOURTH, FURTHER ECONOMIES

Besides the frequent cost-effectiveness of rewards of small absolute size, further economies in the design of rewards can materially limit program expenditures. For example, incentive schemes should, to the extent feasible, generally avoid paying people for what they would do anyhow.

Thus it makes little sense, and it would usually be too costly, to reward people for spacing their children in a society where that practice is already established or is fast becoming so. Also, it is usually apt to be more cost-efficient to pay people for actual results — low fertility — rather than for using the pill, an IUD, or other device(s) whose continuous or regular use would (let us hope) not be verified.

FIFTH, COHORT SPECIFICITY

Expenditures for rewards can also be limited and made more cost-efficient by making rewards "cohort-specific." Though it sounds

---

6. Questionable current state expenditures and undertapped revenue sources are hardly peculiar to nonaffluent nations. Their presence in affluent nations further attests to the latter nations' ability and duty to help.

like gibberish, the concept is important. To make sense of it, we must look at the following fiscal dilemma.

A set of antinatalist incentives generally needs to treat couples who have fewer children more favorably than it treats couples with more children. That is its logic — to encourage low fertility. But recall an accompanying logic. Fair-minded nonretroactivity will usually require that regardless of anyone's actual number of living children, all couples be deemed to be childless as of the program's inception.[7] That logic at least means that couples should pay no fertility fee or tax on their previously conceived children.[8]

The fiscal dilemma gets worse. If nonretroactivity is also applied to rewards, a couple who already has four, five, six, or more children would have to be paid just as much reward for having no additional children as would a couple with only one or two (or even zero) children. Unremedied, that kind of constraint would force the program to choose between two probable fiascos: (1) to offer all couples rewards too small to encourage most young couples to plan small rather than large families, or (2) to bankrupt the program by offering all couples liberal rewards that would usually "overreward" those who hereafter limit their fertility but already have a large family.

The least unacceptable solution to the above dilemma is to offer different reward amounts, or even different rewards, to different "cohorts." A cohort here means those persons born in a given year or longer time period.

How would that solution help? Persons just entering or who are still in the early childbearing years when an incentive program commences do not already have, or are not apt already to have, a large family. Thus larger incentives for future low fertility would overreward but few of them. And they, plus persons who thereafter enter the usual childbearing years, are generally the persons among whom the greatest difference in total (life-time) fertility is possible. Those are the people the incentives most need

---

7. Lest popular awareness of a possible incentive program cause a beat-the-deadline onset of pregnancies, the date of inception probably should be defined as when the public first becomes aware that the program's enactment is a serious possibility. Sometimes imperfect justice is fairer than "perfect" justice.

8. Like their fellow citizens, today's parents could — whatever their fertility — be liable for any new or increased general tax, if one is economically and politically feasible, to finance the program.

to reach. It thus usually makes good sense and necessary economics to offer decidedly larger rewards (though larger may still not be large) to persons who, when the program begins, are not yet past the early usual childbearing or procreative years.[9]

There is at least one exception to the above approach. Because the risk of irreversibility makes voluntary sterilization a questionable option for most young adults, any "reward" therefor (1) should only apply to persons who have two or more children, (2) should, at least as to immediate benefits, essentially be a matter of underwriting costs and risks to the patient,[10] and (3) should *not* be larger for young persons.

Concerning another matter, age may be irrelevant. Provided fertility fees or taxes are nonretroactive, affordable, and otherwise fair, there is no need to limit them to younger couples. Nor is there any economic sense in doing so.

More benefit. Cohort-specific incentives, reward-oriented or not, can also contribute to cost-effectiveness in another way. Because a new mix of incentives could always be offered to those persons who reach childbearing age in a given year, there would be increased opportunity to try different types and amounts of incentives — and then to offer later cohorts incentives that appeared to be most effective in relation to cost.[11]

Cohort-specific incentives have yet another advantage. If, for example,

9. Because persons within a given cohort could be treated equally regardless of each person's past fertility, the principle of nonretroactivity need not be violated.

Were funds very scarce, a cohort-specific incentive rewarding present and future young adults might, for example, apply only to "all women of age 18 and over who reached or reach age 18 after January 1, 1994, but before this incentive is (prospectively) modified or made inapplicable to one or more later cohorts." Were it to take effect in January 1998 the incentive in this example would thus initially cover women then between ages 18 and 22, with the maximum age increasing each year thereafter.

Both good sense and cost containment require some minimum age for reward eligibility. However, children conceived after the program's effective date but before one or both parents reach the designated minimum age should normally count in determining parents' reward entitlements and possible eventual liability for fertility fees or such.

10. Concerning the reimbursement of patients for routine costs, obvious examples are transportation expenses to and from a family planning clinic and lost wages when en route and while receiving care. "In some cases, however, the 'compensation' amount has been high enough to suggest a subterfuge to avoid anti-incentive reactions." John A. Ross and Stephen L. Isaacs, "Costs, Payments, and Incentives in Family Planning Programs: A Review for Developing Countries," *Studies in Family Planning,* Vol. 19, No. 5 (September/October 1988), pp. 270, 280.

Though perfect avoidance of overpayment and underpayment is probably impossible, "reimbursement of [sterilization] expenses removes a serious barrier . . . that would otherwise deter the very poor from making use of this method of birth control." John Cleland and W. Parker Mauldin, "The Promotion of Family Planning by Financial Payments: The Case of Bangladesh," *Studies in Family Planning,* Vol. 22, No. 1 (January/February 1991), pp. 1, 11.

11. Would discrimination between different cohorts be resented? Probably no more than (and perhaps less

having six or more children is the social norm in a given region, an incentive program may well need to reward couples who limit their fertility to, say, four. However, if and when four becomes the new social norm, fiscal soundness will then likely require only rewarding smaller family size. The fairest way to do that is to apply the revised incentive structure only to cohorts who thereafter reach reproductive age.

SIXTH, "BUILDING IN" INCENTIVES

The final reason an adequate set of incentives is within reach of even a poverty-stricken nation could often prove decisive. Assume that a given nation cannot afford to offer low-fertility rewards requiring any sizeable increase in government expenditures. Does that constraint preclude that nation's offering most of its citizens a plausible set of antinatalist incentives?

Reason number six says that, if need be, a government can offer a tolerable set of incentives without having to increase the current level of social expenditures. A government can do that (at very little net administrative expense) by building antinatalist incentives into its existing laws and programs in ways that do not coerce persons into low fertility.

One example of that idea would be Incentive One from the prior chapter. A nation's sad but not-soon-remediable inability to provide a secondary or college education to all qualified young people itself enabled a credible antinatalist incentive: eventually allow applicants from low-fertility families limited priority over those from large households.

Other possibilities: waiting lists and waiting lines. In any but the most pampered society, waiting is a routine part of life. There are goods and services for which one often must wait and for which a longer wait is apt to be a nuisance or a hardship but is not apt to be a disaster or nearly so.

---

than) any discrimination between different locales. The latter is another valid way to experiment with different incentive schemes. It is also a recognition that different kinds of communities (rural versus urban, etc.) are apt to need different specific incentives. Could not people thus be honestly and credibly told that such experimentation and diversity are most probably needed to find a mosaic of incentives that is both sufficiently effective and affordable?

Some adjustment of incentives could occur for a cohort even after its members were already in a given incentive program. The rewards offered those members could fairly be augmented or increased. But promised rewards could not fairly be abolished or decreased for that cohort. And, as always, fertility fees could, subject to ability to pay, be fairly increased only with respect to cohort members' future fertility.

A villager may have to wait in line at a common water supply almost every day. A farmer may often or occasionally have to wait his or her turn for a shared work animal or shared equipment. An urban worker may have to wait years for a new apartment. And he or she may often have to stand in line to buy food or other necessities.

Use the difficulty. The above and other regrettable annoyances and hardships could, *if* they are not severe, be put to valid use. They could be used to create, where one is needed, a credible set of antinatalist incentives that does not require increased state expenditures to pay for rewards. Each incentive would afford "a sensible degree of waiting-list or waiting-line priority" to persons who sufficiently limit their fertility. For lack of a worse acronym, "WLP incentives" might have to do.

What might be a sensible degree of priority? Would it be excessive for low-fertility persons to wait half as long as high-fertility persons? That outcome could be approximated by routinely serving two persons from the former group's waiting list or line after serving one person from the latter's. If that seems excessive, make the ratio three to two. Whatever the ratio, waiting should never be the result of anything but a genuine scarcity of supply or necessary delay in distribution.

COMMENTARY

Though it would be a mix of nonmoney reward for low fertility and nonmoney "taxation" of high fertility, an adequate and reasonable set of WLP incentives should, I believe, still escape the coercive label. In deciding, please remember the considerable disadvantages that low-fertility households suffer in pronatalist societies. One such disadvantage is having fewer children to share "standing-in-line duties" for the household.

What the specific set of WLP incentives could and should be would surely differ from one society to another. Likewise as to whether that set would need to constitute all or only part of a nation's total package of antinatalist incentives. What each set would have in common is that in situations where longer waits or shortage-caused deprivations were not apt to be grievous, low fertility would earn persons a higher priority to receive specified benefits.

There is also a common ethical justification. Though appropriate WLP incentives are unlikely to impose severe shortages upon anyone, they are very likely to help prevent a deluge of future shortages so profoundly tragic that we try to hide them in one banal word: overpopulation.

Recommendations. In every high-fertility nation, each level of government, from the national to the most local, should look at the configuration of state and private-enterprise goods, services, entitlements, and privileges in the society within its political jurisdiction. It should look for fair and reasonable opportunities to build noncoercive WLP antinatalist incentives into the distribution of those goods, services, entitlements, and privileges. Some of the possible incentives may be seemingly trivial or wholly symbolic. But they with other less insubstantial ones may add up to a combination that is both effective and ethically acceptable.

CAUTIONS

Would a set of WLP incentives cause too much resentment and social conflict? As with any substantial set of antinatalist incentives the answer is, "Yes, it would, unless people are first convinced of the urgency of the need for low fertility and for an effective and affordable set of incentives to help achieve that vital goal."

But political acceptance should not beget ethical complacency. In all cases, governments should try to avoid creating an excessive as well as an inadequate set of incentives. When applied to the same individuals or households, a combination of incentives can be coercive even though each separate incentive is not.

In a poor nation any set of incentives that can only redistribute the existing level of goods and services is fraught with danger. Any line between people's emergency and nonemergency needs is hazy at best. And any line between necessities and desired nonnecessities is equally unclear. Thus the danger of moving too far toward coercion on the free-choice-versus-coercion continuum would always be present. Carefully braving that danger is justified only because the dangers of a continued population explosion are so much greater.

With respect to WLP and all other kinds of incentives, here is one plain truth: a government should never contrive or perpetuate any harmful shortage, nor should it ever work less hard to prevent or to correct any harmful shortage, in order somehow to use that shortage to encourage low fertility. One reason no government should ever do any of those things is that to do so would be wrong.

And even were doing so not wrong, in the plausibly relevant decades ahead it will hardly be necessary for governments to contrive, to perpetuate, or otherwise to foster shortages. There will be unhappy shortages without any need for government to abet them in any way. There will also be no shortage of agonizing ethical dilemmas.

SUMMARY

The six affordability reasons discussed in this chapter were hardly a celebration. They do support the view that even if the rich nations are shamefully unwilling to share in the cost, the poor nations could afford to create and to maintain adequate and tolerable systems of antinatalist incentives. A much stronger truth also bears repeating. For the sake of their peoples' future, the governments of low-income, high-fertility nations cannot afford *not* to develop adequate, humane incentives — with or without outside help.

Another truth is that rich nations ought to be helping. Hence the next chapter.

CHAPTER TWENTY-ONE

THE CASE FOR AIDING ANTINATALIST INCENTIVE PROGRAMS

The prior chapter offered six reasons supporting the view that, if need be, low-income high-fertility nations could self-finance a set of direct incentives. Absent real-world context, those six reasons paint, despite already stated cautions, a misleadingly optimistic picture. The necessary context is as follows:

With a reasonable level of international aid to enhance it, a set of incentives in a poverty-stricken nation would be a far happier enterprise. The incentives would be less onerous, more humane. Granted the substantial lack of demarcation between rewards and penalties or fees, an aided set of incentives would be more reward-oriented than would an unaided one. It could offer people positive inducement to low fertility without causing substantial hardship for individuals and the families of individuals who choose not to comply. It could improve the well-being of low-fertility households without sooner or later worsening the situation of high-fertility households.

POLITICAL ACCEPTABILITY

Are direct antinatalist incentives too sensitive a matter to allow for outside aid from the rich, mostly Western, nations? In some developing countries, the answer is likely to remain yes. If Western aid of one or more kinds is apt to engender popular mistrust or resentment in a given nation, such aid to that nation should not be given — and would probably not be wanted. The principle (but such risks would be rarer) also applies to aid from non-Western rich nations.

Though the risk of mistrust or resentment is real, much could be done to reduce it. First, aid for antinatalist incentives should only be offered by one or more international agencies in which developing nations are fully and fairly represented.

Second, subject to international human rights norms (no coercion; no discrimination against racial, religious, ethnic, or tribal minorities; etc.), program design and management should be the province of each recipient nation.

Third, it must be understood that helping low-income, high-fertility nations resolve their population crisis is only one part of a general undertaking to save the planet. Rich nations will need to alter their own behavior (see chapter 23).

BETTER NEWS

In most high-fertility nations, the much happier nature of aided systems of incentives should materially *enhance* their political feasibility. A reward-oriented system is much likelier to win popular acceptance than one that merely or mostly redistributes existing poverty. Its enactment would in most cases pose fewer political risks for any government, strong or weak, democratic or autocratic. By enabling a more reward-oriented approach, appropriate aid would greatly increase both the political and the economic likelihood that governments in most impoverished, high-fertility nations would in fact enact and maintain adequate sets of incentives. That and another effect, reduced risk of coerciveness, together make a compelling case for generous outside help.

EFFICIENCY AND EFFECTIVENESS

An opposing argument. With or without their existing debt burden, the world's low-income nations have an enormous need for general development aid. Because the rich nations' willingness to aid is not unlimited, a decision to channel much or most aidgiving into support of antinatalist incentives would deprive the poor nations of needed development aid.

Response: multipurpose aid. The right response to the above objection is about as happy as realistic public policy ever becomes. There is little if any need to choose between "antinatalist incentives aid" and "development aid." As illustrated by the examples below, the same aid money being used for antinatalist incentives could at the very same time also be used for economic development.

There is further good news. As the examples below should also suggest, the economic development funded by antinatalist incentive programs would be the most beneficial kind of development for societies with an abundance of people. It would tend to be "development with a human face" — people-oriented development that would economically empower the individual person and the small group.[1]

Plus, the lower fertility resulting from antinatalist incentives would, by reducing consumption needs, itself enable further economic development. *Conclusion:* aid monies spent for combined antinatalist-incentives-and-human-development efforts are apt to be — by far — the most efficient and effective development aid monies that could possibly be spent.[2]

EXAMPLES

Though most of the program endeavors listed below may seem familiar from earlier discussion, there is, as already suggested, a large potential difference. With sufficient international aid, each endeavor would only *add to*, rather than merely or partly reallocate, the status quo supply of goods and services. Each would benefit households whose subsequent fertility is low without worsening the future prospects of any household whose subsequent fertility is high. Provided that each is carefully designed to avoid being coercive or otherwise uncivil, the following possible projects are worthy examples:

1. special agricultural development assistance offered free or at reduced cost to farmers who sufficiently limit their procreation;

2. increased educational and employment opportunities, giving priority to children of two-children and one-child families;

---

1. See Henry P. David, "Incentives, Reproductive Behavior, and Integrated Community Development in Asia," *Studies in Family Planning,* Vol. 13, No. 5 (May 1982), pp. 159–73, and Lenni W. Kangas, "Integrated Incentives for Fertility Control," *Science,* Vol. 169, No. 3952 (September 25, 1970), pp. 1278–83.

2. That honor is, however, apt to be happily shared with an equally benevolent and cost-efficient friend: family planning aid.

3. increased educational and employment
    opportunities, with priority for women who
    postpone motherhood or who sufficiently
    limit their fertility;[3]

4. more low-cost housing, with priority for persons who
    opt for low fertility;

5. small business development loans on a sound
    basis, with priority to persons who sufficiently
    limit their fertility.

MORE UTILITY

Besides directly (and indirectly) contributing to economic development and individual well-being while encouraging low fertility, monies supporting a good portion of the above endeavors could later be put to similar, additional good use. Chapter 18 referred to an especially humane antinatalist incentive: a credible commitment to future old-age-subsistence payments for today's and tomorrow's young adults willing to forgo the have-several-children mode of old-age security. That incentive could perhaps endure being called a low-fertility old-age security plan. Monies for the above-listed projects in any aided nation could assist that nation's "low-fertility old-age security plan" in at least two ways:

1. The above-listed projects could often involve
    offering individuals, households, or other small
    groups low-interest loans: agricultural development
    loans, education loans, housing loans, and, as
    explicitly mentioned, small business loans. It
    could be stipulated that all interest payments, and
    all principal repayments after a specified future
    date, would be conservatively invested at market

---

3. One wishes that those and all other new benefits could promptly be offered to everyone regardless of anyone's fertility. And one can believe that the educational and economic empowerment of all women would itself be a benevolent encourager of fertility decline. The problem, however, is how most effectively to use limited funds in the short run to foster a long-term future of universal justice and well-being that, in most high-fertility nations, cannot yet be deemed to be an imminent possibility under any credible scenario. Failure to address that best-use-of-limited-funds problem with honest realism will preclude justice for the long term and will even damage what flawed justice there may be in the short run.

rates to help fund the low-fertility old-age security plan. Thus project monies would, from the start, be encouraging low fertility in that additional way. And they would continue contributing to general economic growth and in due course would help meet the needs of elderly people who will have few or no children to support them.

2. Most of the above-listed projects would help low-fertility individuals or families earn higher incomes than they otherwise would likely have been able to earn. Persons with above-poverty incomes could be required to contribute an affordable percent thereof to their own and/or to their parents' retirement accounts.

ADDED NEED

Clearly, in no impoverished nation would the above two possibilities suffice to assure that all persons who forgo the have-several-children mode of old-age security receive comparably credible and comparably trustworthy substitute protection. Therefore aid for antinatalist incentives should, from its inception, regularly include a generous share for specifically assisting each needy high-fertility nation to do all it can toward this vital goal: to institute a financially sound plan for enabling the young couple or individual who chooses low fertility or childlessness to make that choice without thereby choosing little or no old-age security.

For any old-age-income antinatalist incentive to be as effective as it would be fair and humane, couples would need to believe in the plan's future ability to pay them old-age support with at least as much confidence as they believe that additional children could and would provide such help. Perhaps, akin to an earlier noted South India tea estates example, an affordable sum could be deposited annually to each participant's individual or joint income-accumulating account at a financially sound institution. Diverse international investment of the funds in a good mix of currencies could reduce the risk and fear of hyperinflation.

DONOR AFFORDABILITY

Would widespread aid for antinatalist incentives be too expensive a claim upon rich nations' feeble generosity? Before assuming that it would, we might remember a previously mentioned fiscal mercy: because the material standard of living is so modest in the nations that would need the bulk of the aid, the cost of incentives per individual recipient could usually be kept very small.

Just how inexpensive incentives and even incentives-integrated-with-small-scale-development can be is suggested by the following activities of Community-Based Family Planning Services (CBFPS) in Thailand:

> [V]illages that accepted the CBFPS program [were encouraged] to invest some of their money in a pair of buffalo. Village distributors are responsible for the animals, and registered family planning users can rent them at half the price charged to non-family planning practitioners. . . .
>
> In 1975 CBFPS added a small marketing operation to its existing contraceptive distribution program, allowing people who practice family planning to deposit their nonperishable agricultural products and handicrafts at the house of the distributor. Transportation to markets was then arranged. . . . In some villages, CBFPS sponsored discount dressmaking, hair-dressing, or drug purchases for family planners. In other villages, a farmer who had had a vasectomy could obtain the lifetime services of the "family planning bull."
>
> To simultaneously reduce fertility and provide income-generating activities for villagers, CBFPS launched a contract pig-growing program in one district of Chieng Rai Province in Northern Thailand in August 1978. . . . A family planning acceptor enters into a contract with the CBFPS to take a 15-kilo, two-month-old piglet to be fattened on table scraps and rice crop leavings to 90 kilos. The CBFPS assumes transportation and marketing responsibilities and shares the profits with the contract grower. The woman promises to

continue practicing family planning during the pig's fattening period, which usually requires eight to nine months. If a contract grower breaks the contract by becoming pregnant, she is not penalized and the pig is not taken away, but the family may lose the opportunity to receive another pig in the future. As of December 1981 [a good three years after the program started], no contract grower had given birth. An increasing number of villagers are becoming involved . . . .[4]

Rich nations can afford to help.

4. David, "Integrated Community Development," pp. 167–68. Small-scale development projects can help empower women. See generally May Rihani, *Development as if Women Mattered: An Annotated Bibliography with a Third World Focus,* Overseas Development Council Occasional Paper No. 10 (Washington, D.C.: 1978). When women-oriented development efforts are integrated with family planning incentives, that empowerment is apt to be even greater.

CHAPTER TWENTY-TWO

COMMUNITY INCENTIVES — AND THE FREEDOM OF INDIVIDUAL INCENTIVES

Prior chapters focused on "individual" antinatalist incentives, which grant rewards to and/or impose fees upon the individual person, couple, or household. But as noted in chapter 17, a high-fertility nation can encourage low fertility by also using community incentives. The latter dispense rewards "and penalties" (denied or reduced rewards) to communities larger than the immediate family: kinship groups, whole villages, towns, districts, and perhaps even constituent states.

Whether aided or not, a high-fertility nation could enact or foster community incentives whenever it or one or more of its political entities has or is given scarce resources that can be allocated among smaller, component political or social entities. The entity with power of allocation in any given instance may be the central government itself, or a constituent state, or a district or subdistrict. Each allocating entity would have or receive scarce funds, goods, and/or services for distribution to towns, villages, and other communities within its domain.

PRACTICAL AND MORAL LOGIC

Like most individuals, most communities want more goods and services than scarcity allows.[1] That and the threat of overpopulation set the stage for this nonutopian but sane benevolence: allocate some scarce community benefits so as to encourage low fertility and thereby reduce the likelihood and/or the severity of future tragic shortages. Researcher Judith Jacobsen describes:

---

1. Though it was said while discussing individual incentives, this plea applies to community incentives as well: harmful shortages should never be intentionally (or even negligently) created or prolonged. To do so would indeed be wrong — and unnecessary.

Community incentives reward whole villages with development projects as more and more people in the community use family planning, or as fertility falls. . . . [T]he government agrees to reward a community with a project that will increase its wealth. This might be a well, irrigation, a diesel pump, livestock, a biogas plant, a school, roads, parasite control or low-interest loans. The projects are funded if the community complies with specified family planning or fertility goals, such as contraception practiced by 60 percent of couples, or fertility not exceeding an average of two or three children per family.[2]

As is true of individual incentives, community incentives would be a far happier scenario with substantial international aid. There would be much more help to divide among many more villages, towns, and other communities. And the time needed for all communities to experience improved living conditions would be much shorter.

PLUSES

With or without international aid, community incentives afford nations at least three special advantages. First, the local community itself determines the means by which it will endeavor to reach agreed fertility goals. That process greatly increases the likelihood that the specific means used to encourage individual low-fertility decisions will be psychologically, culturally, and ethically acceptable to the people they are intended to affect.[3]

The second special advantage of community antinatalist incentives is

---

2. Jacobsen, "Promoting Population Stabilization," p. 18. Societal family planning and fertility goals need not, and (per chapter 11) for the sake of client autonomy should not, be applied to family planning programs.

In a society where very high fertility is the current norm, community incentives, like individual antinatalist incentives, might at first reward lower fertility that exceeds two or three children per family.

3. At least the specific means will not be decreed from afar by some central bureaucracy that knows little or nothing about the special nuances of each small community in its overextended domain. Nor will those means be prescribed by some meddlesome book author or other equally ignorant foreigner.

I do not assume that democracy or something akin to democracy prevails in all or even in most of the world's towns, villages, and other local communities. But I am suggesting that the local citizenry is apt to have more input in local decision-making than in larger political decision-making. Because the choice of specific means so obviously requires the input of those whose fertility the measures are meant to affect, the process of locally selecting those means may itself be a step toward local democracy even in communities where the people as yet have little or no say.

their consonance with the "group spirit" that graces traditional society and their ability to appeal to that spirit in behalf of planning smaller families. Community incentives tangibly associate lower fertility rates with the whole community's greater well-being — be it in the form of a new well, a new pump, the new village-owned livestock, the new or better school, or some other improvement. In communities where commonly shared well-being has more everyday-life meaning than many of us autonomous moderns can appreciate,[4] community incentives could be a vital component of a viable low-fertility strategy.

Third, people may well see their local community as being a much more permanent and otherwise more trustworthy aspect of their lives than any larger government could likely seem to be. As Judith Jacobsen puts it, "Few people fear their village will disappear; the same cannot be said of whoever happens to hold national office at the time."[5] Thus real improvements to one's local community may seem, and may be, a more secure reward than would future benefits from the capital city.

MINUSES

Like everything else, community incentives also have their disadvantages. They could be futile in urban and other places if a feeling of community is weak or lacking. Though the incentives may themselves contribute to group spirit and to a belief that the community's well-being can be improved, their doing so is apt to require that social cohesion already exist.

The other main disadvantage is of course the risk of coercion. Although excessive individual incentives also pose that risk, the coercion risked by using community incentives is of a different kind. It is the coercion, or at least the coerciveness, of excessive group pressure — of group spirit overzealously applied. A community might so much want the low-fertility rewards being offered that the community would dominate the individual couple's decision-making.

---

4. Anyone doubting that difference should compare the fraternal love and group concern that describes the bestowal of elder status upon a Masai tribesman with whatever it is that describes the freeway at rush hour.
   5. Jacobsen, "Promoting Population Stabilization," p. 20.

RISK IN CONTEXT

In evaluating the risk of antinatalist social oppressiveness, one should consider the community's status quo. Generalization is difficult because the existing degree of procreative autonomy afforded the individual varies greatly from society to society.

That variance is especially great in the developing world. A modern urban setting may accord individual couples substantial procreative autonomy (subject to the residual influence of grandparents, would-be grandparents, and other relatives adept at applying subtle or not-so-subtle pronatalist pressure). But in tribal or other highly traditional societies, to have several children is apt to be seen not as the couple's choice but as expected social duty. The implicit high-fertility commands of that duty are apt to be relentlessly enforced, consciously and unconsciously, by tenaciously strong extended family and other kinship ties.

It is of course the more traditional societies that most need antinatalist community incentives to counter powerful pronatalist social pressure. As is true of individual incentives, antinatalist community incentives in (forgive my imprecision) suitable amount would tend to increase individual freedom by countering strong pronatalist social pressures in the status quo.[6]

CHOOSING BETWEEN IMPERFECTIONS

Like social science omniscience, perfect freedom does not exist and is not going to happen. Either there is going to be at least a small excess of pronatalist social pressure (witness its abundance in high-fertility societies) or there is going to be at least a small excess of antinatalist social pressure.

In other words, in any nonfictional society, individual fertility decisions are going to be partly controlled by relevant social norms. Couples *can* have more children or fewer children than whatever is the usual number or the usual range. But they will probably suffer subtle or not-so-subtle censure for doing so. They will, at very least, be noticed and wondered about.

Given the inevitability of some social pressure concerning fertility, and given our desire that such pressure not be great enough to dominate

---

6. The individual incentives would probably tend more to counter existing economic pronatalist pressures. The community incentives would probably tend more to counter existing social pronatalist pressures.

the individual, the question — and the answer — become clear. Since nations necessarily risk erring on one side or the other (even if they claim to be doing nothing!), should high-fertility nations in danger of overpopulation (1) more likely risk erring on the side of possibly too much antinatalist group spirit or (2) more likely risk erring on the side of possibly too much pronatalist group spirit?

ADMONITIONS

Let no one misread or misuse the above comments. They do not countenance carelessness toward the risk of reproductive coerciveness, whether antinatalist or pronatalist.

Dear governments of high-fertility nations, please excuse me for again reminding you of what you already know: the risk of reproductive coercion and coerciveness should be kept as small as feasible in all of your population programs. Any lack of care toward or inattention to that concern would be evil. Foolish evil.

It would be foolish evil because, as India's experience in 1976–77 showed, episodes of fertility coercion, even though not widespread, can violate the common as well as the individual good. They can turn the people against desperately needed low-fertility programs, thus prolonging the population explosion and enormously enlarging both the projected population size and the probability of massive tragedy. They can also, by the way, bring down the government.

Tyrants of the left, and tyrants of the right, please take heed. Sufficiently efficacious population programs are too important and too sensitive to be handled in the imperial way you are used to doing other, less important things. The need to end the population explosion may well be your glasnost. You can choose between (1) letting massive overpopulation destroy you and your people or (2) letting the need for expeditiously but humanely ending the population explosion reform you. Choose choice (2).

FURTHER RECOMMENDATIONS

Generally speaking, the most important thing a high-fertility nation's government can do to refrain from unintentionally or intentionally using reproductive coercion is to pre-empt its use with a better idea. Specifically, adopt and implement a feasible set of noncoercive antinatalist measures before the need for low fertility becomes desperate.

Do antinatalist community incentives deserve to be on a nation's list of noncoercive measures? Or are they apt to be as socially coercive as age-old pronatalist pressures that have routinely awarded nonconforming women such damning labels as "old maid" and "barren"?

I *know* that antinatalist community incentives can avoid the social tyranny that the above familiar and contemptuous labels reveal. And I strongly believe that antinatalist community incentives can be kept well within the noncoercive half of the freedom-versus-coercion continuum (see chapter 18), if steps like the following are taken:

1. Ask the women and men in each village, town, district, or other community to adopt realistic fertility reduction goals and to select what they believe are acceptable means of reaching those goals. Relevant principle: women must be fully and fairly represented at all levels of policy formulation and application in all population programs.

2. Preach freedom as an integral part of the program. Continually spread the word, from the highest to the lowest governmental official and among the people, that community goals must be pursued in ways that respect individual fertility freedom.

3. Add credibility to steps 1 and 2 by making clear both at the outset and thereafter that communities will only earn rewards for fertility reduction (or contraceptive prevalence) achieved through democratically decided noncoercive means.

4. The persons who promote responsible family planning among the people should be different people than, and should be sufficiently distinct from, the police, the tax collector, and other "heavy

power wielders" who (no matter how kindly they might be) inherently engender fear.

5. Along with its use of family planning services and population education, each community should use noncoercive individual incentives as a means of encouraging personal compliance with that community's fertility-reduction or contraceptive prevalence goals.

IS STEP FIVE ANTICOERCIVE?

Regarding step 5, how might use of individual incentives to encourage conformity to community low-fertility goals help protect the individual against social pressure? Consider the likely social psychology.

Here, for example, is a village that very much wants the farm development assistance that has been promised it if its fertility rate of about six falls to between three and four children per family. After much public discussion and popular input, the village council decides to recommend as follows: couples with three or more living children should seriously consider voluntary sterilization for husband or wife, and all such couples not opting for sterilization should utilize a reliable-as-possible method of contraception.

Although a strong majority of the villagers favors the new recommendations, a few couples, who intensely want to plan a large family, are very unhappy. What, then, is likely to happen if the village relies solely upon "group spirit," social pressure, to encourage sufficient compliance with its goal? The nonconforming villagers who "fail to do their part" in helping the village lower fertility and obtain valuable agricultural assistance are liable to be looked upon with some degree of scorn. They could even earn for themselves the antinatalist equivalents of "barren," "old maid," and other pronatalist curse words.

Surprising solution. But what if the community uses noncoercive individual incentives (rewards and fees) to help encourage conformity to its fertility reduction goals? Nonconforming behavior that otherwise would be seen as shirking one's duty is apt instead to be seen as, "Here is a couple who wants several children so badly that the couple is willing to pay a significant albeit tolerable price for having them."

That profound change in social perception and the resulting real gain in individual freedom is *not* apt to require that the nonconforming couple or their family suffer great hardship. The mere fact that high-fertility couples are paying a significant, specially imposed cost (e.g., they must rent the village-owned work animal at full rather than at half price) can be enough to preserve their social dignity. Would that pronatalist societies had been so kind.

Symbiosis. Well-designed community and individual incentives are a beneficial combination. Community antinatalist incentives can tilt the balance of social pressure away from having to have a large family. Individual antinatalist incentives can prevent the new balance from being coercively in favor of small families and can counter pronatalist economic pressures.

FREEDOM'S UNEXPECTED ALLY

The above humane effects of individual incentives are not incidental by-products. Those effects exemplify a purpose of any noncoercive antinatalist incentive ("and/or" disincentive). That purpose is to protect freedom.

Used along with family planning services, population education, and any feasible mix of indirect measures, noncoercive direct incentives are in today's population-exploding nations the people's only likely hope for the following freedoms:

1. freedom from coercive antinatalist incentives, which are sure to be needed if governments keep pretending that a fast-worsening population crisis is a nonurgent problem;

2. freedom from absolute reproductive coercion, that last-resort nonsolution that could do as much evil as would continuing to ignore or belittle the exploding-population problem;

3. freedom from the pronatalist economic and social pressures that today pervade most high-fertility societies;

4. freedom from an only partly known array of
   massive risks to human health and survival, and
   of other macro-ecological risks, from a much
   continued population explosion;

5. freedom from the various tyrannies (economic,
   political, and other) that a much continued
   population explosion would visit upon the people
   in most developing nations — and could visit
   upon everyone else; and

6. freedom for a future that would both allow
   the human spirit to flourish and allow humankind to be a caring friend to the planet's
   diversity of life.

Notice that noncoercive antinatalist incentives embody freedom as a means as well as seeking freedom as an end. They, along with family planning and this book's other recommended means, are humanity's last fleeting chance to prevent massive overpopulation without destroying the individual's right not to conform. In a disaster-inviting population explosion, they protect the individual's right to act differently from what needs to be prevailing reproductive behavior.

In a life-and-freedom-threatening population explosion, antinatalist incentives that are on balance noncoercive are thus the opposite of laws that say one cannot have more than x number of children. They are thus also the opposite of forced abortions. They are the opposite of forced sterilizations. They are even the opposite of economic penalties, whenever penalty connotes punitive.

They are the opposite of all those things? Yes. Individual antinatalist incentives say to the individual, "Do you want to plan more children than the average number consistent with soon ending the nation's population explosion? If you want to badly enough to refuse some economic reward and/or to pay an affordable tax or fee, you are free to have your desired number of children without being adjudged 'guilty' or even errant for doing so."

PAYING AS FREEDOM

"Freedom if I pay for it?" Yes. My very act of paying the incentives' price *is* my freedom.

Orwellian nonsense? Every pundit who cannot resist the cheap shot (and most cannot) will indeed call the above freedom Orwellian. But it is not at all Orwellian. Why not? Because some couples paying a reasonable price for having more children, and most other persons deciding to forgo that extra joy and the extra price, are, in the population explosion, both the possibility and the exercise of the dissenters' and the majority's procreative freedom.

What, then, are so many nations, rich and poor, low-fertility and high-fertility, aid donors and aid donees, all doing when they reject or postpone the widespread use of direct incentives and other urgently needed responses to the threat of massive overpopulation? One thing they, we, are thereby doing is diminishing present and future human freedom.

PART III

FOR AND ABOUT
THE FUTURE

CHAPTER TWENTY-THREE

THE GLOBAL BARGAIN, WITH DEMOGRAPHIC ESSENTIALS

What has long been needed, has often been called for,[1] and may even be emerging, is a genuine "planetary partnership," a "global bargain," among all humankind. If it happens, it will begin a new era in relations among the world's nations and among all peoples on earth.

The basis for the global bargain is the simple truth that we all live together on this good earth. The purpose of the bargain is to care for this life-giving planet in ways that will allow humankind, and the vast diversity of other life, a sustainable future. Given man's increasingly heavy impact upon the Garden of Earth, everyone's well-being hence-forth depends upon a viable, earth-caring partnership among all nations, rich, poor, high-fertility, low-fertility, and all degrees between. Viability requires that the partnership also be a road to that most elusive of goals: justice for all.

But what global bargain is needed? As even the following short summary attests, the components need not surprise.

DUTIES OF DEVELOPED NATIONS

1. *"Reindustrialization."* The world's industrialized, afflu-ent nations should agree to reduce sufficiently, in feasible but significant increments, their (our) levels of environmental-ecological harm-doing. Likewise as to their (our) overuse of critically scarce resources.

The goal of that gradual but expeditious-as-feasible economic self-transformation would be for rich nations to do their part in an endeavor needing the participation of all nations: to develop modes of

---

1. See, for example, *The Planetary Bargain: Proposals for a New International Economic Order to Meet Human Needs* (Princeton, N.J.: Aspen Institute for Humanistic Studies, Program on International Affairs, 1976).

economic well-being, including modes of production and consumption, that can be shared with *all* the world's peoples who may want them — without thereby wrecking the earth.

2. *Demographic nonhypocrisy.* Though there are exceptions at both ends of a wide spectrum, in most rich nations fertility is already low, past baby booms have about lost their momentum, and population is headed toward imprecise "zero growth" or negative growth. Nonetheless, to the extent that deliberate policies are now or later become needed to beckon or preserve either low fertility or no-greater-than-approximate-zero growth in rich nations, this is true: rich nations, just like poor and in-between nations, should feel obliged to enact them.[2]

3. *Aidgiving* (per prior chapters). The world's affluent nations need to provide adequate family planning aid to nations with low income and high fertility. Affluent nations also need to give much more aid for environmentally sound economic and human development, emphasizing health, education, job creation, and small-farm and small-business empowerment. (Consider these two truths: first, economic development that cares for people and planet requires sufficient governmental action; second, the major component of development should be private entrepreneurship. Questions: why do leftist ideologues see only the first truth, and why do rightist ideologues see only the second?)

    Aid-recipient governments' use of the aid. In order for development aid to yield an improved rather than

---

2. As suggested in note 2 of chapter 15, immigration policies are — despite heated controversy as to what justice requires — a relevant and sometimes major component of a nation's ability to limit its population growth. See Leon F. Bouvier and Lindsey Grant, *How Many Americans?* (San Francisco: Sierra Club Books, 1994).

a disastrous long-term future, recipient governments should, until low fertility is achieved, offer individuals and communities the funded benefits as antinatalist incentives whenever feasible. Part of "whenever feasible" is that the result not be reproductive coerciveness or worse. Moreover, all kinds of aided endeavors need to be a friend rather than a foe of women's empowerment.

EARTH-CARING DUTIES OF DEVELOPING NATIONS

Like the duties of the developed nations, the developing nations' part of the earth-caring bargain should be no surprise. The developing nations need to avoid the self-destructive folly of repeating, on what would be a demographically far greater scale, the earth-wrecking mistakes of the developed (yes, "misdeveloped") nations. Developing nations thus need to address their already serious pollution problems (to which the West has generously contributed). They need to do that *before* the magnitude of those problems precludes affordable solutions.

And like all other nations, they sorely need to protect their gravely imperiled ecological resources.[3] Finally, lest all other endeavors prove futile, developing nations with fertility above replacement need to attempt a soon-as-humanely-feasible transition to low fertility rates conducive to a viable short-run and long-run future.

SANCTIONS?

Who or what would enforce the global bargain? The most effective enforcement would likely be a combination of (1) nations' common self-interest in building a liveable future and (2) each party's realization that its failure to honor the bargain would encourage comparable or worse failure by others.[4]

---

3. Rich nations should contribute a fair share of the cost. At stake are the planet's major but fast-receding natural storehouses of millions of animal and plant species, unique and irreplaceable biological treasures. At stake are most of the world's remaining natural greeneries and other natural ecosystems, whose progressive destruction threatens all life — but whose conservation would earn their owner-nations ever-increasing wealth, endless thanks, and unrivaled prestige.

4. Mutual self-interest in its observance is why any voluntary international agreement ever works.

The rich nations would know that their own failure to show more environmental, ecological, and resource-conserving care, or their failure to provide significant aid, would tend to lessen the poor nations' ability and willingness to pursue earth-caring goals.[5] The high-fertility, low-income nations would likewise know that *their* showing a substantial lack of resolve would in turn be self-defeating: it would, for example, tend to lessen the rich nations' propensity to self-reform and to provide aid.

A BRIEF CASE FOR AID CONDITIONS

Given the severe resource-use disparities between most developed and most developing nations, where is the justice in making future aid from the former at all conditional upon earth-caring diligence by the latter? The justification for any such *quid pro quo* is the need for the global bargain itself: in a profoundly endangered world, the well-being of everyone, rich and poor, depends upon each nation's moving as fast as it can to policies and practices that sufficiently care for the earth.

Development aid to nations that are willing to protect their forests, wetlands, and other natural ecosystems, and that care about the beleaguered tribal peoples who have long known such places as home, can do lasting good. Development aid to nations that insist upon acting as if they care little or nothing about human or other ecology is not merely a waste of scarce time and money. It is subsidization of harm-doing, whose consequences are apt to be irreversible, massively grievous, or both.

A TOO VITAL CONDITION?

Should a serious commitment to achieving low fertility be a condition for a high-fertility nation to continue receiving development aid? Provided that aidgivers respect each nation's right to design and implement its own specific set of credible and humane antinatalist *means*, the answer has to be yes.

Sages who say that even a nation's fertility *goals* are entirely its own prerogative need to notice that in most high-fertility nations the need for

---

5. Rich Nation A would also know that any shirking by it would tend to encourage rich Nations B and C to shirk that much or more. A stubbornly shirking rich nation would deserve economic sanctions from nonshirking nations with whom it trades.

economic assistance is or will be headed upward. There is no plausible scenario that promises enough economic aid and foreign investment to meet the soaring dire needs of the developing world if the population explosion continues much longer.

Absent an early onset of low fertility, it is most probable that aid-recipient nations' fast-increasing needs will eventually far surpass donor nations' aidgiving capacities. The magnitude of the resulting tragic harm is apt to be immensely greater than if no development aid had been given at all. Thus both sanity and ethics require that aid policies try to help prevent rather than to help instigate that sorrowful outcome.

A serious effort at achieving low fertility should be an aid condition because of the potential good such a condition would foster and the potential harm it would help prevent. Development aid to nations whose governments are willing to use the aid in a development strategy that includes encouraging low fertility can help aided peoples reach a viable future. Development aid to nations *unwilling* to do much about their continuing population explosion is an experiment in recklessness. It is aid that invites, and will most probably contribute to, catastrophe. It is aid to lull recipient nations into a false complacency or at least into a false sense of nonurgency.[6]

A CLAIM TO BE HONORED

The preceding comments point to the most fundamental moral reason that every nation's demographic goals are the world community's proper concern. All nations must avoid overpopulating themselves if every human being is to have a decent chance for physical, mental, and spiritual self-fulfillment.

We cannot say, "Every human being has the right to enough food, water, clothing, fuel, shelter, health care, education, and other scarce resources," and also say, "Each nation has the right to decide how high it wishes its population to grow." Not in the same universe can we honestly say both of those two things.

---

6. The above commentary is not, repeat not, a case against offering development aid. It is a case against offering development aid without sufficient conditions. For further discussion, see chapter 7, "Selective and Conditional Aid," in Michael D. Bayles, *Morality and Population Policy* (University, Ala.: University of Alabama Press, 1980).

To say that every human being has the right to sufficient resources is to affirm that each human being has a profound moral and economic claim upon us all. Despite its profundity, we cannot take that moral-economic claim seriously if we also say that every nation has the right to produce as many claimants as it wishes.

It is because every human being does have a profound moral-economic claim upon the rest of us that each nation's population goals are a proper concern of all other nations. In a world community wanting to recognize each person's moral claim to a liveable share of the earth's scarce resources, no nation's population growth is a purely internal matter.[7]

NEO-EVILS?

Some may still say that a global bargain with a low-fertility component is neocolonialism. Or even neoracism.[8] Yet would it not be supremely condescending for rich nations to fail to call upon high-fertility low-income nations to share fully in the common enterprise of building a sustainable global future?

Would it not be supremely condescending to exempt high-fertility nations, rich or poor, from the newly recognized imperative of every nation's doing what it can to help build a liveable future for all humankind? Would not any such exemption, no matter how narrow or nebulous, be the ultimate subtle neocolonialism, the ultimate subtle neoracism?

Or would it even be subtle? I can think of no greater moral slight to a nation or to a people in today's world than for other nations *not* to try to negotiate it into full participation in a desperately needed common effort at salvaging everyone's Earth.[9]

---

7. Likewise, *on an environmentally and ecologically threatened planet* no nation's population growth is a purely internal matter. If it has become true that the human race is going to sink or swim together, then no nation's population growth is any longer a purely internal matter.

Nor is any other activity that causes or significantly risks causing environmental or ecological risk or harm beyond a nation's borders a purely internal matter. Hence the need for a panoply of adequate internationally agreed strategies to protect the planet's diversity of life.

8. Paradox: those who cast such heinous labels at the goal of global zero population growth are playing fast and loose with the well-being and survival prospects of — most especially — the peoples they are purporting to protect.

9. Notice that *all* nations, rich, poor, high-fertility, low-fertility, will need to be "negotiated," by each other, into that common effort.

INTERVENTION AND INFLUENCE

Or does *any* attempt by developed nations to enter into a partnership with developing nations constitute undue intervention? If so, the prohibition comes a bit late.

To cite a most relevant example, it was, in part, Western intervention that led to the current population explosion. It was partly the West that through the magic wand of modern medicine, facilitated dramatically lower Developing World death rates. It was the affluent West that intervened in that way without also helping the "aided" nations to lower their birth rates enough for their peoples to escape accelerating economic, ecological, and social havoc. Having thus been partly responsible for the developing nations' present demographic crisis, the affluent nations must accept some serious though secondary responsibility for its timely and humane resolution.

Speaking of intervention, the world's rich nations are still busily influencing the lives of the world's high-fertility, low-income peoples. Unfortunately, most of that influence bestows more harm than good. Most of today's foreign aid — and virtually all of today's foreign investment — implicitly says to the host nation, "Continue pretending you have no population crisis. Defer any adequate response until it's too late."

We in the affluent nations also influence the lives of nonaffluent peoples by the extravagant resource-use-and-abuse example we still set. Of all our dubious cultural exports to the developing nations, the most dangerous is our fraudulently soothing but louder-than-words message: humanity can keep on assaulting and plundering the earth's scarce resources as if there were no tomorrow.

What kind. And so the question is not about whether rich nations will influence poor nations. The ongoing industrial-scientific-technological-informational-commercial revolution — and hundreds of millions of records, tapes, reels, bottles, cans, packages, and boxes of Western junk all over the non-Western world — have already answered that one. The question is what kind of influence there mostly shall be.

By what kind I mainly mean what probable consequences. Shall there mostly be influence apt to promote the sustainable well-being of the world's economically distressed, population-exploding peoples? Or shall there be influence conducive to people's eventual cultural destruction and/or physical destitution?

Whatever influence occurs between nations, one constitutive truth is, at long last, clear. The influence should be, must be, a two-way street. The global bargain, the planetary *partnership,* rightly asks much of the developed nations, and it rightly asks much of the developing nations as well.

CHAPTER TWENTY-FOUR

WERE THIS BOOK'S PROPOSALS ATTEMPTED, WHAT WOULD HAPPEN?

Let us imagine the unexpected but possible. The world's nations start to act sensibly. They agree to and begin to implement something like the "global bargain" outlined in the prior chapter. As part of that bargain, each nation above replacement makes achieving no-greater-than-replacement fertility a high-priority goal.

POPULATION POLICY: IMAGINING A FAIRLY SPECIFIC SCENARIO

With nontoken assistance from rich nations where needed, above-replacement-fertility nations, rich and poor, give family planning the resources it deserves. By the end of the next three years, each of today's above-replacement nations is offering an adequate array of family planning services and providing population education to its households.

During the three years such nations are establishing adequate family planning programs, each of the world's high-fertility nations is, with international assistance if needed, also doing these two things: (1) making use of *indirect* antinatalist means to the extent that other compelling claims upon scarce resources allow, and (2) testing various types of *direct* but noncoercive antinatalist incentives "and" disincentives in a diverse array of pilot programs. Once its family planning services are fully available, each high-fertility nation, with feasible international help if needed, then does this good thing: after making a sufficient case to the people, it widely establishes a set or sets of noncoercive individual and community antinatalist incentives "and" disincentives.[1]

With outside funding where needed, by about the year 2000 each

---

1. "Or sets" refers to the likelihood that different communities within the same nation would have (and, I hope, would have devised or helped to devise!) different sets of incentives. That likelihood applies both to individual and to community incentives.

high-fertility nation has a reward-oriented set or sets of antinatalist incentives at least for all couples (and single childbearing-age women) under, say, age 30. The maximum age of persons eligible for a full share of rewards will be raised by one year in each succeeding year.[2]

Regardless of age, parents who can afford it pay an annual fertility tax for children conceived after its enactment. And, if also needed, a set of noncoercive and otherwise tolerable "built-in" or WLP incentives (per chapter 20) also applies to parents of all ages.

DEMOGRAPHIC CONSEQUENCES

Were governments to act in the above fashion, which includes their showing credible political leadership, what demographic changes would result? Although it is not possible to prove the answer beforehand, it is highly probable that fertility rates would fall with extraordinary rapidity.

Given the above-described efforts, a reasonable guess is that, in most high-fertility nations, fertility would fall by about one child per woman each three to four years until approximate replacement is reached. Mainly because the three years just ahead would see family planning programs progressively meeting current unmet need for contraception, the above average pace of decline could be under way about a year from now.

Nations with present fertility of about four children per woman would likely reach approximate replacement rate very soon after the end of the 20th century — meaning within about the next five to eight years. Nations with a present fertility rate of roughly five children per woman would likely reach approximate replacement sometime within the first decade of the 21st century, say within about eight to twelve years hence. Most nations with present fertility of about six children per woman would likely reach approximate replacement rate sometime after 2005 but before 2015.[3]

Though their fertility rates would probably fall rapidly toward and then to replacement or thereabouts, population in today's high-fertility nations

---

2. Though fiscal constraints preclude older persons from receiving rewards, older adults who wish no more children are reimbursed for all costs incident to voluntary sterilization or other long-term contraceptive option.

3. In that and all other cases, the likely time frame for any particular nation would depend upon a host of factors, known and unknown, and thus could differ substantially from other nations with a similar present fertility rate.

would still grow substantially for several decades. That growth would mainly embody the earlier noted demographic momentum already existing in those nations: all have a very high proportion of young people, thus a much enlarged supply of future parents, so, even at low fertility, the prospect of much population growth.[4]

QUALITY-OF-LIFE CONSEQUENCES

In most nations where high fertility was falling, population growth in the decades ahead would seriously tax those nations' economic, environmental-ecological, and social-political-institutional resources. But conditions would be far better than if fertility had remained high. Populations would not be growing at rates nearly as apt to overwhelm nations' ability to cope and to develop. Life is apt to be much kinder than otherwise would be the case.

How would rapidly declining fertility favor the people's well-being? Consider the following factors and effects.[5]

First, economic production. A smaller supply of additional people in today's high-fertility nations would *not* tend to limit those nations' economic output. It would not limit output (or much limit workforce size) in the years just ahead primarily because in those years the added people would of course be infants and children.

It is also unlikely to limit output in later years. In today's high-fertility nations, the children already born and the children (even with rapid fertility decline) sure to be born in the decade just ahead will become part of a congregation of working-age adults much larger than their nations' present supply thereof — a present supply that in most such nations already suffers from massive unemployment and underemployment. In neither the next generation nor beyond are high-fertility nations likely to experience a shortage of workers. Rather, most developing nations will be

---

4. But see chapter 25 concerning the possibility of lessening some of that growth.

5. Although responsibility for the ensuing discussion is mine, that discussion is indebted to the following sources: Gunnar Myrdal, *The Challenge of World Poverty: A World Anti-Poverty Program in Outline* (New York: Pantheon Books, 1970); Gunnar Myrdal, *Asian Drama: An Inquiry into the Poverty of Nations*, Vol. 2 (New York: The Twentieth Century Fund, 1968); and Ansley J. Coale and Edgar M. Hoover, *Population Growth and Economic Development in Low-Income Countries* (Princeton, N.J.: Princeton University Press, 1958). Though those writers' views have been the subject of much controversy in later years, their relevant main ideas have, in my judgment, substantially weathered the storms.

extremely lucky if they can provide jobs for nearly all the would-be workers that even a rapid transition to replacement fertility would still yield.

Second, the dependency ratio. Unlike its having little or no limiting effect upon a developing nation's economic output, declining fertility would begin immediately to make a difference in the number of persons whose needs that output must meet. In doing that, it would be reducing the nation's dependency ratio, meaning the proportion of its people who are wholly or mostly dependent upon the income of one or more other persons.

Though the time for governments to act is fast expiring, economist-sociologist Gunnar Myrdal's words still apply:

> There would be fewer children to support. If the lower fertility were maintained, this decrease in the dependency burden would continue until the children began to reach working age. The decrease in the [relative] population of children would be progressive if the decline in fertility rate were gradually intensified.
>
> A couple of decades hence, when the depleted [i.e., proportionately smaller] age cohorts would have reached adulthood, there would also be a decline in the relative number of people in the reproductive age groups. Still further ahead, if fertility were stabilized at a lower level than the present one, the age distribution would also tend to become stable — at a lower dependency ratio than the present very high one.
>
> . . . [Thus] a decrease in fertility would make people less poor. The income per head would increase.[6]

Third, effects upon consumption needs. Smaller increases in population would soon yield immense differences in necessary consumption from what a continuation of present high fertility would require. For example, in 1985 Kenya's National Council for Population and Development compared two alternative scenarios. One assumed a continuation of the

---

6. Myrdal, *Challenge,* pp. 146–47 (emphasis and footnote deleted; bracketed words mine).

then-current fertility rate of about eight children per woman. The other assumed that fertility would steadily decline to four. The projections showed that "by the year 2010, Kenya would have 38 million people if women had an average of four children, compared with 57 million under higher fertility. With a drop in fertility, 3.2 million fewer tons of the country's staple food, corn, would be required for the population in 2010 . . . ."[7] The 3.2 million tons' savings from what was estimated to be its likely corn requirements without fertility decline would be no less than *twice* Kenya's total corn production in 1980.[8]

Concerning the above example, note three things. First, had it imagined a decline of fertility to replacement, the study would have shown even greater effects. Second, the resulting differences in consumption needs *after* 2010 would be still greater, much greater, because the assumed continued difference in fertility would make a progressively larger difference in population (until, if high fertility persisted, catastrophic mortality cruelly intervened). And third, the study projected the effect of reduced population growth upon needs for only a single commodity, albeit Kenya's basic one. Conclusion: the enormity of the savings in total consumption needs were fertility to decline to replacement would astound the mind and amaze even the most blasé computer.

Fourth, secondary effects. With a lower dependency burden and therefore increased per capita income, people could, in Gunnar Myrdal's words, "eat better[,] . . . be better housed[, and] . . . have a larger share in the educational and health facilities and other benefits provided for in the public budget." Myrdal further explains:

> [A] secondary effect of the higher consumption levels would be to raise productivity by increasing both labor input and labor efficiency. This effect would be most pronounced in the poorest countries, where particularly low levels of nutrition, health, and education depress the duration and efficiency of work, and participation in work, even more than elsewhere.

---

7. Sheila Rule, "African Rift: Birth Control Vs. Tradition," *New York Times,* August 11, 1985, p. 1, col. 5, p. 14, col. 4.
    8. Ibid.

Moreover, at progressively higher levels of income per head, more could be saved or devoted to direct investment . . . [and/or to] "forced savings" through taxation or other means. Both forms of saving would, after some delay, tend to increase income per head still further, with cumulative effects similar to those of the initial rise in income per head due to lower fertility. . . .

Also, relatively more of total national income could then be devoted to raising the living levels of children, with especially beneficial effects on productivity in the long run. Thus public expenditures for educational and training facilities could be increased. Larger efforts could also be devoted to improving health facilities. Better health standards for adults as well as children would result, and still further improvements of labor input and efficiency would be possible. Finally, . . . nearly all these direct and indirect effects of a decline in fertility would facilitate the productive integration of the expanding labor force into the economy.[9]

No wonder, then, that Myrdal can conclude as follows: "[T]he effects of a decline in fertility would be favorable in both economic and more broadly human terms . . . . [T]hese effects are . . . cumulative, gaining momentum over the years. They would also be independent of the man/land ratio: the same causal mechanism must operate in sparsely as in densely populated countries."[10]

CAUTIONS

There are, however, at least four main cautions. *First*, as suggested earlier in this book, low fertility is no guarantor of, nor is it an automatic pilot to, a humane future. What low fertility would do is to make that future a realistic and credible goal. It will allow the emergence of a humane world if nations will complement low fertility with other reasonably wise policies.

---

9. Myrdal, *Asian Drama,* Vol. 2, pp. 1466–67 (footnotes omitted).
10. Ibid., 1467 (emphasis deleted).

Second, Gunnar Myrdal was looking at the developing world of well over two decades ago. Since that time many a developing nation's population has doubled or nearly so. And the explosive growth continues — at much greater absolute magnitudes. Because Myrdal's and others' early pleas for prompt and extensive efforts to lower fertility[11] have in most developing nations remained largely unheeded, the problems in most such nations under any fertility reduction scenario will be greater than he reckoned.[12]

Third, for at least some nations their longstanding past delay in achieving low fertility may mean little or no short-run improvement in economic conditions despite declining fertility. In some of those nations it may, for quite some time, take low fertility, wise economic policies, *and* generous economic aid merely to prevent a worsening of living conditions.[13]

Yet even, indeed especially, in those nations and in the nations that might fit point four below, an earlier comment applies to both the near term and the long term. Living conditions will be far better than would be the case with continued high fertility. The widening differences in living conditions between nonaffluent nations that were rapidly reducing fertility rates and any nonaffluent nations that still were not would belatedly convince even the most comatose government: continued high fertility is inhumane madness.

Fourth, at least some nations may find that though fertility declines to replacement within the hoped for time frame, demographic momentum (see chapter 8) temporarily causes population growth that is too fast and too large for even minimal well-being — with or without generous economic aid. Hence, in part, the next chapter.

---

11. E.g., ibid., 1471–72.

12. That unhappy truth hardly recommends further procrastination.

13. Probably the single greatest challenge will be to provide minimally sufficient or even semisufficient employment for a much larger working-age population.

CHAPTER TWENTY-FIVE

TIMING, TEMPORARY SUBREPLACEMENT, AGE DISTRIBUTION, AND SUPPORT OF THE ELDERLY

The potential problem was raised at the end of the last chapter: even if fertility declines to replacement within the hoped-for time frame, some nations could find that demographic momentum is temporarily causing population growth that is too fast and too large for minimal well-being. That could happen even with generous economic aid.

In nations where such a situation appears likely, their governments may try to lessen momentum-caused population growth. They could make that attempt in either or both of two humane ways.

TIMING

The first way to lessen growth from momentum is to encourage delays in procreation. That includes encouraging people to wait longer before planning a first child and/or to increase spacing between children. Though longer spacing would have the smaller effect on population growth, there are (see chapter 9) vital health benefits to mothers and children from adequate child spacing.

Recall that prevention of adolescent pregnancy is also a vital health matter. Moreover, an increase in the average age of childbearing (mainly caused by later first births) can substantially reduce momentum-caused population growth.

Demographer John Bongaarts offers two examples of that growth reduction potential. If its average age of childbearing gradually but permanently increased by five years over the two and one-half decades from 1995 to 2020, the developing world's population in 2100 could be (though decidedly greater than today's) 1.2 billion less than otherwise expected. Even were the average childbearing age to increase by only 2.5 years, the developing world's population in

2100 could be over a half billion less than would otherwise be likely.[1]

How can delayed procreation be encouraged? Though he mentions increasing the legal age of marriage, Bongaarts rightly emphasizes a happier way to increase the probable age of first pregnancy: improving educational opportunity for women.[2] That endeavor's potential to delay motherhood, to reduce total fertility, and to hasten gender justice makes it a most benevolent goal.

Adding to that endeavor, the mass media and direct incentives could both be appropriately used to encourage delayed parenthood. And, as did chapter 10, Bongaarts rightly recommends another aspect of preventing early pregnancy. Nations, indeed all nations, need seriously "to address the neglected issues of adolescent sexuality and reproductive behavior."[3]

TEMPORARY SUBREPLACEMENT FERTILITY

The second way to lessen momentum-caused population growth is, with mixed thanks to China, more widely known. It is to foster (if they were not already happening) *sub*replacement fertility rates on a temporary basis.

Only one child? A decision to favor subreplacement fertility need not mean, nor should it mean, governmental attempts to insist that all or most couples in a given community have no more than one child, a lesson China learned the hard way. The viable alternative to a one-child policy of reproductive coercion is to use noncoercive means to achieve more modest goals.

Thus a nation's government could use indirect and direct means like those previously discussed, designing incentives "and" disincentives to specially encourage two-children and one-child families. But rather than attempting to make the means strong enough to convert all or most young couples to no-more-than-one-child parenthood, a government should be content with a package able to do two gentler things: (1) persuade a still small but significantly increased minority of couples to

---

1. John Bongaarts, "Population Policy Options in the Developing World," *Science,* Vol. 263 (February 11, 1994), pp. 771, 775.

2. Ibid., 775.

3. Ibid.

plan only one child and (2) persuade a very large majority of couples to plan no more than two children.[4]

I believe that those two goals would be attainable without the use of truly coercive measures. For one thing, focused attempts to encourage one-child families and to widen the increased popularity of two-children families would (unlike in today's Viet Nam) occur after two-children families had become the prevalent size or nearly so, i.e., after fertility had declined to approximate replacement. Also, as earlier argued, appropriately generous international aid would allow a more reward-oriented set of incentives.[5]

CHOICES

Thanks to the normal occurrence of persons who either abstain from sexual intercourse or are otherwise unwilling or unable to have children, it would not be necessary for nearly all couples to limit their family size to one or two offspring. Indeed, if they did, fertility could be too low.

Developing nations should probably not seek temporary subreplacement rates lower than, say, the 1.7 to 2.0 children-per-woman range that today describes Australia, Canada, Singapore, Taiwan, some Caribbean nations, and much of Europe.[6] Besides posing a greater risk of coerciveness in attaining them, fertility rates much below that approximate range would cause temporary but major disruptions in the age structure of a nation's population. And even that range could be too low if youthful mortality was still high.

Any developing nation's governmental decision to encourage temporary subreplacement fertility rates even as moderate as the above often-seen range would likely be a controversial one — both within that nation's

---

4. For yet another approach, see John Bongaarts and Susan Greenhalgh, "An Alternative to the One-Child Policy in China," *Population and Development Review,* Vol. 11, No. 4 (December 1985), pp. 585–617.

5. Thus all advocates who have opposed nontoken population aid to China, to India, and to other distressed nations should note the tendency of that opposition to foster the coercion they rightly abhor.

6. Examples of even lower fertility: Germany, 1.3 children per woman; Greece, 1.4; Hong Kong and Italy, 1.2; Japan, 1.5; Netherlands and South Korea, 1.6; Spain, 1.2. Fertility for Europe as a whole is 1.5 children per woman. PRB, *1995 Data Sheet.* One doubts that Europe's or others' present or future subreplacement fertility rates will continue long enough to approach anything resembling "national extinction." When people sense that more people are needed, they are apt to be glad to help meet that need. Joyously.

government and among the people.[7] For that and other reasons, the question of whether to seek temporary subreplacement fertility and, if yes, the further questions of what approximate rate and duration all belong wholly to each developing nation.

I doubt that any of today's high-fertility nations would choose or need to maintain subreplacement rates long enough to cause any reduction in its 1995 population level. The more probable scenario is that the subreplacement fertility rates sought and achieved (or otherwise experienced) would not be low enough, and would not last long enough, to prevent a substantial increase over today's population. What the rates would do is to moderate somewhat the immensity of expected population increases — and thereby would enhance the affected nations' chances for interim and long-term well-being.

AGE DISTRIBUTION AND SUPPORT OF THE ELDERLY

Picture a society in which everyone is age five, or one where everyone is 75. In either case, you have seen the obvious. Age distribution is of vital importance. We cannot imagine the future results of fertility decline without looking at its effect upon a population's age structure.

Start with the status quo. As earlier noted, a high-fertility-engendered population's age distribution is heavily skewed toward the young. In Latin America an average of 34 percent of the people are under age 15. In Asia, excluding China, the proportion under age 15 averages 36 percent. In Africa it averages an astounding 45 percent.[8] Yet in all three of those regions, the proportion of persons over 65 averages 5 percent or less: 5 percent in Latin America and Asia, and only 3 percent in Africa.[9]

Thus besides its being deemed mainly a family matter, support of the elderly in a high-fertility nation is a numerically small problem. But even that usually tractable situation is essentially precarious. The (again no

7. Thus some old advice applies. The people should be both apprised of the justifying facts and consulted as to the proposed policy and its implementation.
8. PRB, *1995 Data Sheet*. The proportions of course vary from nation to nation.
9. Ibid.

pun intended) relative ease of supporting the elderly depends upon each succeeding generation's being more numerous than the prior one. And adequate actual support of course depends upon each succeeding generation's economic productivity.

Therefore, unless one imagines that already distressed nations can continue doubling their populations without inviting economic and ecological collapse, one is apt to agree: the high-fertility, low-income nations' elderly are, like the rest of their citizenry, caught in a demographic updraft that, with too much further ascent, portends a great and awful crashing down.

NEEDED TRANSITION

It would thus make sense for high-fertility nations to move rapidly to replacement fertility, whatever the resulting changes in the proportion of dependent elderly. But what resulting changes would occur? During a high-fertility nation's transition to replacement rate, its proportion of persons over age 65 would begin gradually to increase. That proportion would continue to increase until (assuming both the attainment and the continuation of replacement fertility) the population finally reached zero growth — by, in most cases, the late 21st century.

Even then, the percentage of elderly people in a developing nation's population would not be great. Assuming a life expectancy of 70 years (which in most developing nations would represent at least some gain in longevity), only about 15 percent of a stationary population will consist of persons age 65 or older. Even with a life expectancy of 75 years, only about 17 percent of the citizenry will be age 65 or older.[10]

PROGNOSIS

The age distribution effects of fertility decline to replacement contain both good news and bad news concerning today's high-fertility, low-income nations' future ability to support all the age groups, young and old, that are likely to be economically dependent. The good news is that the

---

10. Both examples are my rough interpolations from Ansley J. Coale and Paul Demeny, with Barbara Vaughan, *Regional Model Life Tables and Stable Populations, Second Edition* (New York: Academic Press, 1983), as updated by Ansley Coale and Guang Guo in *Population Bulletin of the United Nations*, No. 30 (1991). I thank Professor Coale for his kind advice.

increased proportion of probably dependent elderly will be countered by an even greater decrease in the proportion of persons under age 15. Thus, as Myrdal promised, the fertility decline's *net* effect upon the society's probable dependency ratio — the total proportion of persons apt to be economically dependent — will be to diminish that ratio.

More good news is that most of the decrease in the proportion of dependent young would occur a few decades *before* most of the increase in the ratio of probably dependent elderly to usual-working-age adults. That happy sequence of events would thus provide three or so decades whose especially light dependency burden would help enable the educational expenditures and the other economic investment needed to build an economy adequate to support all persons in those and in later decades. That excellent opportunity bodes well for a nation's future elderly as well as for all other age groups.

The bad news in the age distribution changes resulting from replacement fertility is that the per person subsistence needs of the elderly (who would be relatively more numerous) average about double those of children (who would be relatively less numerous). Even so, with the expeditious attainment of replacement fertility, today's low-income nations are apt to be much better able to support their elderly citizens (and all their other citizens!) than is at all likely if their population explosion is needlessly prolonged.[11]

Equally important, an expeditious attainment of replacement fertility (and, if necessary in the worst cases, a temporary, nonexcessive dose of subreplacement rates) should eventually enable every nation to support all its elderly and all its other citizens on a sustainable basis. Even so, for some interim period after fertility has declined to replacement (or to temporary subreplacement), with the proportion of dependent elderly to usual-working-age adults substantially increased, the going could be very rough. At least some still-low-income nations may still

---

11. For some reasons for that improved prognosis, see the "Quality-of-Life Consequences" section in chapter 24. The *probable* ecological, economic, and other human costs of yet more delay in nations' reducing fertility to replacement would be much greater than the age distribution problems of rapid fertility decline. And the *possible* costs of such delay would be far, far greater. No nation will be able to reduce fertility nearly rapidly enough to cause itself anything approaching the problems — and the tragedy — that it would invite by continuing high fertility for even longer than is already inevitable.

require temporary help toward meeting their elderly and/or other citizens' needs.

Standby support. Whether or not the above later need for aid materializes, this is true: any low-income nation that will credibly and expeditiously attempt rapid fertility decline to replacement (or to any temporarily lower rate) deserves a substantial aid commitment both for the transition to replacement and for the subsequent time needed to build a viable economy. That long-term aid offer should be a part of the global bargain endorsed in chapter 23.[12]

TEMPORARY SUBREPLACEMENT FERTILITY: A SECOND LOOK

The above discussion may now help explain an earlier voiced caution against any nation's attempting too low a temporary subreplacement fertility rate.[13] *Point one* is that any temporary subreplacement fertility will, in due course, temporarily raise a nation's percentage of elderly to a level above what replacement fertility would cause.

In other words, when the children of subreplacement fertility reach the usual-working-age years, there would be fewer of them to support the then-elderly prior generation than if fertility had not fallen below replacement.[14] A similar effect would also follow any increase in the average age of childbearing even if lifetime fertility stayed at replacement rate.[15]

Point two is that the lower the subreplacement fertility rate, and the longer it lasts, the greater the temporary increase in the percentage of elderly citizens in the population. That is thus a valid reason (besides the

---

12. Warning to reluctant aidgivers: it is most probable that, unless unprecedented magnitudes of human need were allowed to go unmet, far more aid would be required were fertility to remain high.

13. There is a conclusive case against any "permanent" subreplacement fertility rate. *If* subreplacement fertility lingered on and on and on (an if that will not happen nor nearly so), a nation would finally unbreed itself into actual extinction.

Granted, extinction of even the whole human race may occur from any number of causes, known and unknown. But absent some environmental pollutant or other mad science that makes reproduction unlikely or impossible, humankind's exit will not happen from low fertility.

14. For example, with a total fertility rate of 1.7 experienced for 15 years (followed by continuous replacement rate) a nation's proportion of elderly could eventually exceed 20 percent before falling back to the proportion of elderly for a stationary population (about 15 percent, assuming a 70-year life expectancy). See World Bank, *World Development Report 1984* (New York: Oxford University Press), p. 104, for the above example in connection with China.

15. Therefore the rest of this chapter substantially also applies to that previously discussed method of lessening momentum-caused population growth.

risk of coerciveness) both against too many years of subreplacement fertility and against any fertility rate too far below replacement. Either of the latter would add to the eventual temporary increase in the proportion of (probably dependent) elderly.[16]

In deciding what if any subreplacement rate to seek, and in deciding how long to encourage its continuation, a still-distressed-nation's government would need to balance two partly obscure sets of consequences. Set one consists of the probable and possible harms of not further limiting population growth by x amount.

Set two consists of the probable and possible temporary age distribution difficulties that y amount of subreplacement fertility for z years (and any increase in the average age of childbearing) would cause. Such balancing would require Solomonic wisdom and empirical sophistication.[17]

Argument against my position: Nations should not encourage subreplacement fertility because there is no reliable way to guard against excessive success. In other words, fertility could easily fall too far below replacement or remain below replacement too long.

My response: Substantial risk of a significant difference between desired and attained fertility exists with *any* societal fertility goal. (And absent the demise of reproductive freedom, some difference is — be thankful — virtually certain.) Thus an above-replacement nation's deciding to seek "replacement but not a lower fertility rate" takes (among other risks) the considerable risk that its fertility will remain significantly above replacement. For a nation approaching overpopulation, the latter risk is apt to threaten much graver harm than does any risk of an oversuccessful encouragement of subreplacement rates.

---

16. Too low a subreplacement rate or too long a time of significantly subreplacement fertility entails a related disadvantage. There would be a larger dose of all the "age distribution adjustments" that will occur before and well after fertility eventually stabilizes in (one hopes) a fairly narrow range surrounding the only long-term-tenable fertility rate: replacement. Substantial changes in a population's age structure require a succession of costly social and economic adjustments (fewer schools and teachers needed, more schools and teachers needed; fewer nursing homes and nurses needed, more nursing homes and nurses needed; etc.). But adjustment costs of age distribution changes are also yet another eventual price of fertility that is too far *above* replacement or that remains above replacement too long.

17. The balancing could need, for example, to remember this convoluted truth: though further moderation of population growth would later mean a numerically smaller working-age population than would otherwise occur (but still much larger than today's), a lessening of dysfunctional population growth is apt to yield a workforce that is more economically productive, more able to support society's dependent persons, than a larger working-age population would be. That is true both during any interim and thereafter.

MORE ABOUT STANDBY SUPPORT

We again visit the future. Despite their fertility's fall to replacement, some nations are experiencing or approaching overpopulation. But they are able to mitigate or prevent that tragedy by achieving temporary subreplacement fertility rates (and/or by increasing the average age of childbearing).

Though such success, full or partial, would be far less costly — in every sense — than failure, it is apt to foreshadow an earlier suggested possible cost. The temporarily high proportion of dependent elderly persons that would occur well after subreplacement fertility rates (or any increased average childbearing age) had begun could easily constitute, for a limited time, an additional future aid need.

The just-stated likely possibility is a valid reason for an especially generous long-term aid commitment to low-income nations who utilize subreplacement fertility as a temporary emergency measure (or who accompany replacement fertility with delayed childbearing) to limit their population explosion. That contingent enhancement of the rich nations' long-term aid offer should be a part of the earlier proposed global bargain.

Generous aid commitments? Long-term aid offers? Am I dreaming a politically impossible dream? Please defer your answer until the next and final chapter.

CHAPTER TWENTY-SIX

TOWARD A PEACEFUL WORLD OF JUSTICE AND WELL-BEING: ARE WE WILLING?

There is a practical question at the heart of the matter. Why would the world's rich nations be willing to commit generous sums of aid under this book's scenario when, under the status quo, they fail to give nearly enough aid to meet the poor nations' unmet basic needs?

In attempting to answer, I must mention two things about the people of the rich nation to which I belong, the United States of America. Though I feel I know the people of the United States better than I know other peoples, my bet is that the following two things are just as true of other peoples as well.

HEAD VERSUS HEART

First, people in the United States have big hearts. They care. When they see or hear of persons in need, they want to respond in a helpful way. And often they do. They can be immensely generous, even sacrificially so.

Second, they have heads on their shoulders. They do not want their good deeds to do more harm than good. Nor do they want their good deeds to be futile.

And so merely watching the evening news can put them through moral torture — even if there is no genocidal warfare that day. When folks in the United States see or read of families starving in Africa, of children needing medical care in Asia, or of young people being denied sufficient schooling and job opportunity in Latin America, the thoughtful head and the sympathetic heart are torn apart from each other.

What is it the mind consciously or unconsciously realizes, which sunders the mind from the heart? The rich-nation people cannot help but know, even if subliminally, a truth the heart dares not acknowledge: unless the developing world's population explosion is soon ended, there will be far more hunger, far more untreated sickness, and many more young lives that are denied a chance to develop in body and mind. That will happen despite our kind help; and even, in part, because of it.

So what do we U.S. Americans do? Some of us turn away and do (give) nothing. But that is too heartless for most. Most of us respond in some token way. Most of us give only enough to claim feeble reassurance that we are still human beings with humane feelings. We do not give nearly our potential share in the total common effort needed to enable a humane life and world for others and for ourselves. Our head tells us that, unless sufficient steps are soon taken to prevent massively tragic overpopulation, our help is liable to do more eventual harm than immediate good.

SAINTS HEAVENLY AND EARTHLY

But some give all they can anyhow. Some devote their all despite the seemingly certain futility in their doing so. They are called saints.

Though I do admire those saintly souls (albeit from a safe distance), I do not think it at all useful to expect the rest of us to become saints of their heavenly ilk. After all, we have been invited to join their blessed ranks for centuries upon centuries. The overwhelming majority of us have politely, but fervently, refused.

If the rest of us are destined to become any kind of saint at all, we are, I believe, destined to become very earthly saints.[1] We could be willing, even happy, to do our part toward building a humane future for all — if we could see a plausibly viable path to that elusive goal. If the head could see, the heart would say yes.

It is all people's capacity for earthly sainthood that causes me to believe that rich-nation peoples would be willing to aid the world's poor-nation peoples in the ways proposed in this book. Even the most tough-minded reluctant taxpayer should be able to recognize a once-in-an-eon bargain. *The aid he or she would be asked to help pay for offers exactly what the status quo cannot offer: a realistic chance of a sustainable future of well-being for the entire human race — and for the vast diversity of other life with whom we also share this wondrous planet.*

Yes, this book asks for, among other things, a generous long-term aid commitment from the rich nations, just as it also asks (see chapter 23)

---

1. But that too is a heavenly enterprise.

much of the poor nations. But it does not propose perpetual aidgiving. It does not ask the rich nations to throw their precious wealth into a seemingly infinite abyss.

AID SCENARIO SUMMARY

As has already been implied, the long-term but not endless aidgiving being asked of the world's rich nations would essentially consist of two phases. *Phase one*, recall, would be the aid needed to help low-income, high-fertility nations achieve sufficiently low fertility, and otherwise to increase their ecological stewardship, rapidly and humanely.[2] It would also mean helping them pursue other feasible goals in health, education, gender equity, employment, and other economic development.[3]

Phase two would be the aid needed to help not-yet-prosperous nations continue their development efforts after low fertility had been achieved but while their populations were still growing.[4] It would include (1) helping those nations to support their elderly and other needy persons during what (recall chapter 25) might be called the "age distribution adjustment years" and (2) helping those nations to move closer to their goal of well-being for all their people on a self-sustaining, ecologically sound, continuing basis.

Hard road, right direction. There is no politically and economically realistic level of aidgiving and private investment inflow that would make life easy for the developing nations during the above transition. But, unlike the disastrous future that continued high fertility would have wrought, with low fertility and sensible economic policies nonaffluent people's material well-being would in time be credibly heading upward rather than cruelly tumbling down. Humankind would be progressing toward that long-thought impossible goal: justice for all.

---

2. Recall also that increased ecological stewardship would likewise be expected of the world's rich nations.

3. Further recall that the same aid could often serve multiple goods. For example: aid expenditures to create jobs as incentives to low fertility could (1) help meet the critical need for more jobs, (2) contribute to fertility decline, (3) increase women's freedom, and (4) contribute to general economic growth. The wages could be fairly taxed to support old-age assistance or to meet other social needs. The job program in each nation or district could be administered by an entity whose stock and earnings were owned by a pension fund to serve the future elderly who would most need help — those who have the fewest or no children. The fund could thus be operating two antinatalist incentive programs at the same time, one offering jobs and one offering future old-age assistance.

4. As but partly illustrated by the prior footnote's example, phase one aid would already have been contributing to phase two goals in a variety of ways.

AND IMAGINE THE INTANGIBLE

Something else would also be happening, both in the developing and in the developed nations. Given that people do not nearly live by bread alone, this something else could be even more beneficent than sorely needed gains in material well-being. And it surely surpasses the latter in being impossible to describe before it happens.

To try to describe it, think about its virtual opposite: overpopulation. The sorrowful essence of that sad concept is not the shortages of food and other material necessities, poignant and deadly though such shortages are. Nor do the abuses more and more humans inflict upon each other and upon the rest of nature capture the essence of overpopulation. They are not why we can hardly bear to use the word.

The sorrowful essence of overpopulation is what "too many people" does to the socially perceived and the self-perceived value of each human being. Overpopulation is intrinsically at war with the preciousness of every person.

In contrast, imagine this. Before it is too late, human population is ending its numerical growth, and sufficient other steps are being taken to conserve the wondrous diversity of life that graces this planet. Humankind is working together to salvage the whole Garden of Earth and to use it in ways that meet all people's needs on a sustainable basis.

In the economically richest and in the economically poorest nations on earth, and in all nations between those extremes, a common revolution of mind and heart would be under way: *the dream of a viable future for all would be becoming a credible vision for all.* People, all people, would be able to see that they and their children do indeed have a decent place in that future and a worthy role to play in helping to get there.[5]

One need not think of human beings as being unduly future-oriented to imagine how the rebirth of the above dream would give new meaning, new dignity, new purpose, new joy, to each person's present individual and communal life. One need only imagine — there is no need to count — the ways.

---

5. The dream, the vision, equally belongs to persons who are and to persons who are not the biological parent of one or more children. No one is really childless. We all have children. Everyone even has grandchildren — if the world lasts that long.

Just imagine. Imagine that gentle but profound revolution. Imagine that reunion of the head and the heart. All over the world.

Then demand and support the policies that would help it happen.

Because the literature on population and related subjects is both vast and ever growing, numerous excellent and important sources, old and new, are missing from this abbreviated list.

Abdalla, Raqiya Haji Dualeh. *Sisters in Affliction: Circumcision and Infibulation of Women in Africa.* London: Zed Press, 1982.

Abernethy, Virginia D. *Population Politics: The Choices That Shape Our Future.* New York: Plenum Press, 1993.

Adlakha, Arjun, Mohamed Ayad, and Sushil Kumar. "The Role of Nuptiality in Fertility Decline: A Comparative Analysis," in *Demographic and Health Surveys (DHS) World Conference Proceedings,* Vol. 2, 1991, pp. 947–64.

Barnett, Patricia G. *Incentives for Family Planning?* Washington, D.C.: Population Crisis Committee, 1992.

Bayles, Michael D. *Morality and Population Policy.* University, Ala.: University of Alabama Press, 1980.

Berelson, Bernard and Jonathan Lieberson. "Government Efforts to Influence Fertility: The Ethical Issues," *Population and Development Review,* Vol. 5, No. 4 (December 1979), pp. 581–613.

Bicego, George T. and J. Ties Boerma. "Maternal Education and Child Survival: A Comparative Analysis of DHS Data," in *DHS World Conference Proceedings,* Vol. 1, 1991, pp. 177–204.

Bongaarts, John. "The KAP-Gap and the Unmet Need for Contraception," *Population and Development Review,* Vol. 27, No. 2 (June 1991), pp. 293–313.

―――. "Population Policy Options in the Developing World," *Science*, Vol. 263 (February 11, 1994), pp. 771–76.

Bongaarts, John and Judith Bruce. "The Causes of Unmet Need for Contraception and the Social Content of Services," *Studies in Family Planning,* Vol. 26, No. 2 (March/April 1995), pp. 57–75.

Bongaarts, John and Susan Greenhalgh. "An Alternative to the One-Child Policy in China," *Population and Development Review,* Vol. 11, No. 4 (December 1985), pp. 585–617.

Bongaarts, John, W. Parker Mauldin, and James F. Phillips. "Demographic Impact of Family Planning Programs," *Studies in Family Planning,* Vol. 21, No. 6 (November/December 1990), pp. 299–310.

Bos, Eduard, My T. Vu, Ernest Massiah, and Rodolfo A. Bulatao. *World Population Projections, 1994–95 Edition.* Baltimore: The Johns Hopkins University Press, published for the World Bank, 1994.

Bouvier, Leon F. and Lindsey Grant. *How Many Americans?* San Francisco: Sierra Club Books, 1994.

Bracher, Michael and Gigi Santow. "Premature Discontinuation of Contraception in Australia," *Family Planning Perspectives,* Vol. 24 (1992), pp. 58–65.

Brass, William and Carole L. Jolly. *Population Dynamics of Kenya.* Washington, D.C.: National Academy Press, 1993.

Bratton, Susan Power. *Six Billion and More: Human Population Regulation and Christian Ethics.* Louisville, Ky.: Westminster/John Knox Press, 1992.

Bronstein, Audrey. *The Triple Struggle: Latin American Peasant Women.* London: WOW Campaigns Ltd., 1982.

Brown, Lester R. and Hal Kane. *Full House: Reassessing the Earth's Population Carrying Capacity.* New York: W.W. Norton, 1994.

Brown, Lester R. et al. *State of the World 1995: A Worldwatch Institute Report on Progress Toward a Sustainable Society.* New York: W.W. Norton (published annually).

Bruce, Judith. "Fundamental Elements of the Quality of Care: A Simple Framework," *Studies in Family Planning,* Vol. 21, No. 2 (March/April 1990), pp. 61–91.

Calabresi, Guido and Philip Bobbitt. *Tragic Choices.* New York: W.W. Norton, 1978.

Caldwell, John C. "Mass Education as a Determinant of the Timing of Fertility Decline," *Population and Development Review,* Vol. 6, No. 2 (June 1980), pp. 225–55.

———. *Theory of Fertility Decline.* London: Academic Press, 1982.

Callahan, Daniel, and Phillip G. Clark, eds. *Ethical Issues of Population Aid: Culture, Economics and International Assistance.* New York: Irvington, 1981.

Cassen, Robert. "Population Policy: A New Consensus," *Policy Essay No. 12.* Washington, D.C.: Overseas Development Council, 1994.

Cassen, Robert and contributors. *Population and Development: Old Debates, New Conclusions.* New Brunswick, N.J.: Transaction Publishers and Overseas Development Council, 1994.

Church, Cathleen A. and Judith S. Geller. "Lights! Camera! Action! Promoting Family Planning with TV, Video, and Film," *Population Reports,* Series J, No. 38. Baltimore: Population Information Program, The Johns Hopkins University, December 1989.

———. "Voluntary Female Sterilization: Number One and Growing," *Population Reports,* Series C, Number 10. Baltimore: Population Information Program, The Johns Hopkins University, November 1990.

Cleland, John and John Hobcraft. *Reproductive Change in Developing Countries: Insights from the World Fertility Survey.* Oxford University Press, 1985.

Cleland, John and W. Parker Mauldin. "The Promotion of Family Planning by Financial Payments: The Case of Bangladesh," *Studies in Family Planning,* Vol. 22, No. 1 (January/February 1991), pp. 1–18.

Cleland, John and Germán Rodríguez. "The Effect of Parental Education on Marital Fertility in Developing Countries," *Population Studies,* Vol. 42 (1988), pp. 419–42.

Cleland, John and Jerome K. van Ginneken. "Maternal Education and Child Survival in Developing Countries: The Search for Pathways of Influence," *Social Science and Medicine,* Vol. 27, No. 12 (1988), pp. 1357–68.

Cleland, John and Christopher Wilson. "Demand Theories of the Fertility Transition: An Iconoclastic View," *Population Studies,* Vol. 41, No. 1 (1987), pp. 5–30.

Coale, Ansley J. "The Demographic Transition," in *International Population Conference 1973.* Liège: International Union for the Scientific Study of Population, pp. 53–72.

———. "The History of the Human Population," *Scientific American,* Vol. 231, No. 3 (September 1974), pp. 41–51.

Coale, Ansley J. and Paul Demeny, with Barbara Vaughan. *Regional Model Life Tables and Stable Populations, Second Edition.* New York: Academic Press, 1983.

Coale, Ansley J. and Edgar M. Hoover. *Population Growth and Economic Development in Low-Income Countries.* Princeton, N.J.: Princeton University Press, 1958.

Cochrane, Susan H. "Effects of Education and Urbanization on Fertility," in Rodolfo A. Bulatao and Ronald D. Lee, eds., *Determinants of Fertility in Developing Countries,* Vol. 2. New York: Academic Press, 1983, pp. 587–626.

Conly, Shanti R. and J. Joseph Speidel. *Global Population Assistance: A Report Card on the Major Donor Countries.* Washington, D.C.: Population Action International, 1993.

Conning, Arthur M. and Albert M. Marckwardt. "Analysis of WFS Data in Colombia, Panama, Paraguay and Peru: Highlights from the CELADE Research and Training Seminar," *WFS Occasional Papers No. 25,* 1982.

Daly, Herman E. and John B. Cobb, Jr. *For the Common Good: Redirecting the Economy Toward Community, the Environment, and a Sustainable Future.* Boston: Beacon Press, 1989.

David, Henry P. "Incentives, Reproductive Behavior, and Integrated Community Development in Asia," *Studies in Family Planning,* Vol. 13, No. 5 (May 1982), pp. 159–73.

Deevey, Edward S. Jr. "The Human Population," *Scientific American,* Vol. 203, No. 3 (September 1960), pp. 195–204.

Demeny, Paul. "Bucharest, Mexico City, and Beyond," *Population and Development Review,* Vol. 11, No. 1 (March 1985), pp. 99–106.

Dixon-Mueller, Ruth. *Population Policy and Women's Rights: Transforming Reproductive Choice.* Westport, Conn.: Praeger, 1993.

230
ENDING THE EXPLOSION

Easterlin, Richard A. and Eileen M. Crimmons. *The Fertility Revolution: A Supply-Demand Analysis.* University of Chicago Press, 1985.

Ehrlich, Paul R. and Anne H. *The Population Explosion.* New York: Simon and Schuster, 1990.

Ezeh, Alex Chika. "The Influence of Spouses Over Each Other's Contraceptive Attitudes in Ghana," *Studies in Family Planning,* Vol. 24, No. 3 (May/June 1993), pp. 163–74.

"Fertility Decline in Bangladesh: An Emerging Family Planning Success Story," *Asia-Pacific Population & Policy,* March 1992.

Feyisetan, Bamikale and Anne R. Pebley. "Premarital Sexuality in Urban Nigeria," *Studies in Family Planning,* Vol. 20, No. 6 (November/December 1989), pp. 343–54.

Finkle, Jason L. and C. Alison McIntosh, eds. *The New Politics of Population: Conflict and Consensus in Family Planning.* New York: The Population Council, 1994.

Finnigan, Oliver D. III and T. H. Sun. "Planning, Starting, and Operating an Educational Incentives Project," *Studies in Family Planning,* Vol. 3, No. 1 (January 1972), pp. 1–7.

Frank, Odile and Geoffrey McNicoll. "An Interpretation of Fertility and Population Policy in Kenya," *Population and Development Review,* Vol. 13, No. 2 (June 1987), pp. 209–43.

Freedman, Ronald. "Theories of Fertility Decline: A Reappraisal," *Social Forces,* Vol. 58 (September 1979), pp. 1–17.

————. "Family Planning Programs in the Third World," *The Annals of the American Academy of Political and Social Science,* Vol. 510 (July 1990), pp. 33–43.

Freedman, Ronald and Ann K. Blanc. "Fertility Transition: An Update," *International Family Planning Perspectives,* Vol. 18, No. 2 (June 1992), pp. 44–50, 72.

Gallant, Roy A. *The Peopling of Planet Earth: Human Population Growth Through the Ages.* New York: Macmillan, 1990.

Garrett, Laurie. *The Coming Plague: Newly Emerging Diseases In A World Out Of Balance.* New York: Farrar, Straus and Giroux, 1994.

Gilluly, Richard H. and Sidney H. Moore. "Radio — Spreading the Word on Family Planning," *Population Reports,* Series J, No. 32. Baltimore: Population Information Program, The Johns Hopkins University, September-October 1986.

Goldberg, Howard I., Fara G. M'Bodji, and Jay S. Friedman. "Fertility and Family Planning in One Region of Senegal," *International Family Planning Perspectives,* Vol. 12, No. 4 (December 1986), pp. 116–22.

Goldfarb, Johanna, M.D., and Edith Tibbetts. *Breastfeeding Handbook.* Hillside, N.J.: Enslow Publishers, 1989.

Graham-Smith, Sir Francis, ed. *Population — the Complex Reality: A Report of the Population Summit of the World's Scientific Academies.* Golden, Colo.: North American Press, 1994.

Green, Ronald Michael. *Population Growth and Justice: An Examination of Moral Issues Raised by Rapid Population Growth.* Missoula, Mont.: Scholars Press, 1976.

Gupte, Pranay. *The Crowded Earth: People and the Politics of Population.* New York: W.W. Norton, 1984.

Handwerker, W. Penn. "Women's Power and Fertility Transition: The Cases of Africa and the West Indies," *Population and Environment,* Vol. 13, No. 1 (Fall 1991), pp. 55–78.

Hardaway, Robert M. *Population, Law, and the Environment.* Westport, Conn.: Praeger, 1994.

Hardin, Garrett. "The Tragedy of the Commons," *Science,* Vol. 162, No. 3859 (December 13, 1968), pp. 1243–48.

————. *Living Within Limits: Ecology, Economics, and Population Taboos.* New York: Oxford University Press, 1993.

Hartmann, Betsy. *Reproductive Rights and Wrongs: The Global Politics of Population Control,* Rev. Ed. Boston: South End Press, 1995.

Hatcher, Robert A., M.D., et al. *Contraceptive Technology,* 15th Rev. Ed. New York: Irvington, 1992.

Heer, David M. "Infant and Child Mortality and the Demand for Children," in Rodolfo A. Bulatao and Ronald D. Lee, eds., *Determinants of Fertility in Developing Countries,* Vol. 1. New York: Academic Press, 1983.

Hern, Warren, M.D. "Family Planning, Amazon Style," *Natural History,* Vol. 101, No. 12 (December 1992), pp. 31–36.

Hines, Norman E. *Medical History of Contraception.* New York: Schocken Books, 1970; first published 1936.

Hobcraft, John. "Child Spacing and Child Mortality," in *DHS World Conference Proceedings,* Vol. 2, 1991, pp. 1157–81.

Inkeles, Alex. *Exploring Individual Modernity.* New York: Columbia University Press, 1983.

Jacobsen, Judith. "Promoting Population Stabilization: Incentives for Small Families," *Worldwatch Paper No. 54,* June 1983.

Jacobson, Jodi L. "Planning the Global Family," *Worldwatch Paper No. 80,* December 1987.

Kangas, Lenni W. "Integrated Incentives for Fertility Control," *Science,* Vol. 169, No. 3952 (September 25, 1970), pp. 1278–83.

Kennedy, Paul. *Preparing for the Twenty-First Century.* New York: Vintage Books, 1993.

Ki, Paik Hyun. *A Field Try-Out of Population Education Curriculum Materials for Teacher Education Programmes — An Experimental Study: A Case of the Philippines.* Bangkok: Asia Regional Office of the United Nations Educational, Scientific and Cultural Organization, 1973.

Kritz, Mary M. and Douglas T. Gurak. "Women's Economic Independence and Fertility Among the Yoruba," in *DHS World Conference Proceedings,* Vol. 1, 1991, pp. 89–111.

Lande, Robert E. "New Era for Injectables," *Population Reports,* Series K, No. 5. Baltimore: Population Information Program, The Johns Hopkins University, August 1995.

Lande, Robert E. and Judith S. Geller. "Paying for Family Planning," *Population Reports,* Series J, Number 39. Baltimore: Population Information Program, The Johns Hopkins University, November 1991.

Lapham, Robert J. and George B. Simmons, eds. *Organizing for Effective Family Planning Programs.* Washington, D.C.: National Academy Press, 1987.

Liskin, Laurie, Ellen Benoit, and Richard Blackburn. "Vasectomy: New Opportunities," *Population Reports,* Series D, No. 5. Baltimore: Population Information Program, The Johns Hopkins University, March 1992.

Liskin, Laurie and Richard Blackburn, with Rula Ghani. "Hormonal Contraception: New Long-Acting Methods," *Population Reports,* Series K, No. 3. Baltimore: Population Information Program, The Johns Hopkins University, March-April 1987.

Liskin, Laurie and Ward Rinehart, with others. "Minilaparotomy and Laparoscopy: Safe, Effective, and Widely Used," *Population Reports,* Series C, No. 9. Baltimore: Population Information Program, The Johns Hopkins University, May 1985.

Lloyd, Cynthia B. and Serguey Ivanov. "The Effects of Improved Child Survival on Family Planning Practice and Fertility," *Studies in Family Planning,* Vol. 19, No. 3 (May/June 1988), pp. 141–61.

Lynam, Pamela, Leslie McNeil Rabinovitz, and Mofoluke Shobowale. "Using Self-Assessment to Improve the Quality of Family Planning Clinic Services," *Studies in Family Planning,* Vol. 24, No. 4 (July/August 1993), pp. 252–260.

Mason, Karen Oppenheim. "The Impact of Women's Social Position on Fertility in Developing Countries," *Sociological Forum,* Vol. 2, No. 4 (Fall 1987), pp. 718–45.

Mauldin, W. Parker. "Contraceptive Use in the Year 2000," in *DHS World Conference Proceedings,* Vol. 2, 1991, pp. 1373–93.

Mauldin, W. Parker and Bernard Berelson. "Conditions of Fertility Decline in Developing Countries, 1965–75," *Studies in Family Planning,* Vol. 9 (1978), pp. 90–147.

Mazur, Laurie Ann, ed. *Beyond the Numbers.* Covelo, Calif.: Island Press, 1994.

McCann, Margaret F. et al. "Breast-Feeding, Fertility, and Family Planning," *Population Reports,* Series J, No. 24. Baltimore: Population Information Program, The Johns Hopkins University, March 1984.

McCauley, Ann P. and Judith S. Geller. "Decisions for Norplant Programs," *Population Reports,* Series K, No. 4. Baltimore: Population Information Program, The Johns Hopkins University, November 1992.

McCauley, Ann P., Bryant Robey, Ann K. Blanc, and Judith S. Geller. "Opportunities for Women Through Reproductive Choice," *Population Reports,* Series M, No. 12. Baltimore: Population Information Program, The Johns Hopkins University, July 1994.

McLaren, Angus. *A History of Contraception: From Antiquity to the Present Day.* Oxford: Basil Blackwell, 1990.

Meadows, Donella H., Dennis L. Meadows, Jørgen Randers. *Beyond the Limits: Confronting Global Collapse, Envisioning a Sustainable Future.* Post Mills, Vt.: Chelsea Green, 1992.

Moffett, George D. *Critical Masses: The Global Population Challenge.* New York: Viking Penguin, 1994.

Myers, Norman. *Ultimate Security: The Environmental Basis of Political Stability.* New York: W.W. Norton, 1993.

Myrdal, Gunnar. *Asian Drama: An Inquiry into the Poverty of Nations,* Vol. 2. New York: The Twentieth Century Fund, 1968.

————. *The Challenge of World Poverty: A World Anti-Poverty Program in Outline.* New York: Pantheon Books, 1970.

National Research Council, Committee on Population, Working Group on Population and Development, *Population Growth and Economic Development: Policy Questions.* Washington, D.C.: National Academy Press, 1986.

Noonan, John T. Jr. *Contraception: A History of Its Treatment by the Catholic Theologians and Canonists.* Cambridge, Mass.: Belknap Press, 1986.

Novak, Michael, ed. *The Experience of Marriage: The Testimony of Catholic Laymen.* New York: Macmillan, 1964.

Oppong, Christine. "Women's Roles, Opportunity Costs, and Fertility," in Rodolfo A. Bulatao and Ronald D. Lee, eds., *Determinants of Fertility in Developing Countries,* Vol. 1. New York: Academic Press, 1983, pp. 547–89.

Phillips, James F. and John A. Ross, eds. *Family Planning Programmes and Fertility.* Oxford: Clarendon Press, 1992.

Piotrow, Phyllis Tilson. *World Population Crisis: The United States Response.* New York: Praeger, 1973.

Piotrow, Phyllis Tilson et al. "Mass Media Family Planning Promotion in Three Nigerian Cities," *Studies in Family Planning,* Vol. 21, No. 5 (September/October 1990), pp. 265–74.

The Planetary Bargain: Proposals for a New International Economic Order to Meet Human Needs. Princeton, N.J.: Aspen Institute for Humanistic Studies, Program on International Affairs, 1976.

Pohlman, Edward. *Incentives and Compensations in Birth Planning,* Monograph 11. Chapel Hill, N.C.: Carolina Population Center, University of North Carolina, 1971.

Population Crisis Committee (now Population Action International). "Country Rankings of the Status of Women: Poor, Powerless, and Pregnant," *Population Briefing Paper,* No. 20. Washington, D.C.: June 1988.

————. "Access to Affordable Contraception," *1991 Report on World Progress Towards Population Stabilization.* Washington, D.C.: 1991.

Population Reference Bureau. *1995 World Population Data Sheet.* Washington, D.C.

Poston, Dudley L. Jr. and David Yaukey, eds. *The Population of Modern China.* New York: Plenum Press, 1992.

Preston, Samuel H., ed. *The Effects of Infant and Child Mortality on Fertility.* New York: Academic Press, 1978.

Pritchett, Lant H. "Desired Fertility and the Impact of Population Policies," *Population and Development Review,* Vol. 20, No. 1 (March 1994), pp. 1–55.

Pritchett, Lant H. et al. "The Impact of Population Policies: An Exchange," *Population and Development Review,* Vol. 20, No. 3 (September 1994), pp. 611–30.

Rawls, John. *A Theory of Justice.* Cambridge, Mass.: Harvard University Press, 1971.

Riddle, John M. *Contraception and Abortion from the Ancient World to the Renaissance.* Cambridge, Mass.: Harvard University Press, 1992.

Ridker, Ronald G. "The No-Birth Bonus Scheme: The Use of Savings Accounts for Family Planning in South India," *Population and Development Review,* Vol. 6, No. 1 (March 1980), pp. 31–46.

Rihani, May. *Development as if Women Mattered: An Annotated Bibliography with a Third World Focus.* Overseas Development Council Occasional Paper No. 10 (Washington, D.C.: 1978).

Rinehart, Ward, Adrienne Kols, and Sidney H. Moore. "Healthier Mothers and Children Through Family Planning," *Population Reports,* Series I, Number 27. Baltimore: Population Information Program, The Johns Hopkins University, May-June 1984.

Roberts, Godfrey, ed. *Population Policy: Contemporary Issues.* New York: Praeger, 1990.

Robey, Bryant, Phyllis Tilson Piotrow, and Cynthia Salter. "Family Planning Lessons and Challenges: Making Programs Work," *Population Reports,* Series J, No. 40. Baltimore: Population Information Program, The Johns Hopkins University, August 1994.

Robey, Bryant, Shea O. Rutstein, Leo Morris, and Richard Blackburn. "The Reproductive Revolution: New Survey Findings," *Population Reports,* Series M, Number 11. Baltimore: Population Information Program, The Johns Hopkins University, December 1992.

Rodríguez, Germán and Ricardo Aravena. "Socio-economic Factors and the Transition to Low Fertility in Less Developed Countries: A Comparative Analysis," in *DHS World Conference Proceedings,* Vol. 1, 1991, pp. 39–72.

Ross, John A. and Stephen L. Isaacs. "Costs, Payments, and Incentives in Family Planning Programs: A Review for Developing Countries," *Studies in Family Planning,* Vol. 19, No. 5 (September/October 1988), pp. 270–83.

Ross, John A., W. Parker Mauldin, Steven R. Green, and E. Romana Cooke. *Family Planning and Child Survival Programs as Assessed in 1991.* New York: The Population Council, 1992.

Ross, John A., W. Parker Mauldin, and Vincent C. Miller. *Family Planning and Population: A Compendium of Statistics.* New York: The Population Council, 1993.

Rule, Sheila. "African Rift: Birth Control Vs. Tradition," *New York Times,* August 11, 1985, p. 1.

Rutstein, Shea Oscar. "The Impact of Breastfeeding on Fertility," in *DHS World Conference Proceedings,* Vol. 2, 1991, pp. 897–924.

Santow, Gigi. "Coitus Interruptus in the Twentieth Century," *Population and Development Review,* Vol. 19, No. 4 (December 1993), pp. 767–92.

Sen, Gita, Adrienne Germain, and Lincoln C. Chen. *Population Policies Reconsidered: Health, Empowerment, and Rights.* Boston: Harvard University Press, 1994.

Simon, Julian L. *The Ultimate Resource.* Princeton, N.J.: Princeton University Press, 1981.

Sinding, Steven W. "Getting to Replacement: Bridging the Gap Between Individual Rights and Demographic Goals," paper presented at IPPF Family Planning Congress, October 23–25, 1992, Delhi, India.

Singh, Susheela and John Casterline. "The Socio-Economic Determinants of Fertility," in John Cleland and John Hobcraft, *Reproductive Change in Developing Countries: Insights from the World Fertility Survey.* Oxford University Press, 1985, pp. 199–222.

Sowers, MaryFran et al. "Changes in Bone Density with Lactation," *JAMA,* Vol. 269, No. 24 (June 23/30, 1993), pp. 3130–35.

Standing, Guy. "Women's Work Activity and Fertility," in Rodolfo A. Bulatao and Ronald D. Lee, eds., *Determinants of Fertility in Developing Countries,* Vol. 1. New York: Academic Press, 1983, pp. 517–46.

Steinfels, Peter. "Papal Birth-Control Letter Retains Its Grip," *New York Times,* August 1, 1993, p. 1.

Stokes, Bruce. "Men and Family Planning," *Worldwatch Paper No. 41,* December 1980.

Szreter, Simon. "The Idea of Demographic Transition and the Study of Fertility Change: A Critical Intellectual History," *Population and Development Review,* Vol. 19, No. 4 (December 1993), pp. 659–701.

Tobias, Michael. *World War III: Population and the Biosphere at the End of the Millennium.* Santa Fe, N. Mex.: Bear and Company, 1994.

Treiman, Katherine and Laurie Lisken. "IUDs — A New Look," *Population Reports,* Series B, No. 5. Baltimore: Population Information Program, The Johns Hopkins University, March 1988.

Trussell, James, Robert A. Hatcher, et al. "Contraceptive Failure in the United States: An Update," *Studies in Family Planning,* Vol. 21, No. 1 (January/February 1990), pp. 51–59.

Turner, B.L. II, ed. *The Earth as Transformed by Human Action: Global and Regional Changes in the Biosphere over the Past 300 Years.* Cambridge University Press, 1990.

United Nations. *Programme of Action of the International Conference on Population and Development.* New York: 1994.

United Nations Children's Fund. *The State of the World's Children, 1996.* Oxford University Press.

United Nations Department of International Economic and Social Affairs. *Variations in the Incidence of Knowledge and Use of Contraception: A Comparative Analysis of World Fertility Survey Results for Twenty Developing Countries,* ST/ESA/Series R/40. New York: 1981.

————. *Fertility Behavior in the Context of Development: Evidence from the World Fertility Survey,* Population Studies No. 100. New York: 1987.

————. *Long-range World Population Projections: Two Centuries of Population Growth, 1950–2150.* New York: 1992.

United Nations Development Programme. *Human Development Report, 1993.* New York: Oxford University Press.

United Nations Population Fund. *Background Note on the Resource Requirements for Population Programmes in the Years 2000–2015.* New York: July 13, 1994.

————. *Contraceptive Use and Commodity Costs in Developing Countries, 1994–2005,* Technical Report No. 18. New York: 1994.

Veatch, Robert M. "Governmental Population Incentives: Ethical Issues at Stake," *Studies in Family Planning,* Vol. 8, No. 4 (April 1977), pp. 100–08.

Wang, C. M. and S. T. Chen. "Evaluation of the First Year of the Educational Savings Program in Taiwan," *Studies in Family Planning,* Vol. 4, No. 7 (July 1973), pp. 157–61.

Wann, David. *Biologic: Environmental Protection by Design.* Boulder, Colo.: Johnson Books, 1990.

Warwick, Donald P. *Bitter Pills: Population Policies and their Implementation in Eight Developing Countries.* Cambridge University Press, 1982.

Westoff, Charles F. "Reproductive Preferences: A Comparative View," *DHS Comparative Studies No. 3,* February 1991.

Westoff, Charles F. and Luis Hernando Ochoa. "Unmet Need and the Demand for Family Planning," *DHS Comparative Studies No. 5,* July 1991.

Westoff, Charles F. and Germán Rodríguez. "The Mass Media and Family Planning in Kenya," *DHS Working Papers,* No. 4, August 1993.

Wilson, Edward O. *The Diversity of Life.* Cambridge, Mass.: The Belknap Press, 1992.

Wogaman, J. Philip, ed. *The Population Crisis and Moral Responsibility.* Washington, D.C.: Public Affairs Press, 1973.

World Commission on Environment and Development. *Our Common Future.* Oxford University Press, 1987.

Wright, Robin and Doyle McManus. *Flashpoints: Promise and Peril in a New World.* New York: Alfred A. Knopf, 1991.

Seven Locks Press Current Offerings

The Other Victim

How Caregivers Survive a Loved
One's Chronic Illness
by Alan Drattell

Paper
0-929765-43-5 $17.95

A comprehensive discussion of strategies for coping with the physical,
mental and emotional problems faced by caregivers, including real life stories.

Citistates

How Urban American Can Prosper
in a Competitive World
by Neal R. Peirce
with Curtis W. Johnson
and John Stuart Hall

Cloth
0-929765-16-8 $24.95
Paper
0-929765-34-6 $18.95

"Neal Peirce is the best writer on urban affairs in the country."
- **Henry Cisneros**, Secretary of Housing & Urban Development

National Public Radio

Cast of Characters
by Mary Collins
Photographs by Jerome Liebling

Cloth
0-929765-19-2 $39.95

*"...informative, charming, even compelling. It tells the story of a special institution
and special people.*
- **Doug Bennett**, former NPR President

Continued

ORDER FORM

Book Title	Quantity	Reference No.	Cost
Total			

CA Residents add 7.75% sales tax   Shipping: $4.00 for the first book, $1.00 for each add'l title

❑ **Check or money order enclosed.**   ❑ **Bill me.**   *Charge my*   ❑ **Visa**   ❑ **Mastercard**

Card #   Exp Date   Signature
(   )

Name   Phone

Address   City   State   Zip

When you order with this form your order will be shipped Freight Free.
Address and Phone Numbers on back

On Board with the Duke

John Wayne and the
Wild Goose
by Captain Bert Minshell with
Clark Sharon

Cloth
0-929765-13-3

$39.95

John Wayne's yacht, *The Wild Goose*, provides the backdrop as the ship's
Captain chronicles family activities, stories of famous quests and a revealing
glimpse of Wayne.

Organizing for Social Change
2nd Edition

A Manual for Activists
by Kim Bobo, Jackie Kendall, Steve
Max

Paper
0-929765-41-9

$19.95

An updated and complete manual for grassroots organizers working for
social, political and economic change at any level of government.

Please call or write for a complete catalogue.

- -

SEVEN LOCKS PRESS
PO Box 25689 Santa Ana, CA 92799

Phone: **800-354-5348** or **714-545-2526**
Fax: **714-545-1572**